Garfield
EATS AND RUNS

BY JIM DAVIS

Ballantine Books ● New York

A Ballantine Books Trade Paperback Original

Published in the United States by Ballantine Books, an imprint of Random House,
a division of Penguin Random House LLC, New York.

BALLANTINE and the HOUSE colophon are registered trademarks of Penguin Random House LLC.

ISBN 978-0-425-28572-5
Ebook ISBN 978-0-425-28573-2

Printed in China on acid-free paper

randomhousebooks.com

9 8 7 6 5 4 3 2 1

GARFIELD'S 40TH BIRTHDAY EXTRAVAGANZA!

SPECIAL NEW BOOK
CELEBRATING GARFIELD'S EPIC 40TH BIRTHDAY!
JUNE 19, 2018

The big year is finally here! Garfield, the original party animal, is aging disgracefully and celebrating wildly! Hey, what do you expect from the mischievous fat cat who is so good at being bad?

Join the party, as celebrity cartoonists and fans alike pay homage to the famous feline. Even Broadway legend Lin-Manuel Miranda, a lifelong Garfield lover, gets into the act by composing the book's foreword.

This commemorative collection of birthday comic strips—plus a ton of other festive fun—is a gift for Garfield fans of all ages!

AGE HAPPENS
Garfield
HITS THE BIG 4-0

BY JIM DAVIS

Foreword by Lin-Manuel Miranda, Pulitzer Prize-winning creator of *Hamilton*

garfield.com
GARFIELD®
www.facebook.com/garfield
SCHLURP
Distributed by Universal Uclick
JIM DAVIS 10-18
MMMMMMMMMMMM
PUMPKIN SPICE LATTE
MMMMMMMMMMMMM
© 2015 PAWS, INC. All Rights Reserved.

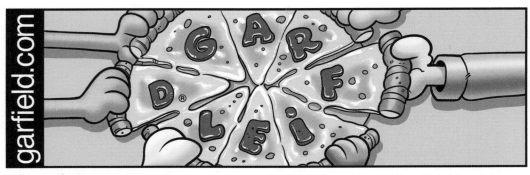

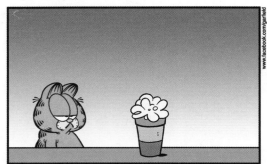

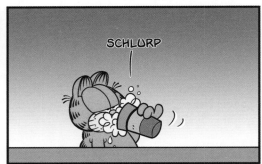

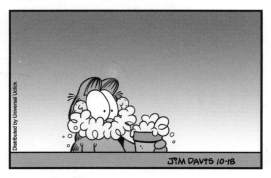

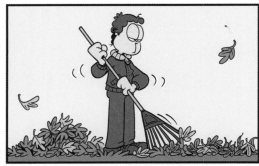

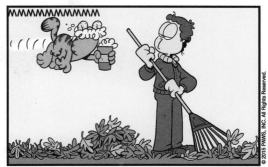

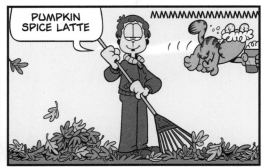

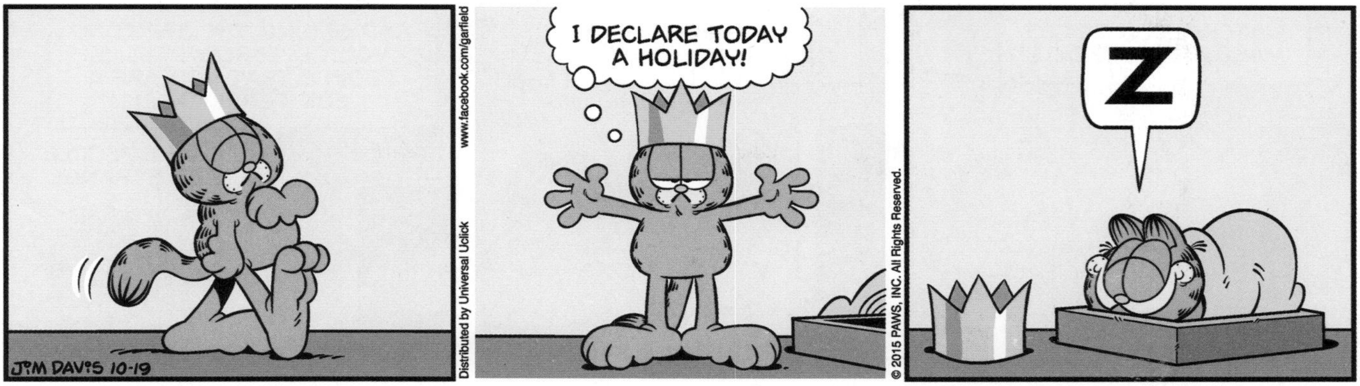
JIM DAVIS 10-19
Distributed by Universal Uclick www.facebook.com/garfield
I DECLARE TODAY A HOLIDAY!
© 2015 PAWS, INC. All Rights Reserved.
Z

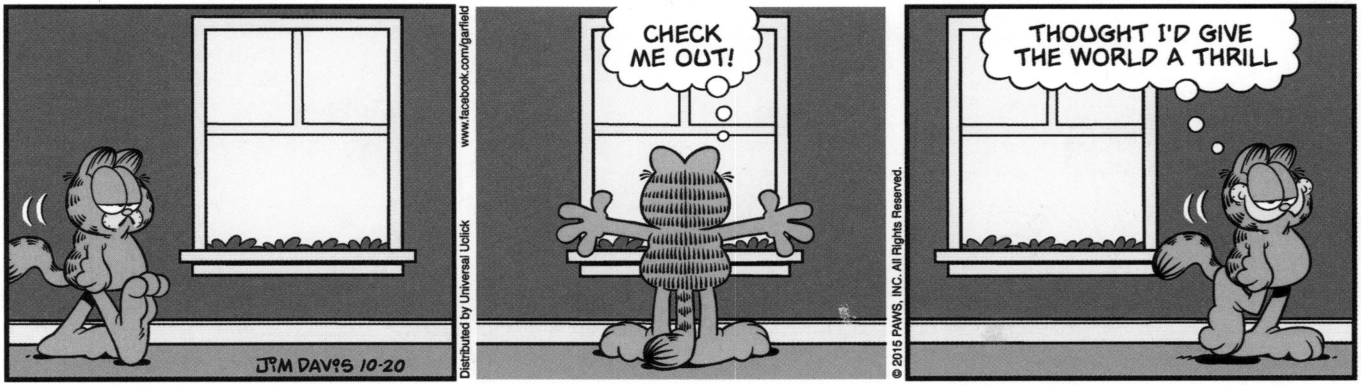
JIM DAVIS 10-20
Distributed by Universal Uclick www.facebook.com/garfield
CHECK ME OUT!
© 2015 PAWS, INC. All Rights Reserved.
THOUGHT I'D GIVE THE WORLD A THRILL

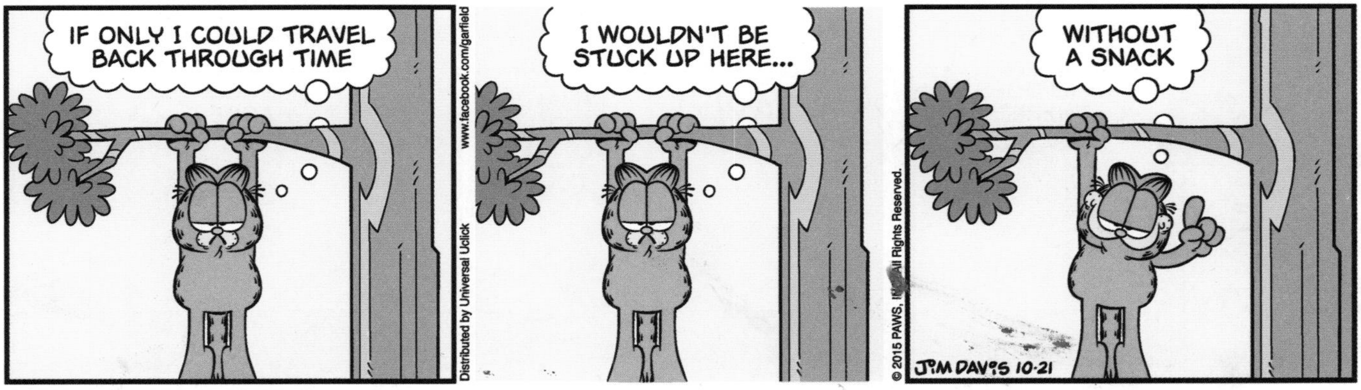
IF ONLY I COULD TRAVEL BACK THROUGH TIME
Distributed by Universal Uclick www.facebook.com/garfield
I WOULDN'T BE STUCK UP HERE...
© 2015 PAWS, INC. All Rights Reserved.
WITHOUT A SNACK
JIM DAVIS 10-21

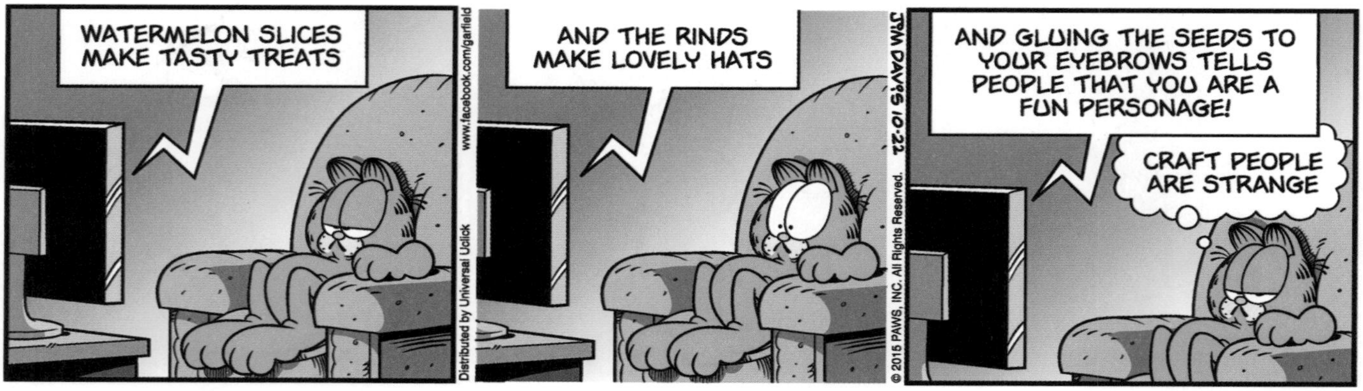
WATERMELON SLICES MAKE TASTY TREATS
www.facebook.com/garfield
Distributed by Universal Uclick
AND THE RINDS MAKE LOVELY HATS
JIM DAVIS 10-22
© 2015 PAWS, INC. All Rights Reserved.
AND GLUING THE SEEDS TO YOUR EYEBROWS TELLS PEOPLE THAT YOU ARE A FUN PERSONAGE!
CRAFT PEOPLE ARE STRANGE

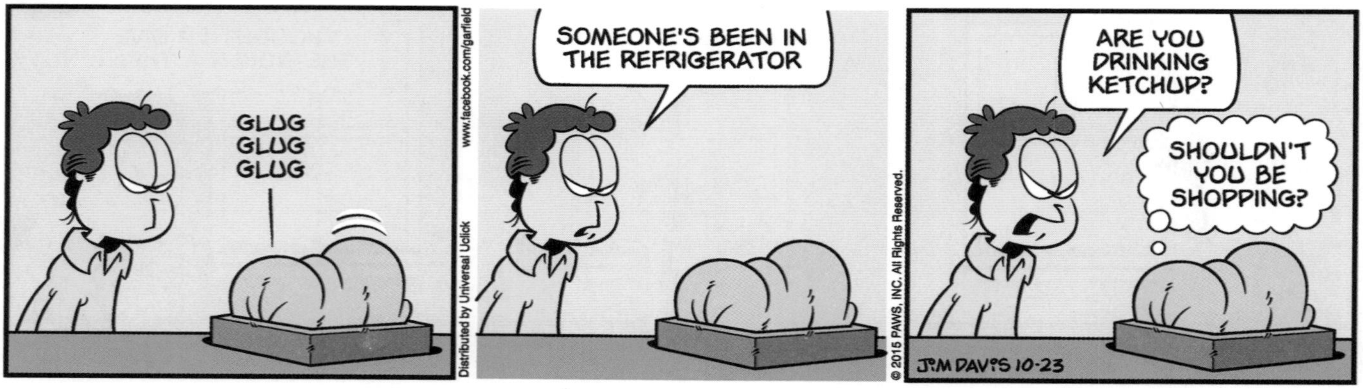
GLUG GLUG GLUG
www.facebook.com/garfield
Distributed by Universal Uclick
SOMEONE'S BEEN IN THE REFRIGERATOR
© 2015 PAWS, INC. All Rights Reserved.
ARE YOU DRINKING KETCHUP?
SHOULDN'T YOU BE SHOPPING?
JIM DAVIS 10-23

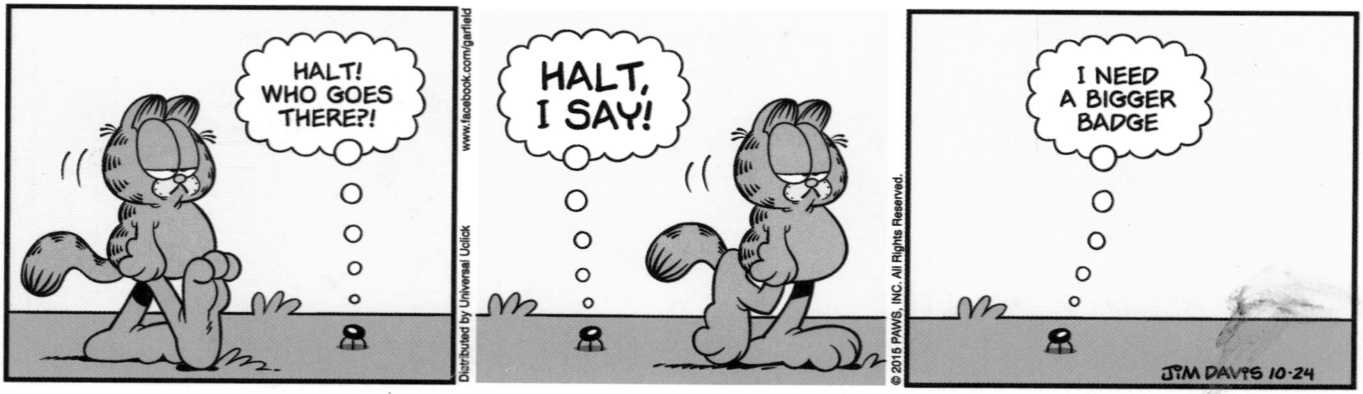
HALT! WHO GOES THERE?!
www.facebook.com/garfield
Distributed by Universal Uclick
HALT, I SAY!
© 2015 PAWS, INC. All Rights Reserved.
I NEED A BIGGER BADGE
JIM DAVIS 10-24

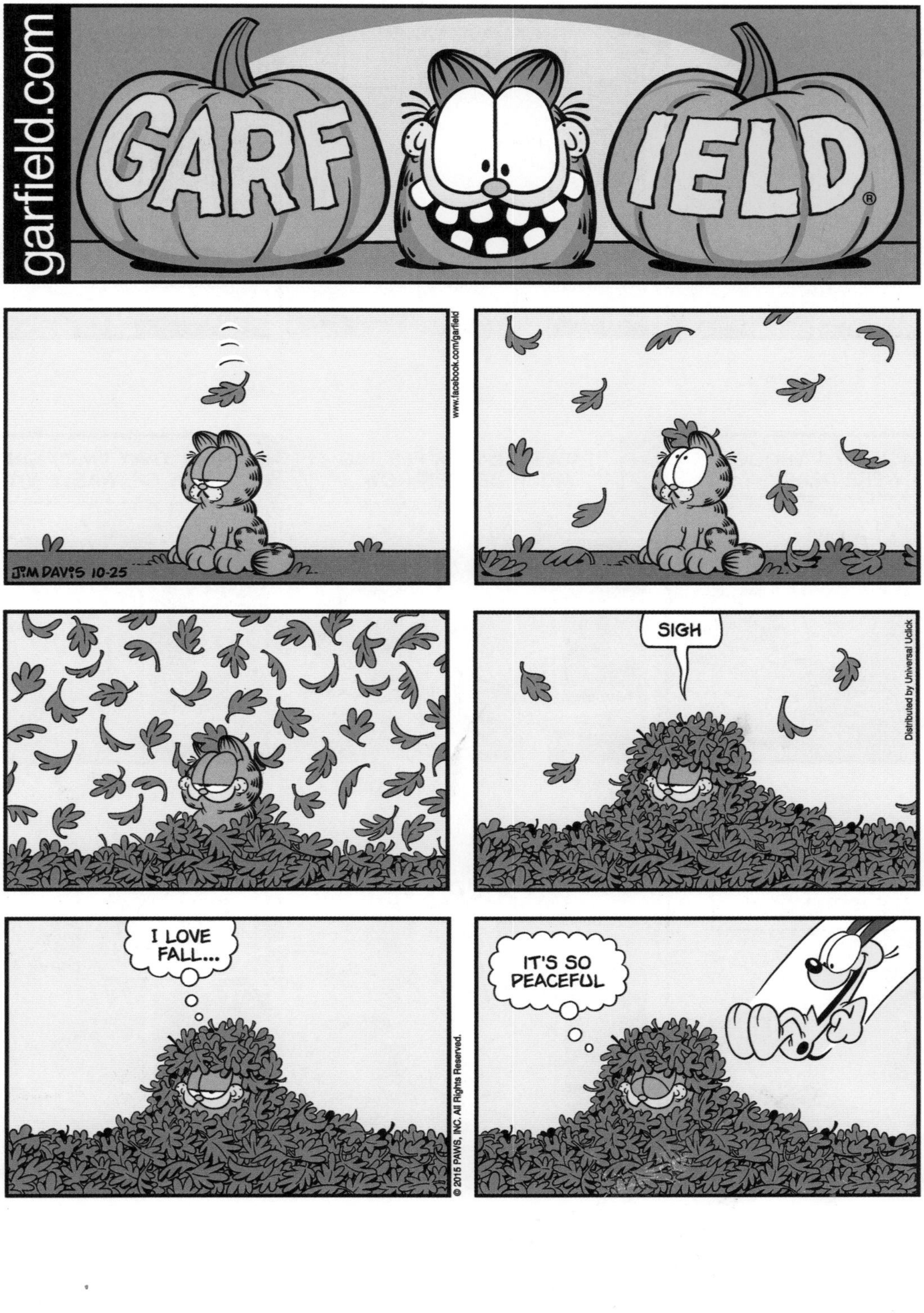
garfield.com
GARF IELD®
www.facebook.com/garfield
JIM DAVIS 10-25
SIGH
Distributed by Universal Uclick
I LOVE FALL...
© 2015 PAWS, INC. All Rights Reserved.
IT'S SO PEACEFUL

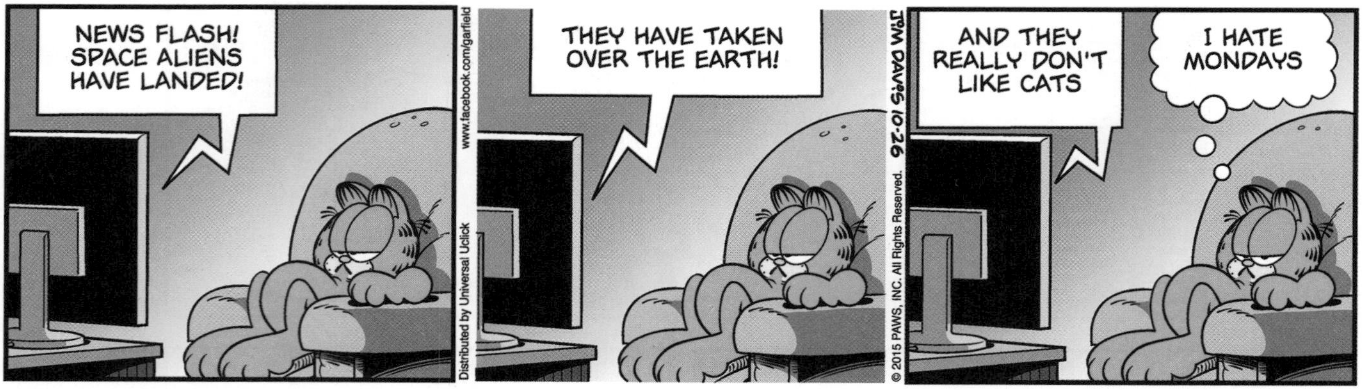
NEWS FLASH! SPACE ALIENS HAVE LANDED!
THEY HAVE TAKEN OVER THE EARTH!
AND THEY REALLY DON'T LIKE CATS
I HATE MONDAYS
Distributed by Universal Uclick www.facebook.com/garfield
© 2015 PAWS, INC. All Rights Reserved.

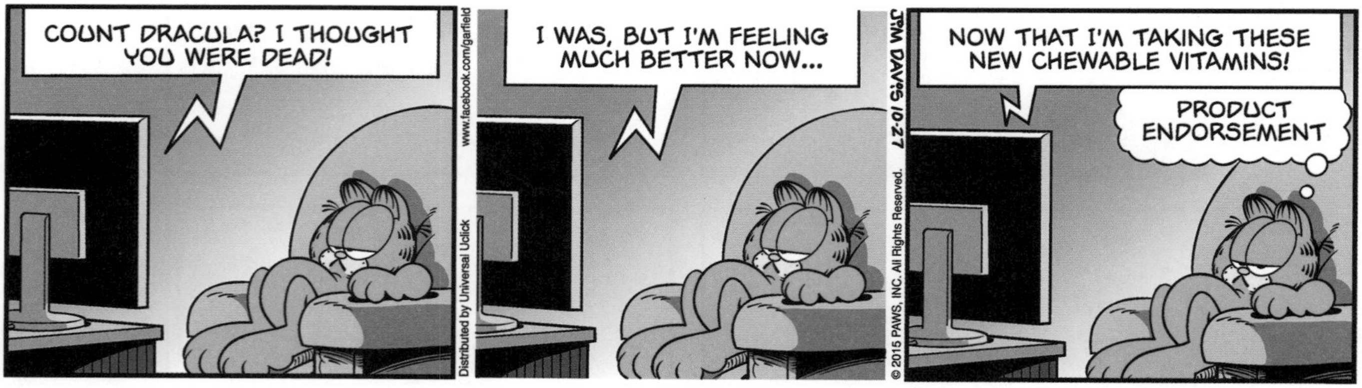
COUNT DRACULA? I THOUGHT YOU WERE DEAD!
I WAS, BUT I'M FEELING MUCH BETTER NOW...
NOW THAT I'M TAKING THESE NEW CHEWABLE VITAMINS!
PRODUCT ENDORSEMENT
Distributed by Universal Uclick www.facebook.com/garfield
© 2015 PAWS, INC. All Rights Reserved.

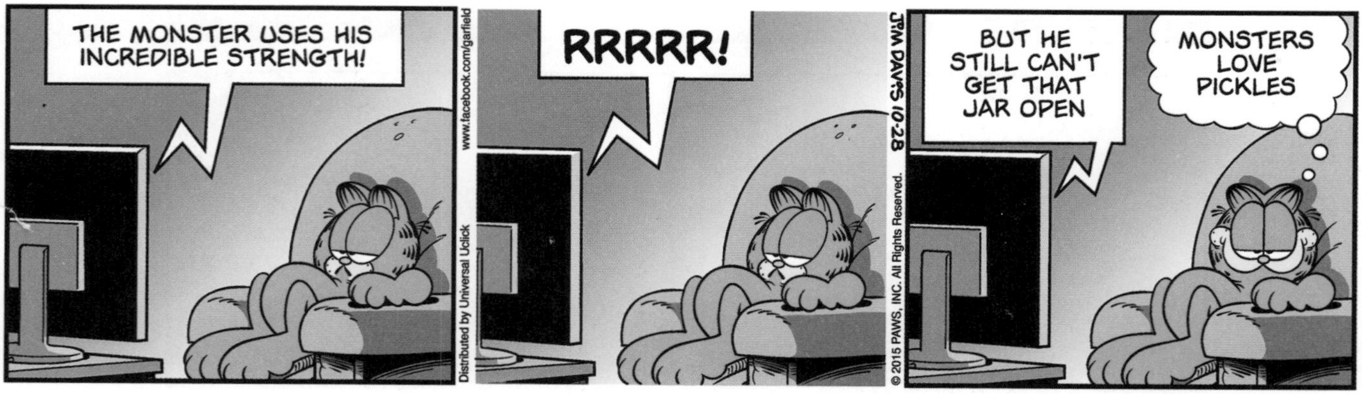
THE MONSTER USES HIS INCREDIBLE STRENGTH!
RRRRR!
BUT HE STILL CAN'T GET THAT JAR OPEN
MONSTERS LOVE PICKLES
Distributed by Universal Uclick www.facebook.com/garfield
© 2015 PAWS, INC. All Rights Reserved.

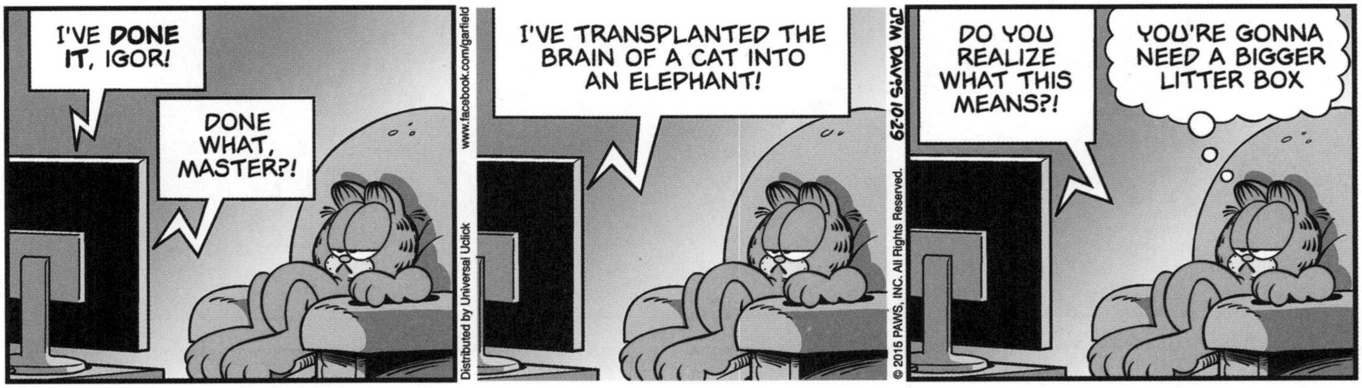
I'VE DONE IT, IGOR!
DONE WHAT, MASTER?!
I'VE TRANSPLANTED THE BRAIN OF A CAT INTO AN ELEPHANT!
JIM DAVIS 10-29
DO YOU REALIZE WHAT THIS MEANS?!
YOU'RE GONNA NEED A BIGGER LITTER BOX

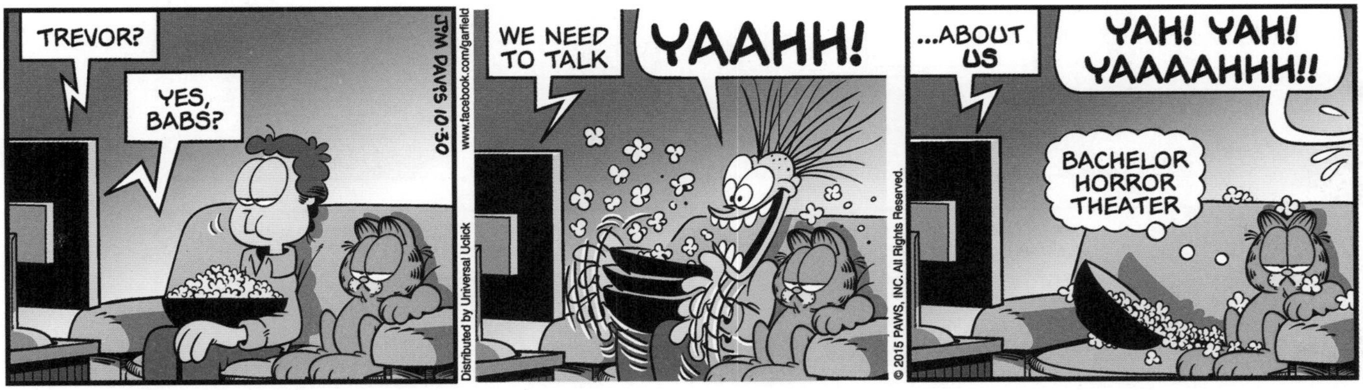
TREVOR?
YES, BABS?
JIM DAVIS 10-30
WE NEED TO TALK
YAAHH!
...ABOUT US
YAH! YAH! YAAAAHHH!!
BACHELOR HORROR THEATER

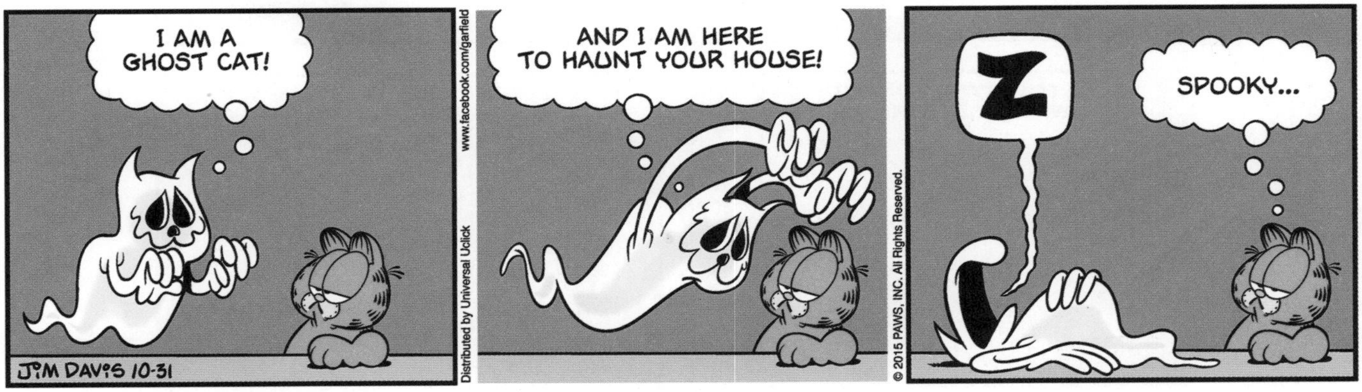
I AM A GHOST CAT!
JIM DAVIS 10-31
AND I AM HERE TO HAUNT YOUR HOUSE!
Z
SPOOKY...

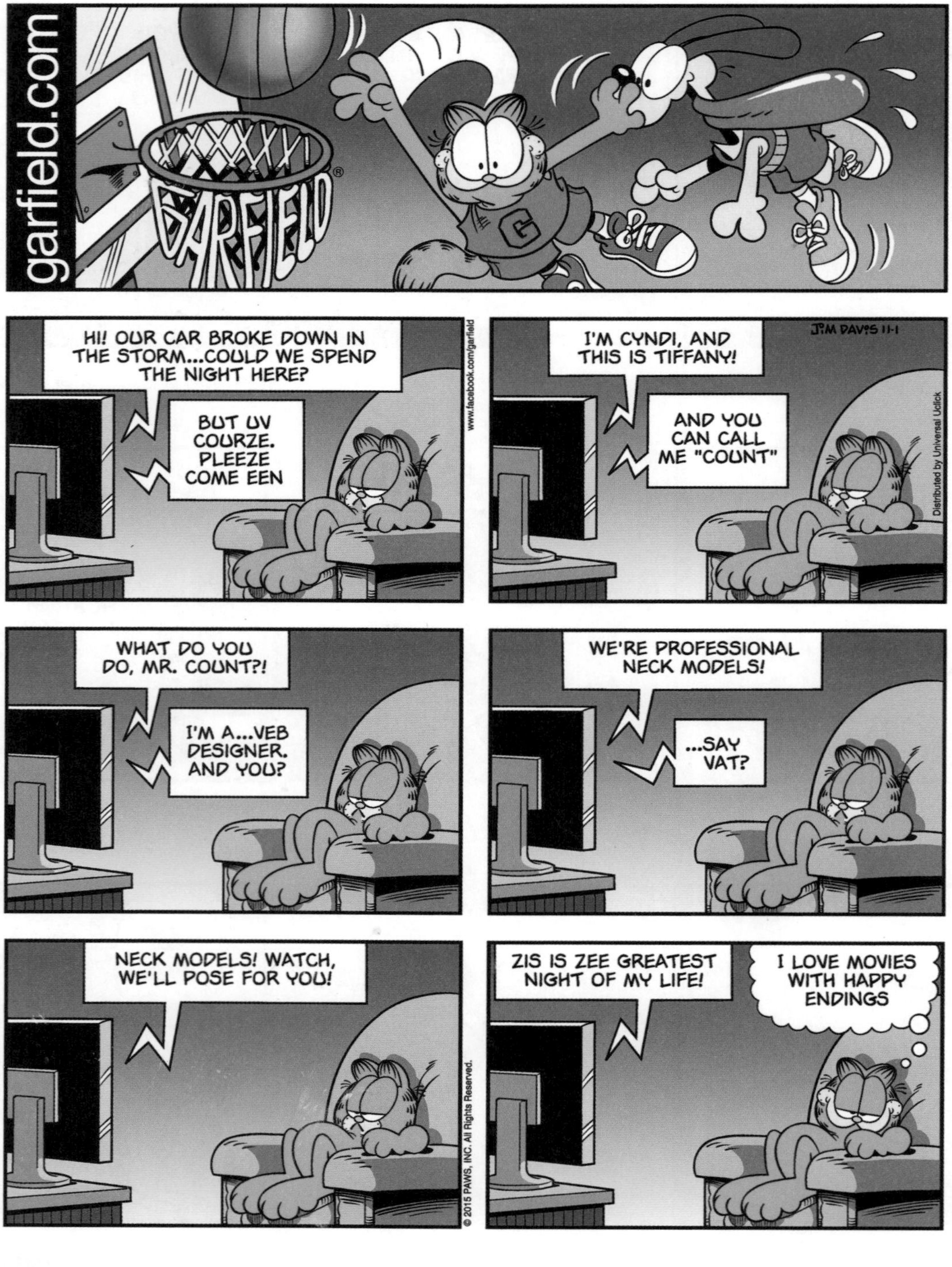
garfield.com
GARFIELD®
HI! OUR CAR BROKE DOWN IN THE STORM...COULD WE SPEND THE NIGHT HERE?
BUT UV COURZE. PLEEZE COME EEN
www.facebook.com/garfield
I'M CYNDI, AND THIS IS TIFFANY!
AND YOU CAN CALL ME "COUNT"
JIM DAVIS 11-1
Distributed by Universal Uclick
WHAT DO YOU DO, MR. COUNT?!
I'M A...VEB DESIGNER. AND YOU?
WE'RE PROFESSIONAL NECK MODELS!
...SAY VAT?
NECK MODELS! WATCH, WE'LL POSE FOR YOU!
© 2015 PAWS, INC. All Rights Reserved.
ZIS IS ZEE GREATEST NIGHT OF MY LIFE!
I LOVE MOVIES WITH HAPPY ENDINGS

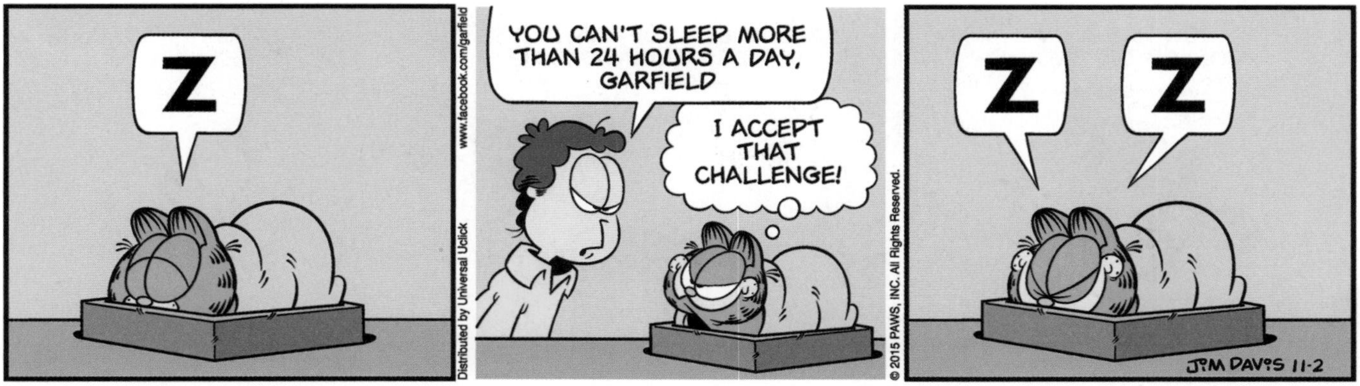
Z
YOU CAN'T SLEEP MORE THAN 24 HOURS A DAY, GARFIELD
I ACCEPT THAT CHALLENGE!
Z
Z
Distributed by Universal Uclick www.facebook.com/garfield
© 2015 PAWS, INC. All Rights Reserved.
JIM DAVIS 11-2

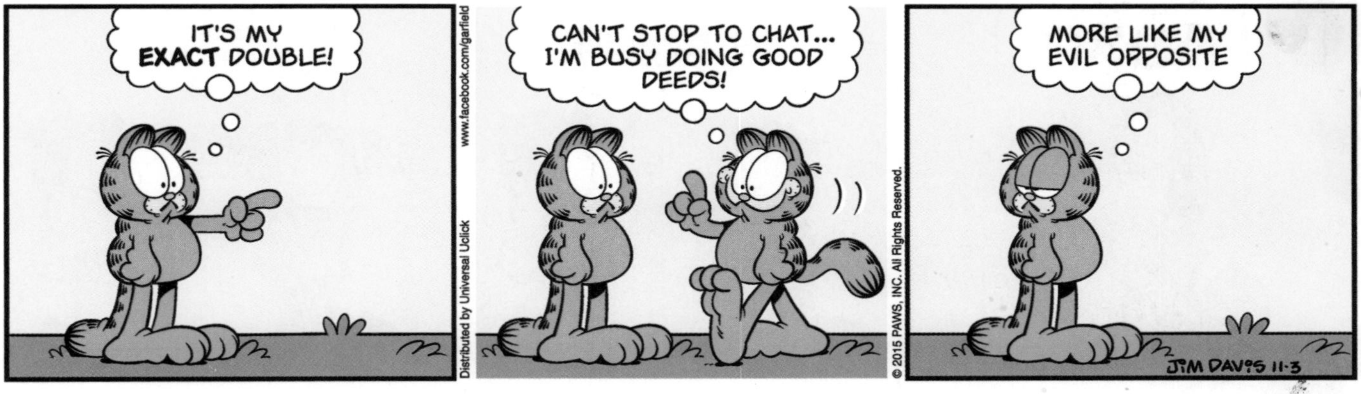
IT'S MY EXACT DOUBLE!
CAN'T STOP TO CHAT... I'M BUSY DOING GOOD DEEDS!
MORE LIKE MY EVIL OPPOSITE
Distributed by Universal Uclick www.facebook.com/garfield
© 2015 PAWS, INC. All Rights Reserved.
JIM DAVIS 11-3

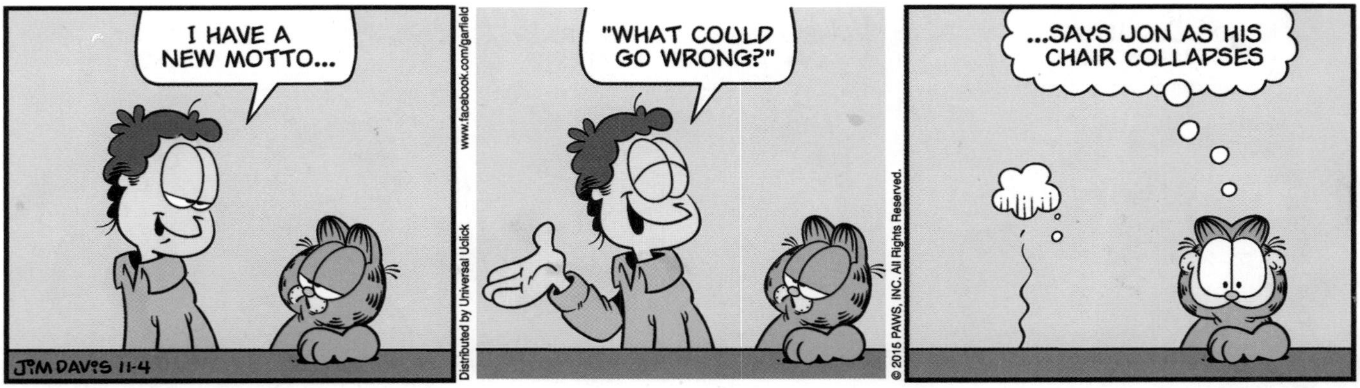
I HAVE A NEW MOTTO...
"WHAT COULD GO WRONG?"
...SAYS JON AS HIS CHAIR COLLAPSES
Distributed by Universal Uclick www.facebook.com/garfield
© 2015 PAWS, INC. All Rights Reserved.
JIM DAVIS 11-4

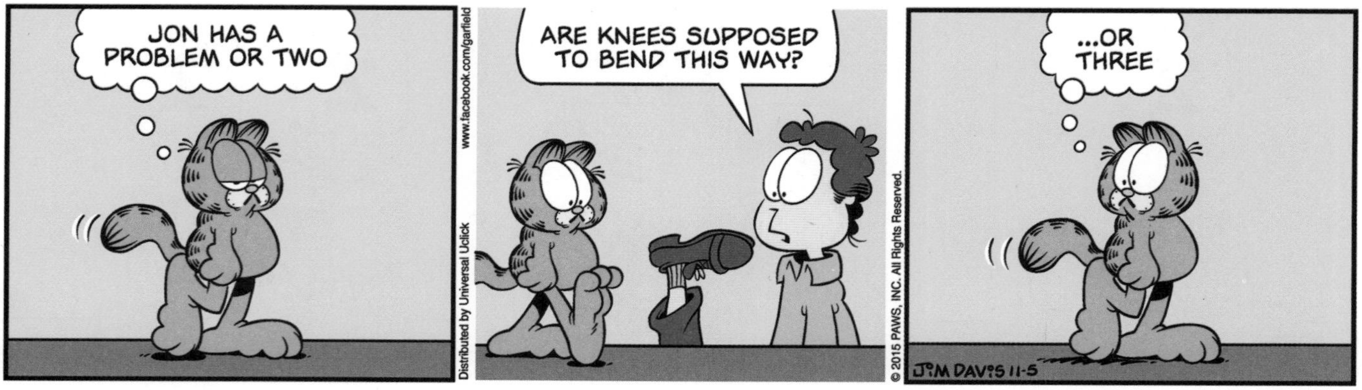
JON HAS A PROBLEM OR TWO
ARE KNEES SUPPOSED TO BEND THIS WAY?
...OR THREE
JIM DAVIS 11-5
Distributed by Universal Uclick
www.facebook.com/garfield
© 2015 PAWS, INC. All Rights Reserved.

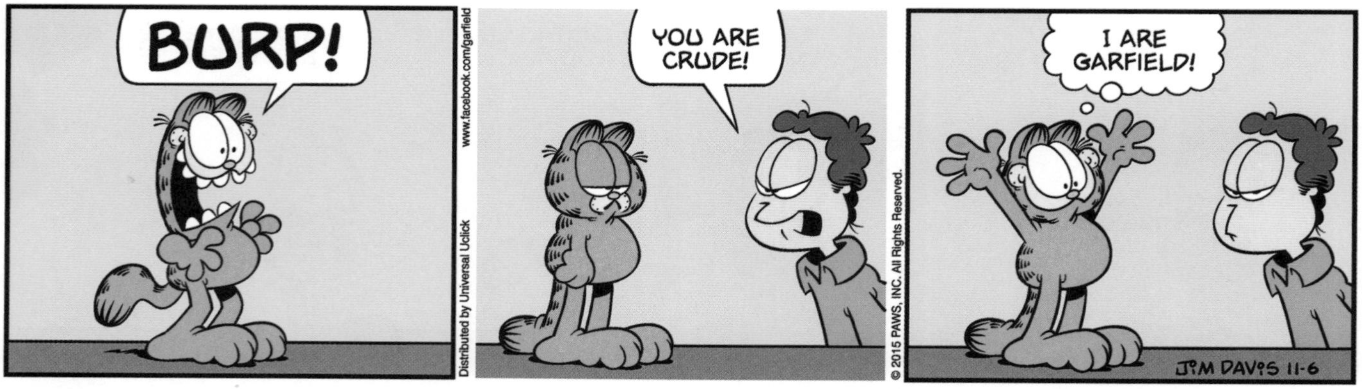
BURP!
YOU ARE CRUDE!
I ARE GARFIELD!
JIM DAVIS 11-6
Distributed by Universal Uclick
www.facebook.com/garfield
© 2015 PAWS, INC. All Rights Reserved.

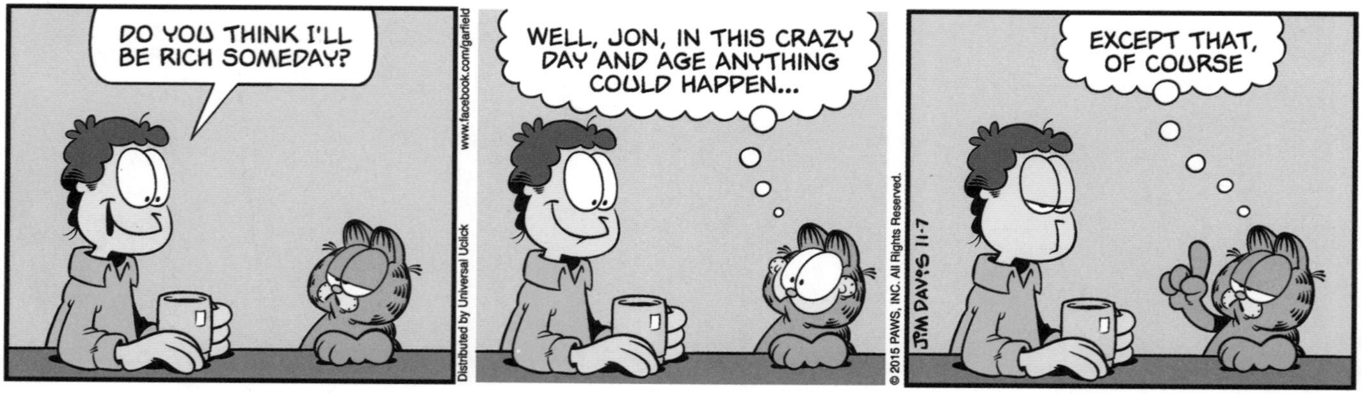
DO YOU THINK I'LL BE RICH SOMEDAY?
WELL, JON, IN THIS CRAZY DAY AND AGE ANYTHING COULD HAPPEN...
EXCEPT THAT, OF COURSE
JIM DAVIS 11-7
Distributed by Universal Uclick
www.facebook.com/garfield
© 2015 PAWS, INC. All Rights Reserved.

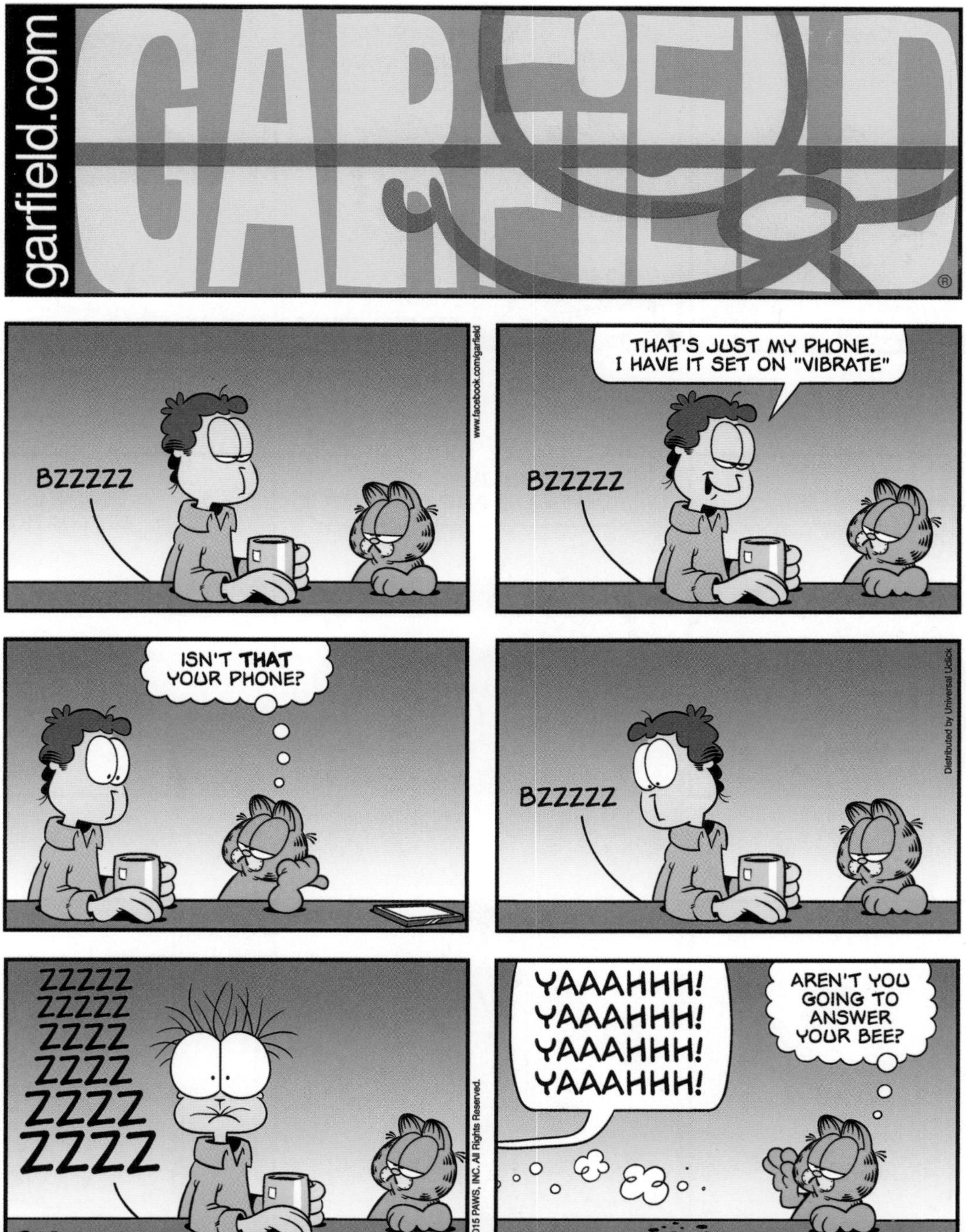
garfield.com
GARFIELD
www.facebook.com/garfield
BZZZZZ
BZZZZZ
THAT'S JUST MY PHONE. I HAVE IT SET ON "VIBRATE"
ISN'T **THAT** YOUR PHONE?
BZZZZZ
Distributed by Universal Uclick
ZZZZZ ZZZZZ ZZZZ ZZZZ ZZZZ ZZZZ
JIM DAVIS 11-8
© 2015 PAWS, INC. All Rights Reserved.
YAAAHHH! YAAAHHH! YAAAHHH! YAAAHHH!
AREN'T YOU GOING TO ANSWER YOUR BEE?

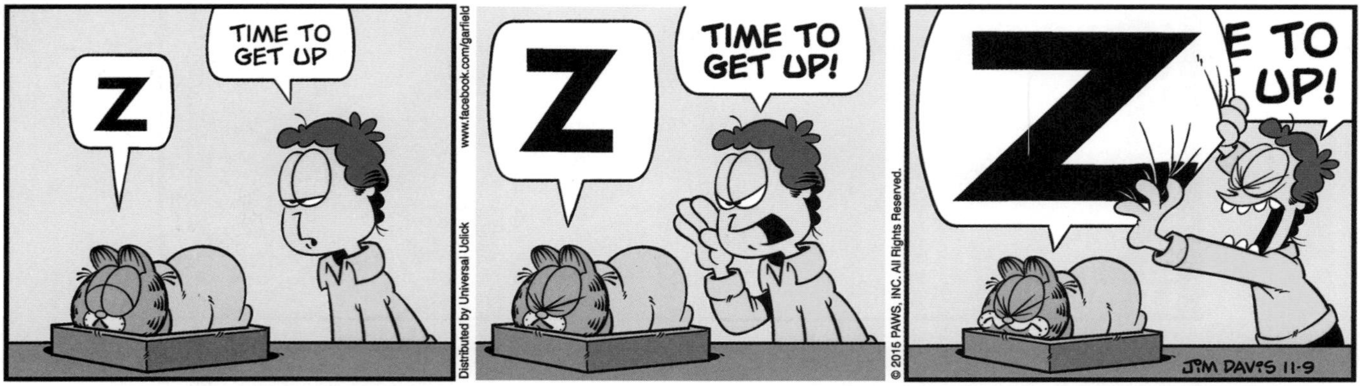
Z
TIME TO GET UP
Z
TIME TO GET UP!
Z
E TO
UP!
JIM DAVIS 11-9
Distributed by Universal Uclick www.facebook.com/garfield
© 2015 PAWS, INC. All Rights Reserved.

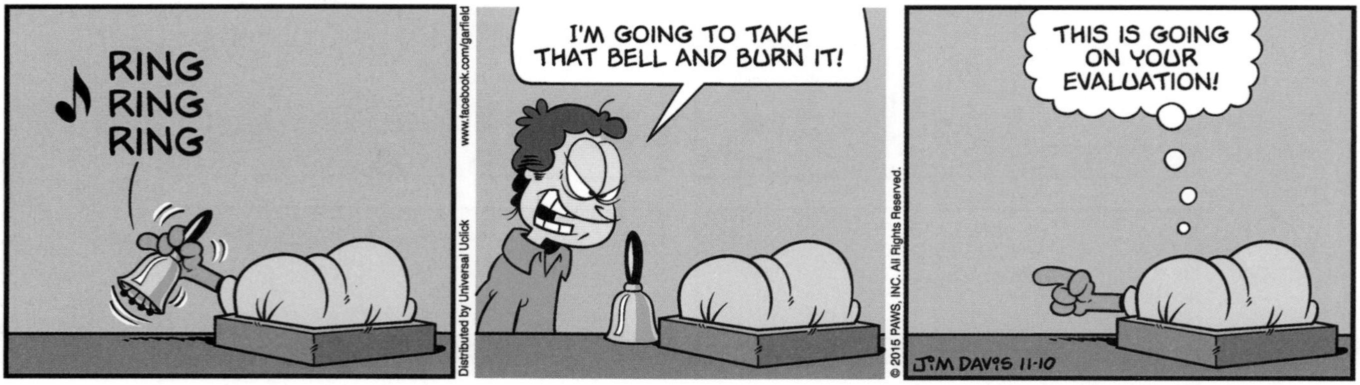
RING
RING
RING
I'M GOING TO TAKE THAT BELL AND BURN IT!
THIS IS GOING ON YOUR EVALUATION!
JIM DAVIS 11-10
Distributed by Universal Uclick www.facebook.com/garfield
© 2015 PAWS, INC. All Rights Reserved.

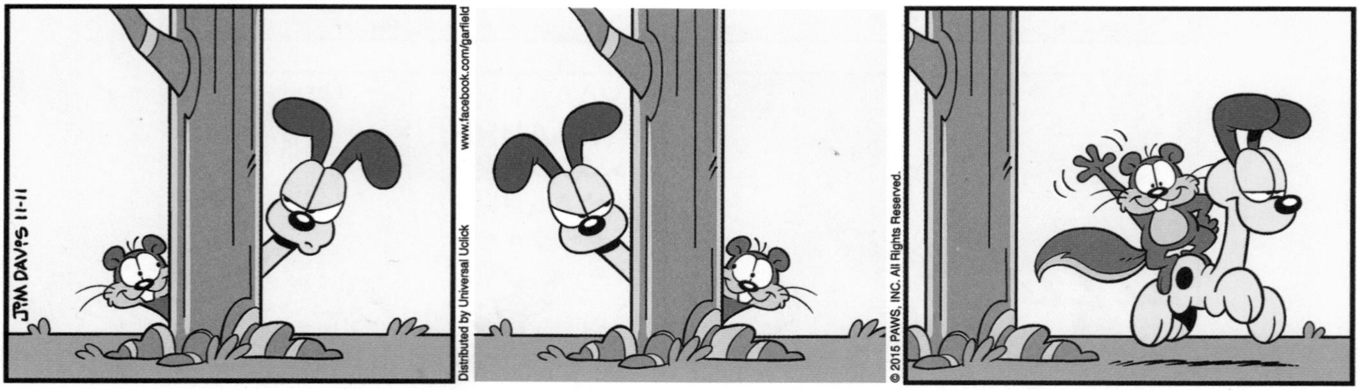
JIM DAVIS 11-11
Distributed by Universal Uclick www.facebook.com/garfield
© 2015 PAWS, INC. All Rights Reserved.

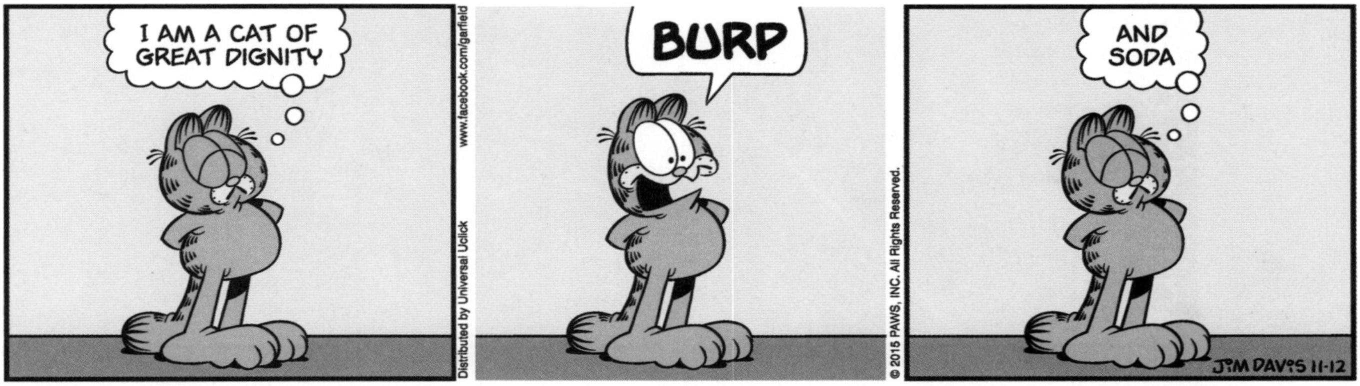
I AM A CAT OF GREAT DIGNITY
BURP
AND SODA
JIM DAVIS 11-12
Distributed by Universal Uclick
www.facebook.com/garfield
© 2015 PAWS, INC. All Rights Reserved.

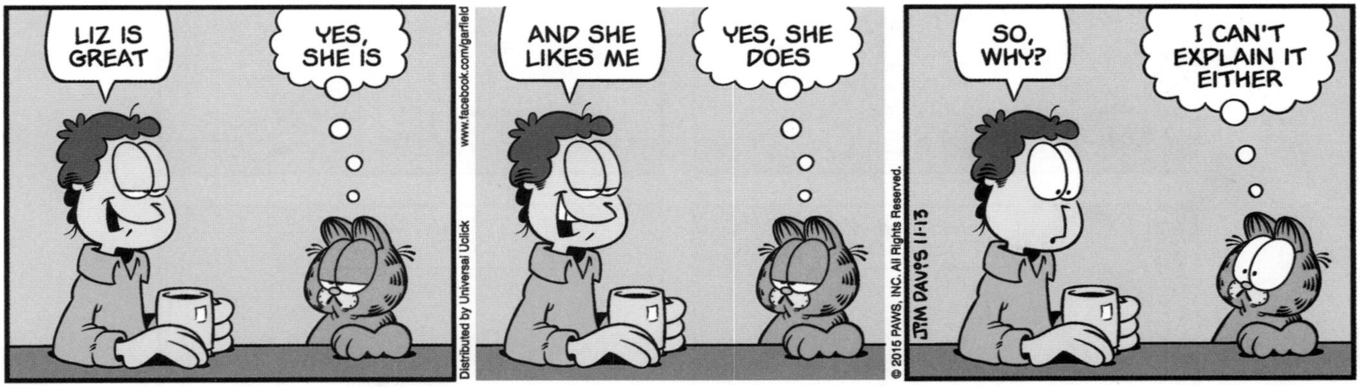
LIZ IS GREAT
YES, SHE IS
AND SHE LIKES ME
YES, SHE DOES
SO, WHY?
I CAN'T EXPLAIN IT EITHER
JIM DAVIS 11-13
Distributed by Universal Uclick
www.facebook.com/garfield
© 2015 PAWS, INC. All Rights Reserved.

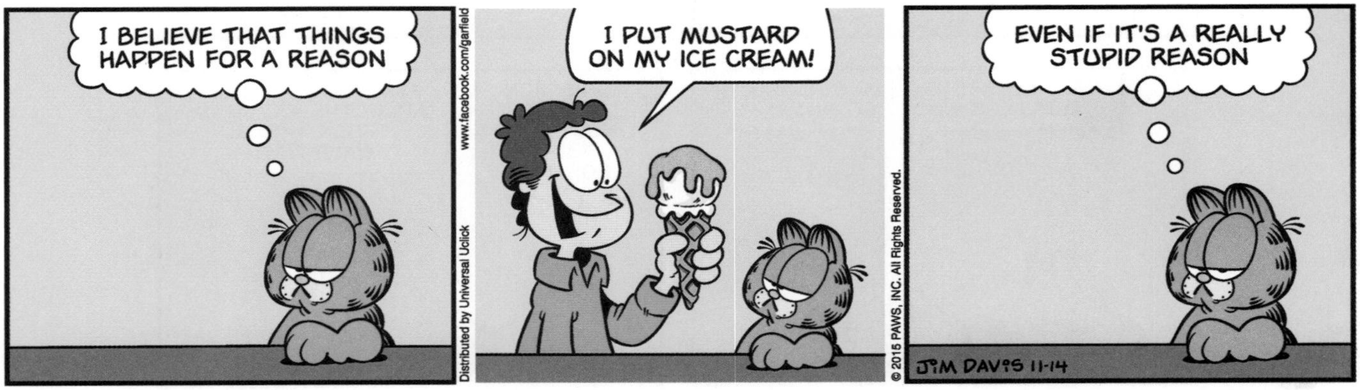
I BELIEVE THAT THINGS HAPPEN FOR A REASON
I PUT MUSTARD ON MY ICE CREAM!
EVEN IF IT'S A REALLY STUPID REASON
JIM DAVIS 11-14
Distributed by Universal Uclick
www.facebook.com/garfield
© 2015 PAWS, INC. All Rights Reserved.

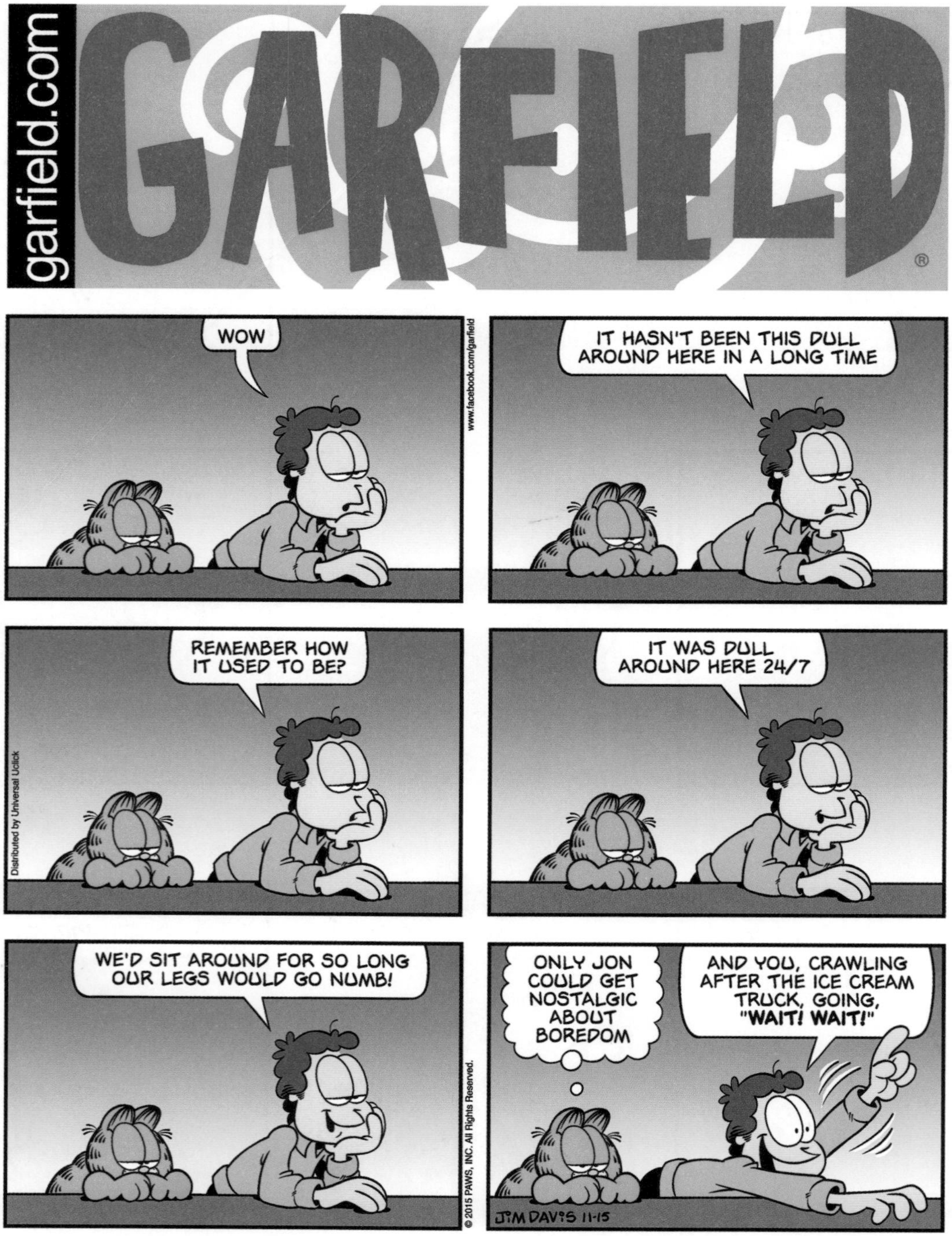
garfield.com
GARFIELD
www.facebook.com/garfield
WOW
IT HASN'T BEEN THIS DULL AROUND HERE IN A LONG TIME
REMEMBER HOW IT USED TO BE?
IT WAS DULL AROUND HERE 24/7
Distributed by Universal Uclick
WE'D SIT AROUND FOR SO LONG OUR LEGS WOULD GO NUMB!
AND YOU, CRAWLING AFTER THE ICE CREAM TRUCK, GOING, "WAIT! WAIT!"
ONLY JON COULD GET NOSTALGIC ABOUT BOREDOM
© 2015 PAWS, INC. All Rights Reserved.
JIM DAVIS 11-15

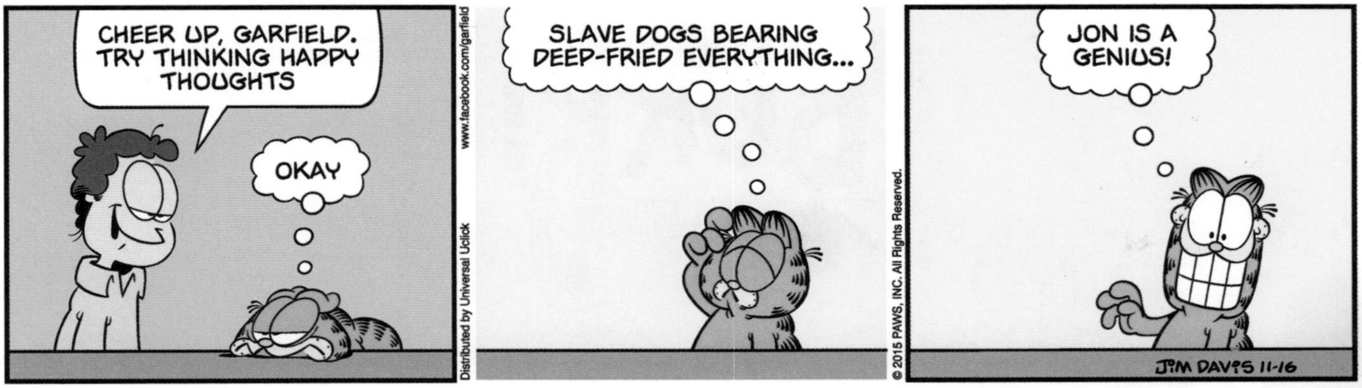
CHEER UP, GARFIELD. TRY THINKING HAPPY THOUGHTS
OKAY
Distributed by Universal Uclick www.facebook.com/garfield
SLAVE DOGS BEARING DEEP-FRIED EVERYTHING...
© 2015 PAWS, INC. All Rights Reserved.
JON IS A GENIUS!
JIM DAVIS 11-16

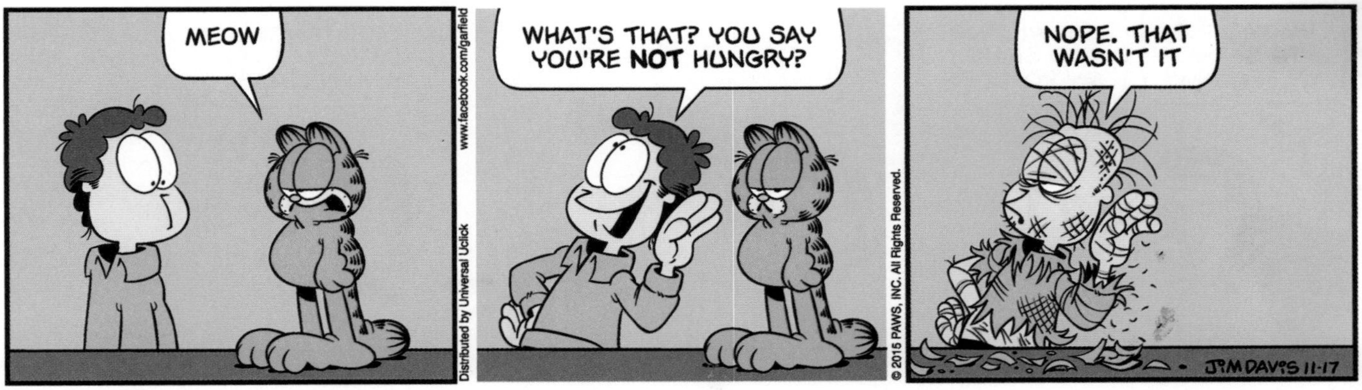
MEOW
Distributed by Universal Uclick www.facebook.com/garfield
WHAT'S THAT? YOU SAY YOU'RE **NOT** HUNGRY?
© 2015 PAWS, INC. All Rights Reserved.
NOPE. THAT WASN'T IT
JIM DAVIS 11-17

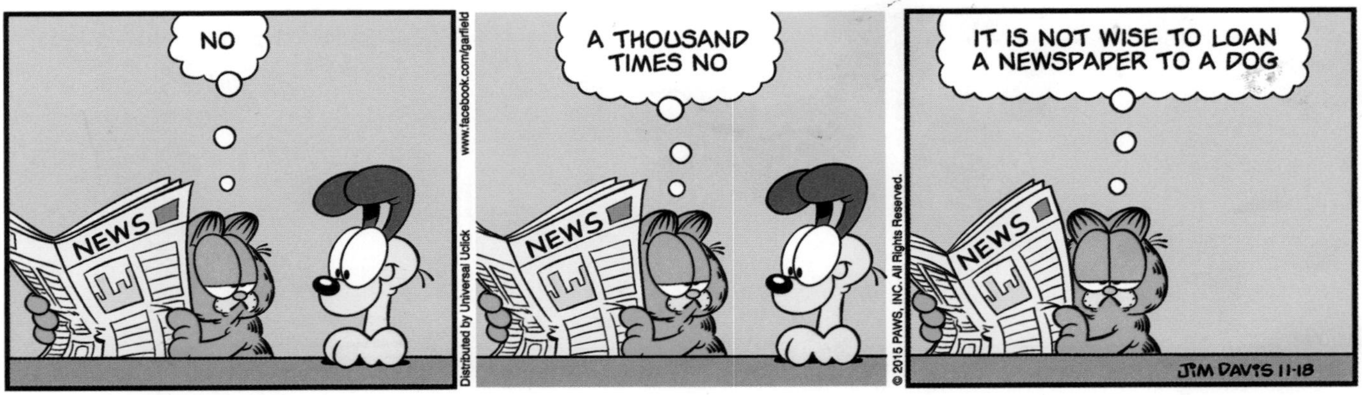
NO
NEWS
Distributed by Universal Uclick www.facebook.com/garfield
A THOUSAND TIMES NO
NEWS
© 2015 PAWS, INC. All Rights Reserved.
IT IS NOT WISE TO LOAN A NEWSPAPER TO A DOG
NEWS
JIM DAVIS 11-18

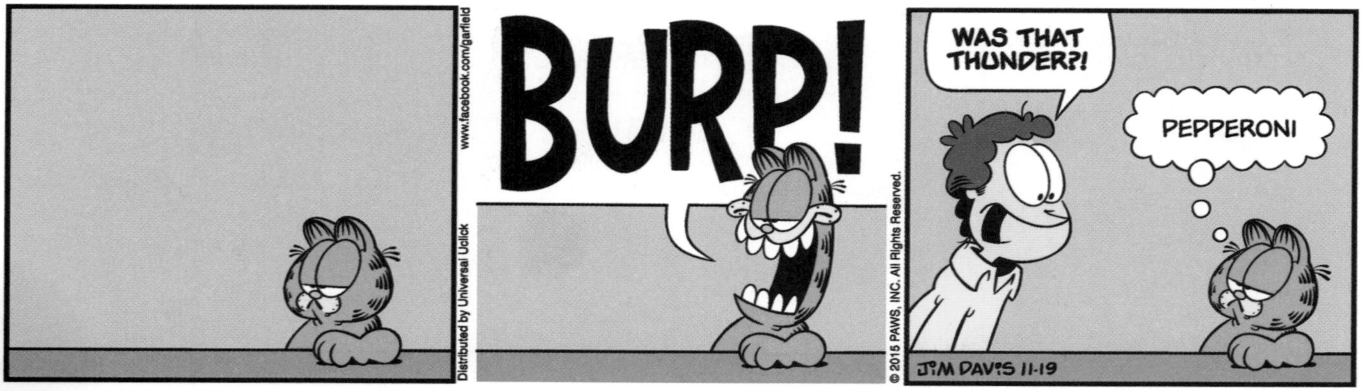
Distributed by Universal Uclick
www.facebook.com/garfield
BURP!
WAS THAT THUNDER?!
PEPPERONI
© 2015 PAWS, INC. All Rights Reserved.
JIM DAVIS 11-19

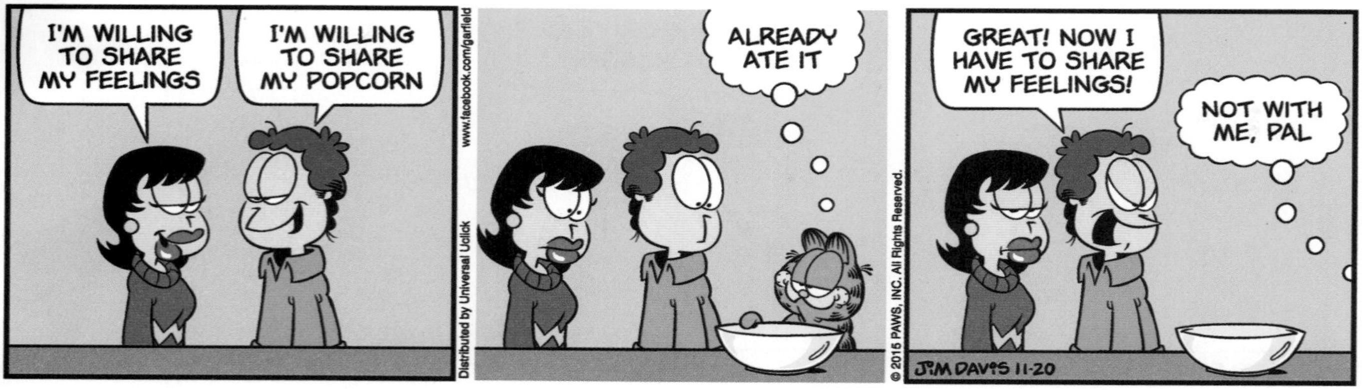
I'M WILLING TO SHARE MY FEELINGS
I'M WILLING TO SHARE MY POPCORN
Distributed by Universal Uclick
www.facebook.com/garfield
ALREADY ATE IT
GREAT! NOW I HAVE TO SHARE MY FEELINGS!
NOT WITH ME, PAL
© 2015 PAWS, INC. All Rights Reserved.
JIM DAVIS 11-20

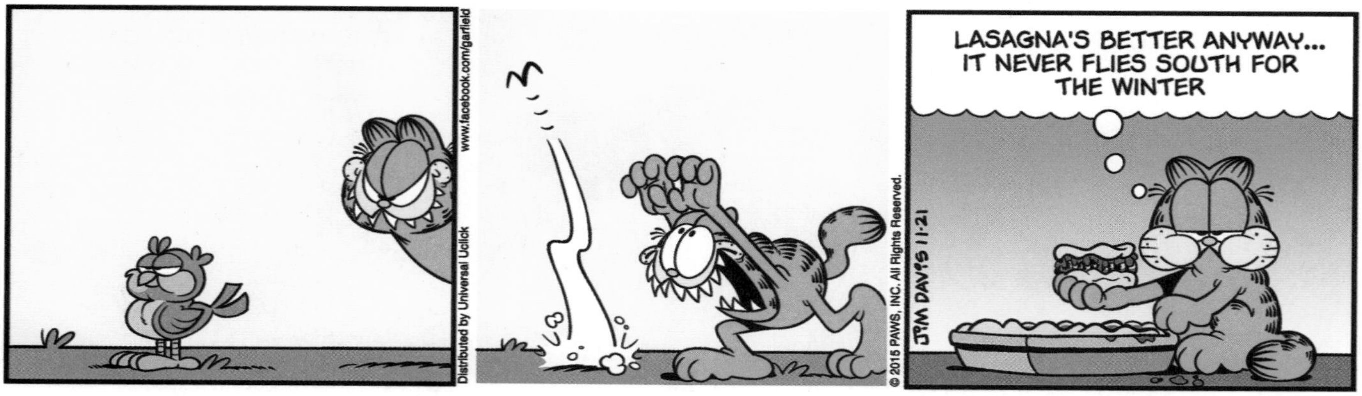
Distributed by Universal Uclick
www.facebook.com/garfield
LASAGNA'S BETTER ANYWAY... IT NEVER FLIES SOUTH FOR THE WINTER
© 2015 PAWS, INC. All Rights Reserved.
JIM DAVIS 11-21

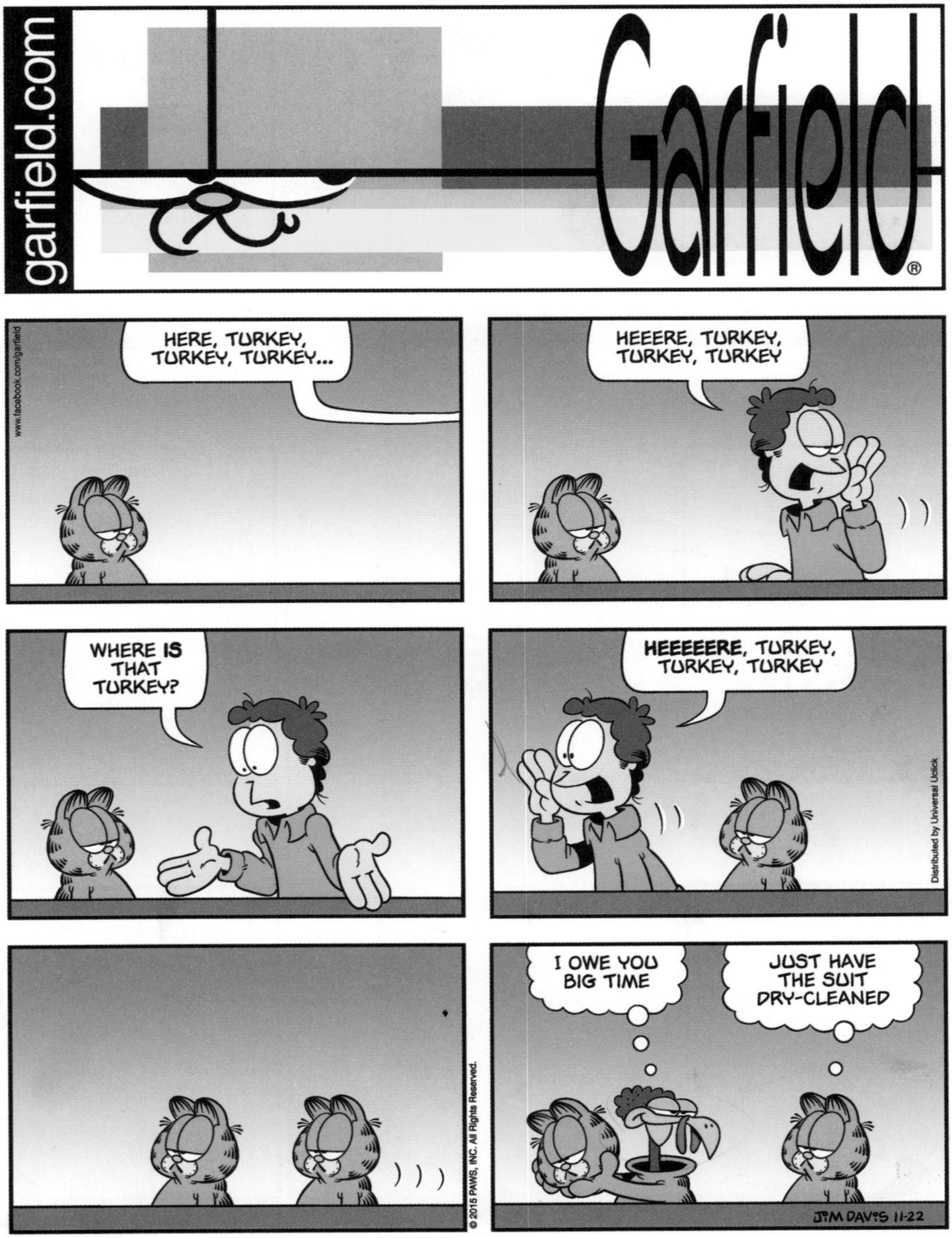
garfield.com
Garfield®
www.facebook.com/garfield
HERE, TURKEY, TURKEY, TURKEY...
HEEERE, TURKEY, TURKEY, TURKEY
WHERE IS THAT TURKEY?
HEEEEERE, TURKEY, TURKEY, TURKEY
Distributed by Universal Uclick
© 2015 PAWS, INC. All Rights Reserved.
I OWE YOU BIG TIME
JUST HAVE THE SUIT DRY-CLEANED
JIM DAVIS 11-22

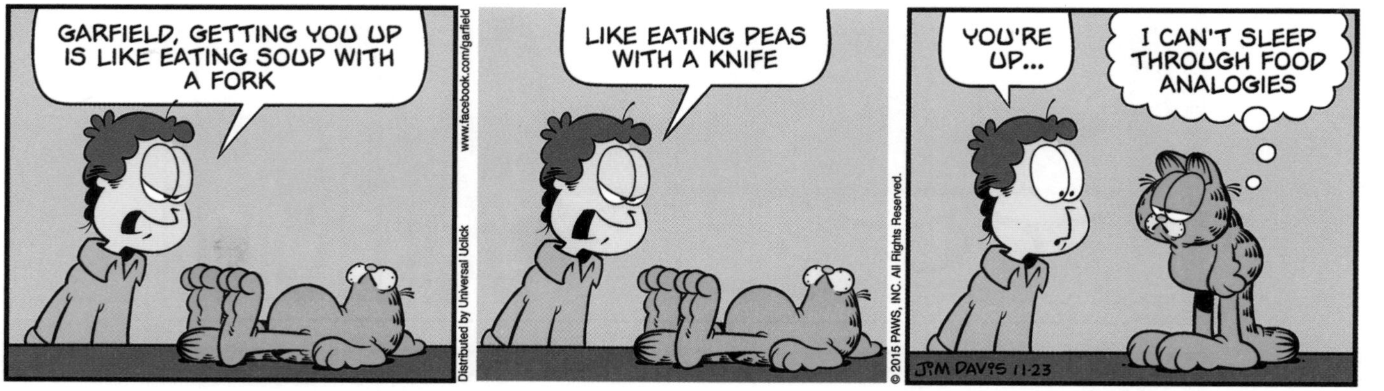
GARFIELD, GETTING YOU UP IS LIKE EATING SOUP WITH A FORK
Distributed by Universal Uclick www.facebook.com/garfield
LIKE EATING PEAS WITH A KNIFE
© 2015 PAWS, INC. All Rights Reserved.
YOU'RE UP...
I CAN'T SLEEP THROUGH FOOD ANALOGIES
JIM DAVIS 11-23

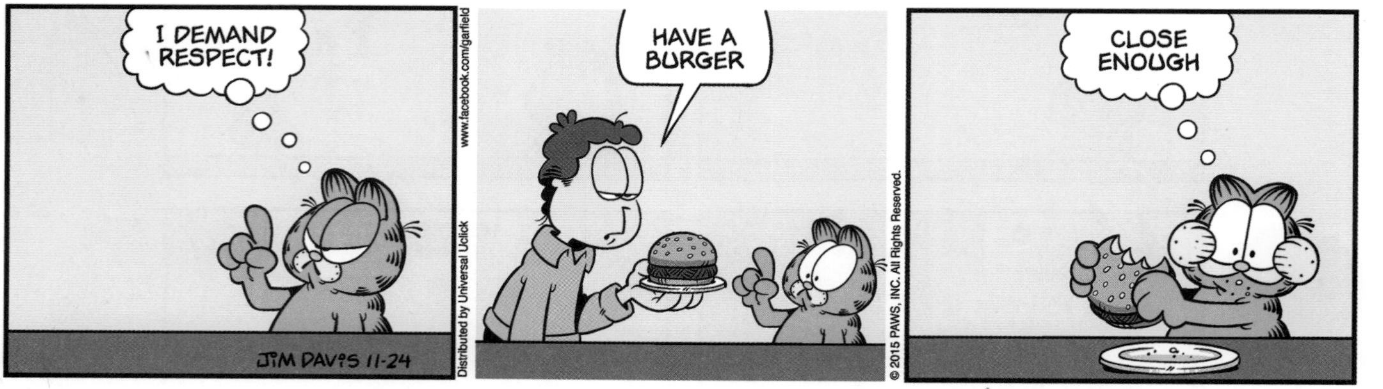
I DEMAND RESPECT!
JIM DAVIS 11-24
Distributed by Universal Uclick www.facebook.com/garfield
HAVE A BURGER
© 2015 PAWS, INC. All Rights Reserved.
CLOSE ENOUGH

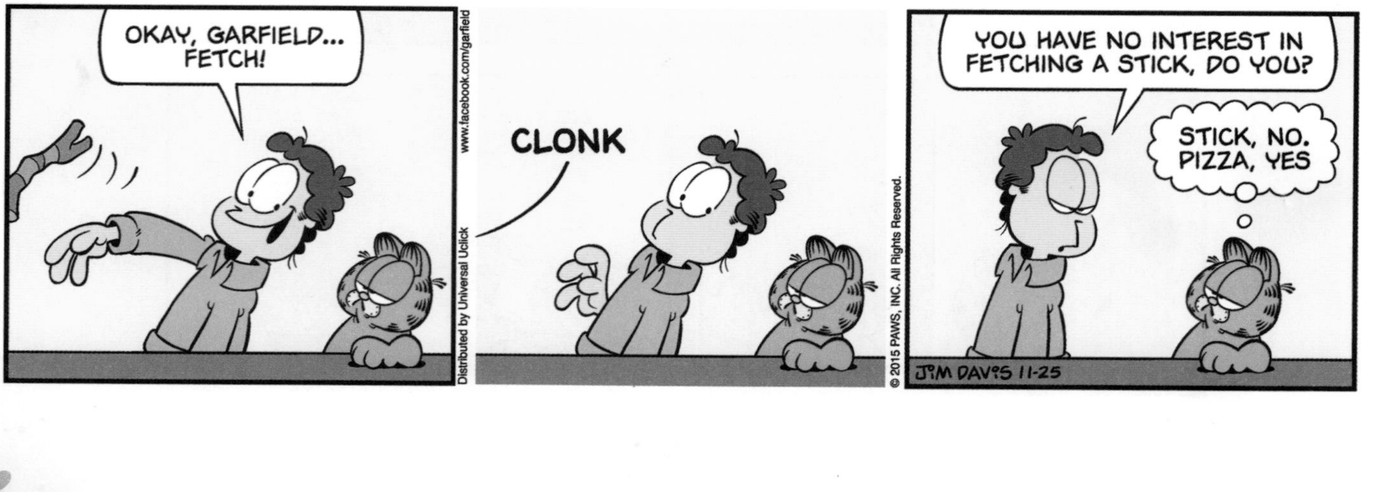
OKAY, GARFIELD... FETCH!
Distributed by Universal Uclick www.facebook.com/garfield
CLONK
© 2015 PAWS, INC. All Rights Reserved.
YOU HAVE NO INTEREST IN FETCHING A STICK, DO YOU?
STICK, NO. PIZZA, YES
JIM DAVIS 11-25

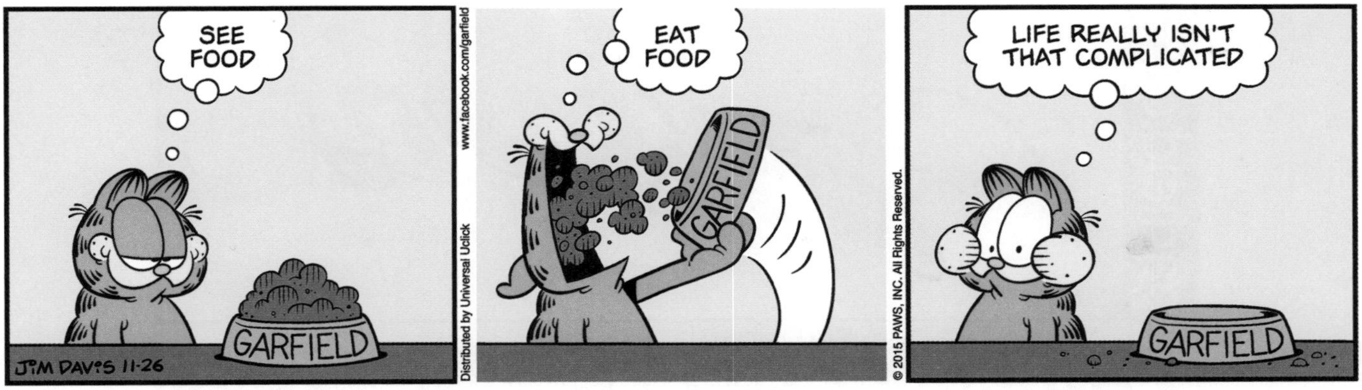
SEE FOOD
GARFIELD
JIM DAVIS 11-26
Distributed by Universal Uclick
www.facebook.com/garfield
EAT FOOD
GARFIELD
© 2015 PAWS, INC. All Rights Reserved.
LIFE REALLY ISN'T THAT COMPLICATED
GARFIELD

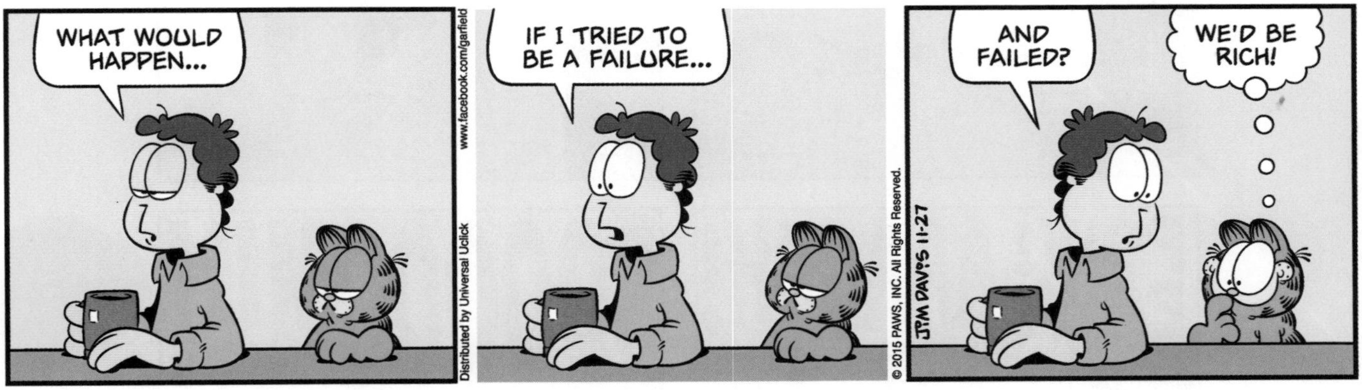
WHAT WOULD HAPPEN...
Distributed by Universal Uclick
www.facebook.com/garfield
IF I TRIED TO BE A FAILURE...
© 2015 PAWS, INC. All Rights Reserved.
JIM DAVIS 11-27
AND FAILED?
WE'D BE RICH!

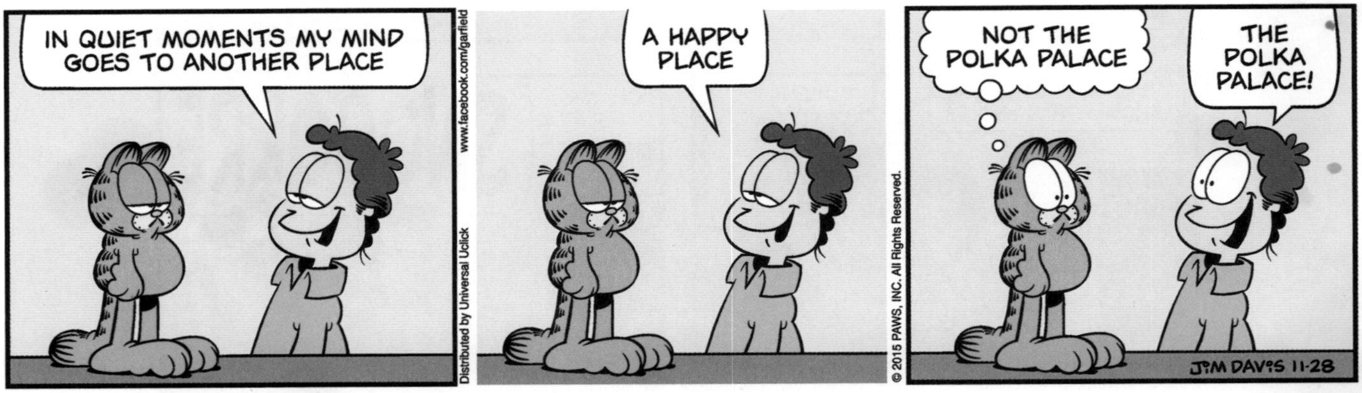
IN QUIET MOMENTS MY MIND GOES TO ANOTHER PLACE
Distributed by Universal Uclick
www.facebook.com/garfield
A HAPPY PLACE
© 2015 PAWS, INC. All Rights Reserved.
NOT THE POLKA PALACE
THE POLKA PALACE!
JIM DAVIS 11-28

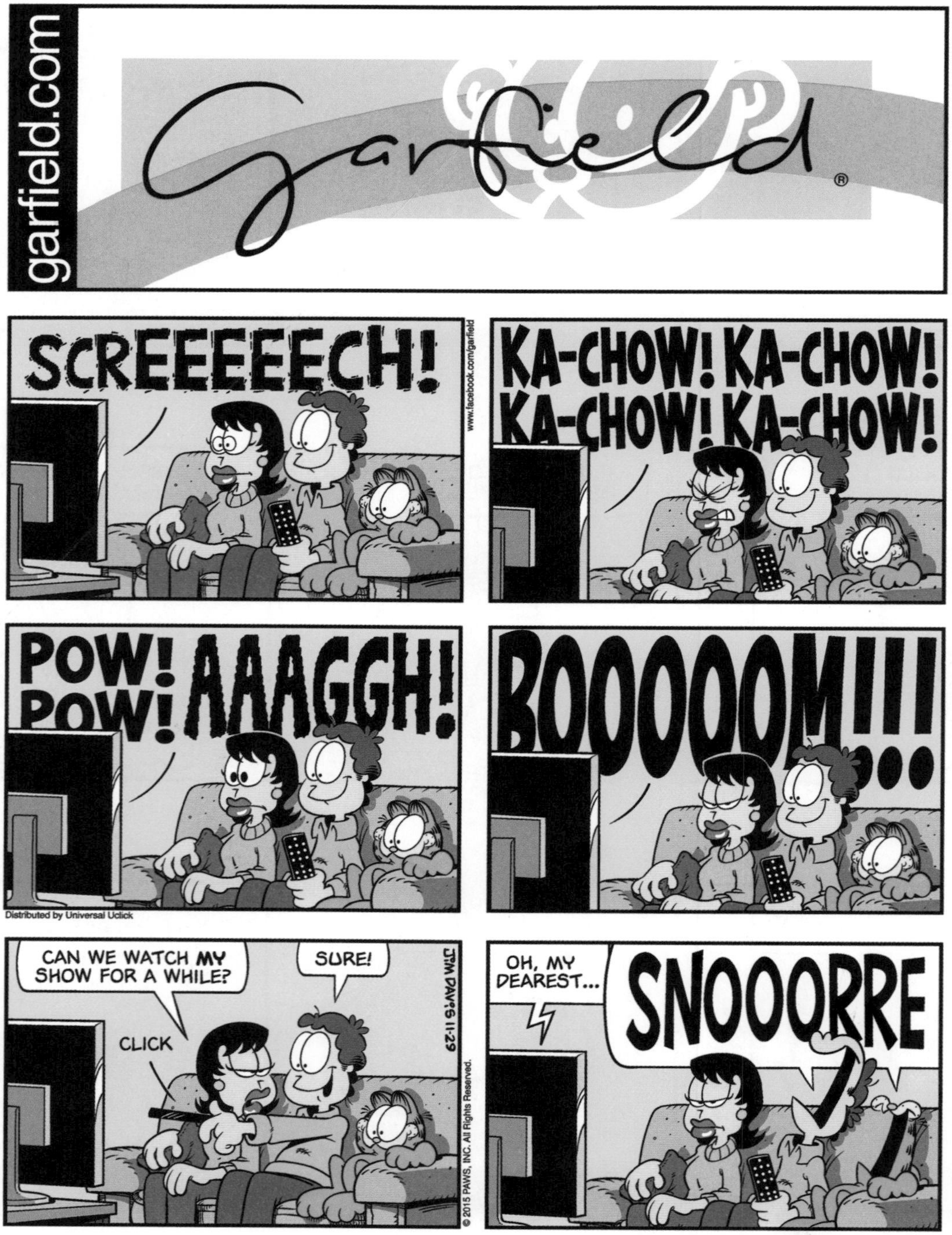
garfield.com
Garfield®
SCREEEEEECH!
www.facebook.com/garfield
KA-CHOW! KA-CHOW!
KA-CHOW! KA-CHOW!
POW! POW!
AAAGGH!
BOOOOOM!!!...
Distributed by Universal Uclick
CAN WE WATCH MY SHOW FOR A WHILE?
SURE!
CLICK
JIM DAVIS 11-29
© 2015 PAWS, INC. All Rights Reserved.
OH, MY DEAREST...
SNOOORRE

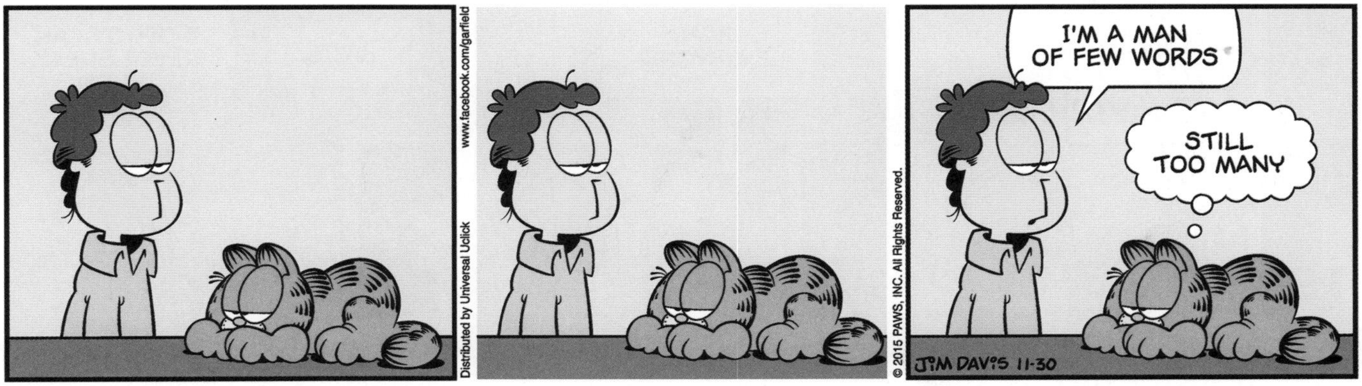
Distributed by Universal Uclick www.facebook.com/garfield
© 2015 PAWS, INC. All Rights Reserved.
I'M A MAN OF FEW WORDS
STILL TOO MANY
JIM DAVIS 11-30

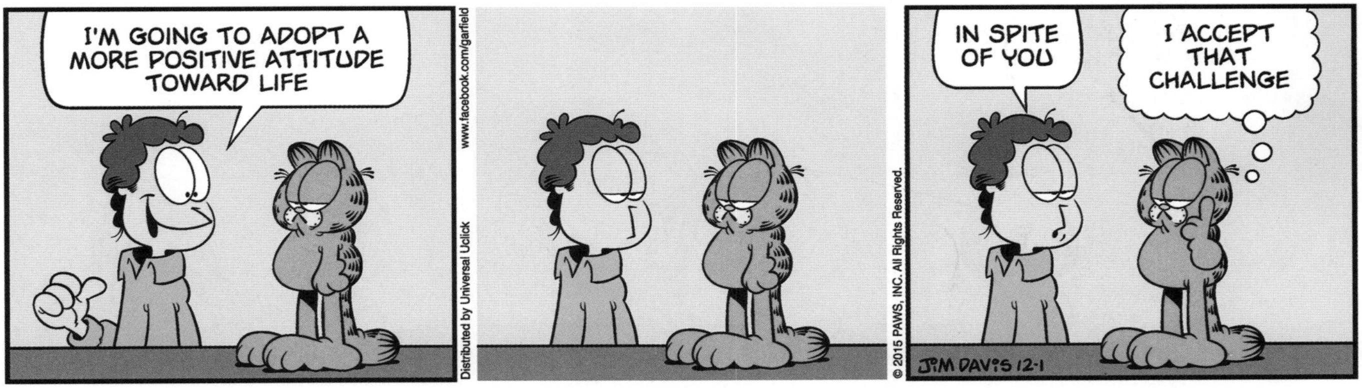
I'M GOING TO ADOPT A MORE POSITIVE ATTITUDE TOWARD LIFE
Distributed by Universal Uclick www.facebook.com/garfield
© 2015 PAWS, INC. All Rights Reserved.
IN SPITE OF YOU
I ACCEPT THAT CHALLENGE
JIM DAVIS 12-1

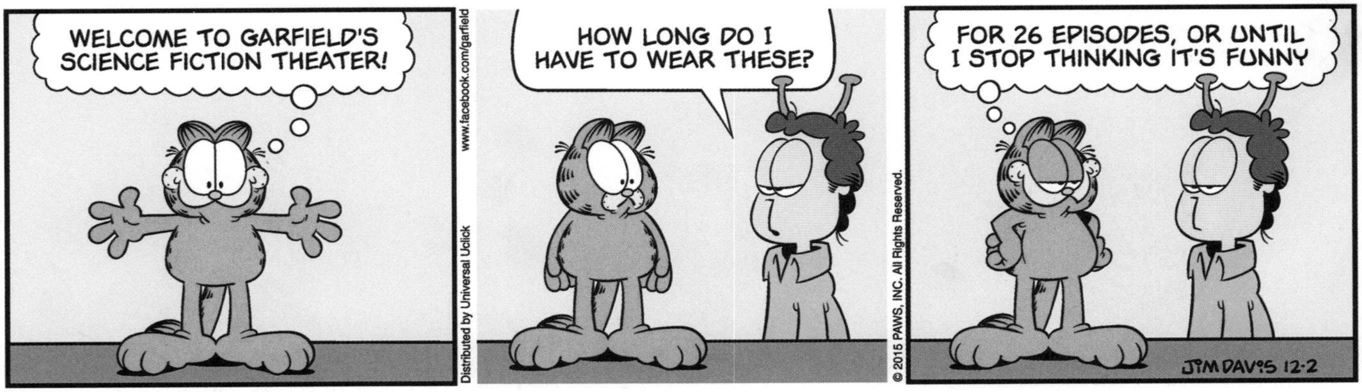
WELCOME TO GARFIELD'S SCIENCE FICTION THEATER!
Distributed by Universal Uclick www.facebook.com/garfield
HOW LONG DO I HAVE TO WEAR THESE?
© 2015 PAWS, INC. All Rights Reserved.
FOR 26 EPISODES, OR UNTIL I STOP THINKING IT'S FUNNY
JIM DAVIS 12-2

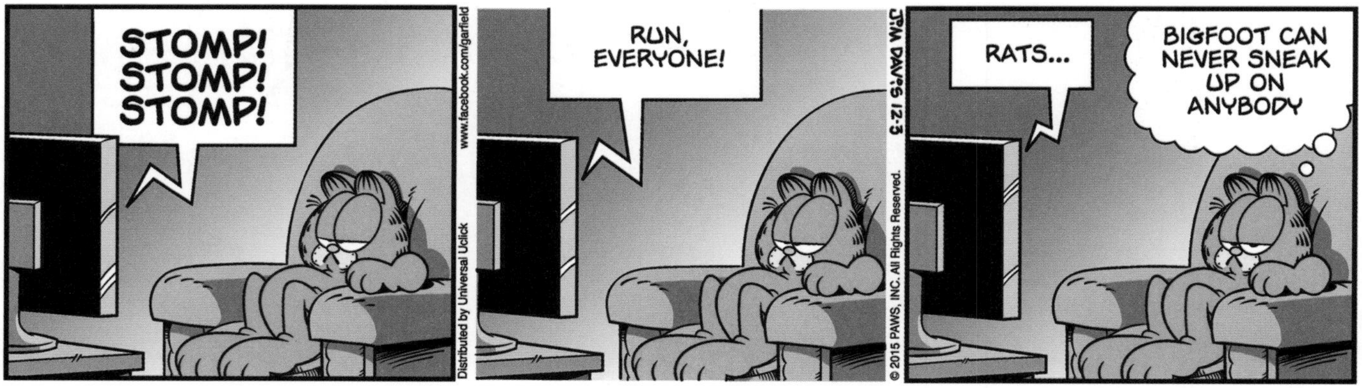
STOMP! STOMP! STOMP!
RUN, EVERYONE!
RATS...
BIGFOOT CAN NEVER SNEAK UP ON ANYBODY
Distributed by Universal Uclick www.facebook.com/garfield
JIM DAVIS 12-3
© 2015 PAWS, INC. All Rights Reserved.

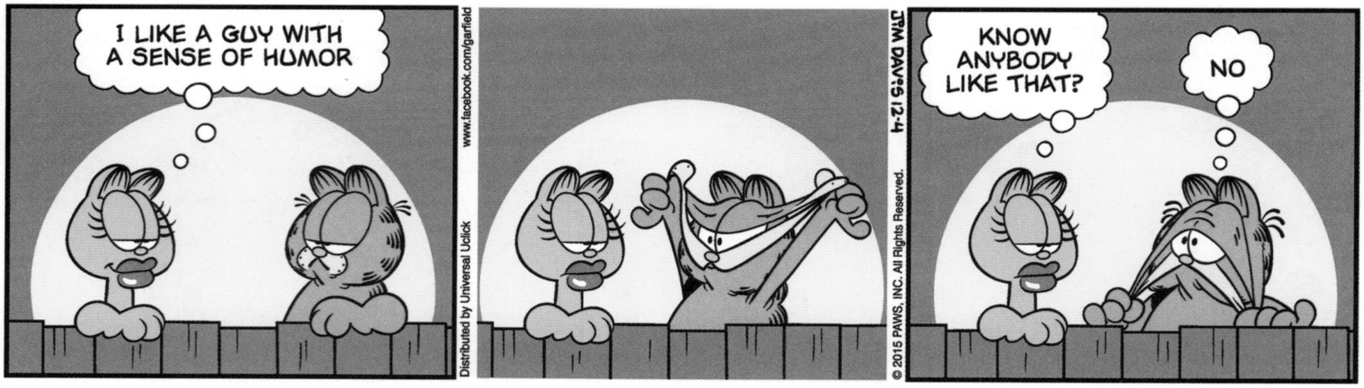
I LIKE A GUY WITH A SENSE OF HUMOR
KNOW ANYBODY LIKE THAT?
NO
Distributed by Universal Uclick www.facebook.com/garfield
JIM DAVIS 12-4
© 2015 PAWS, INC. All Rights Reserved.

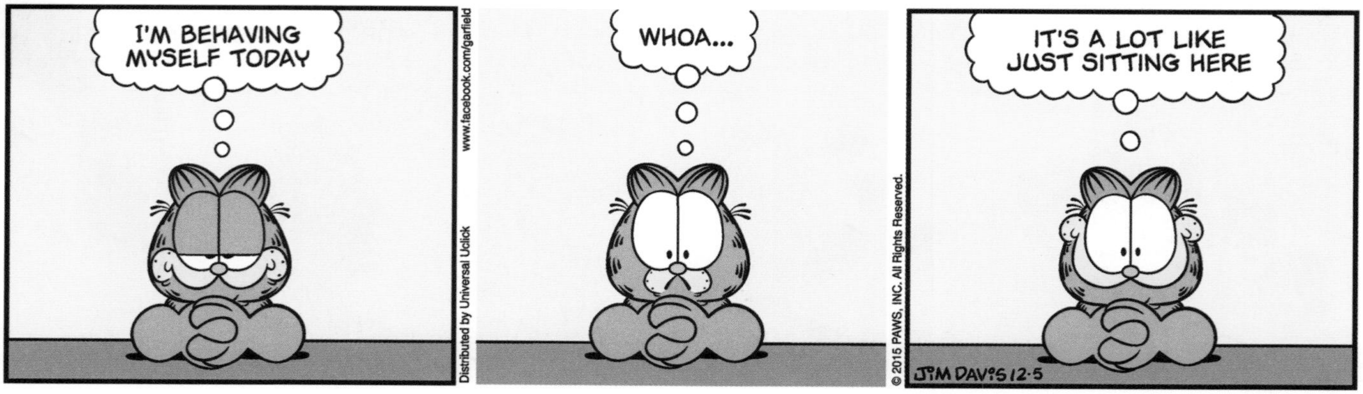
I'M BEHAVING MYSELF TODAY
WHOA...
IT'S A LOT LIKE JUST SITTING HERE
Distributed by Universal Uclick www.facebook.com/garfield
© 2015 PAWS, INC. All Rights Reserved.
JIM DAVIS 12-5

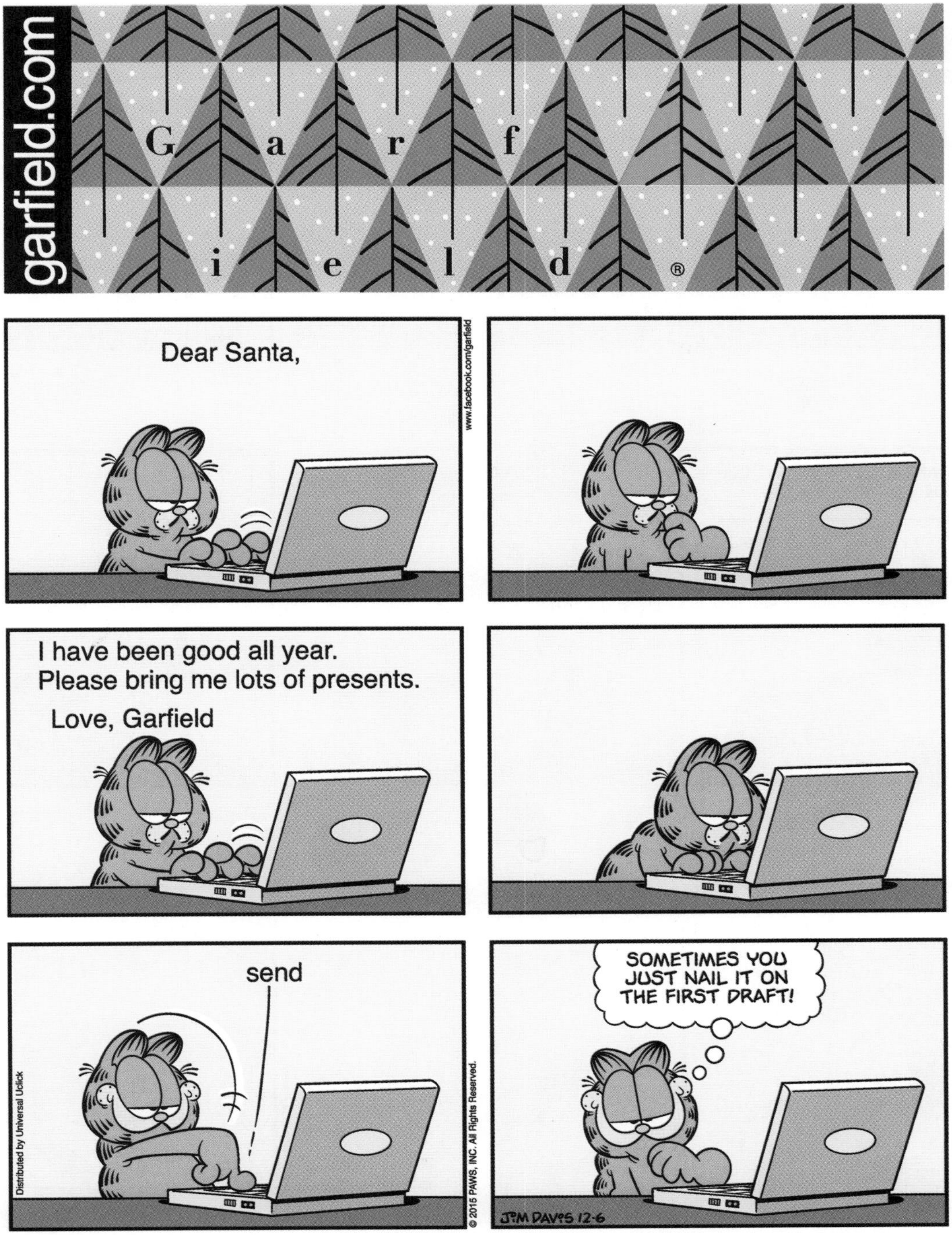
garfield.com
Garfield®
www.facebook.com/garfield
Dear Santa,
I have been good all year.
Please bring me lots of presents.
Love, Garfield
send
SOMETIMES YOU JUST NAIL IT ON THE FIRST DRAFT!
Distributed by Universal Uclick
© 2015 PAWS, INC. All Rights Reserved.
JIM DAVIS 12-6

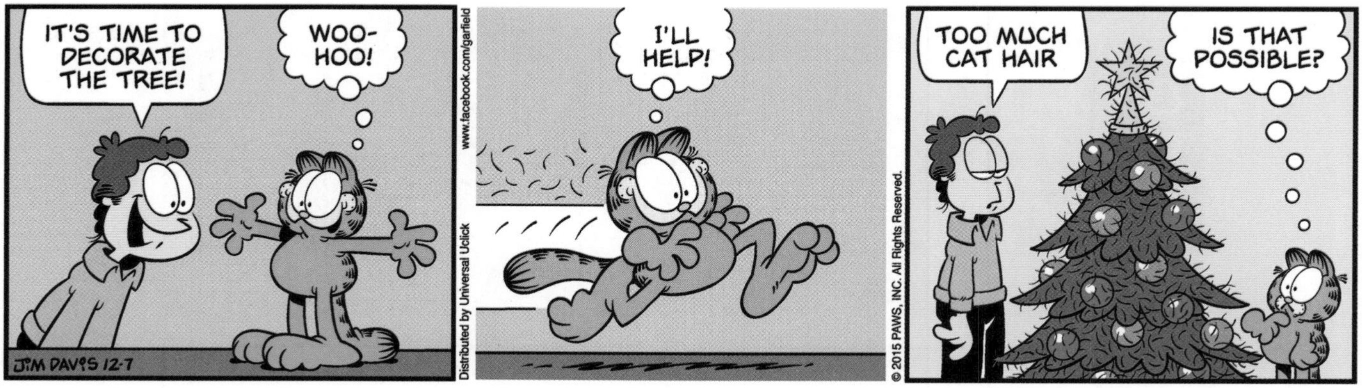
IT'S TIME TO DECORATE THE TREE!
WOO-HOO!
I'LL HELP!
TOO MUCH CAT HAIR
IS THAT POSSIBLE?
JIM DAVIS 12-7
www.facebook.com/garfield
Distributed by Universal Uclick
© 2015 PAWS, INC. All Rights Reserved.

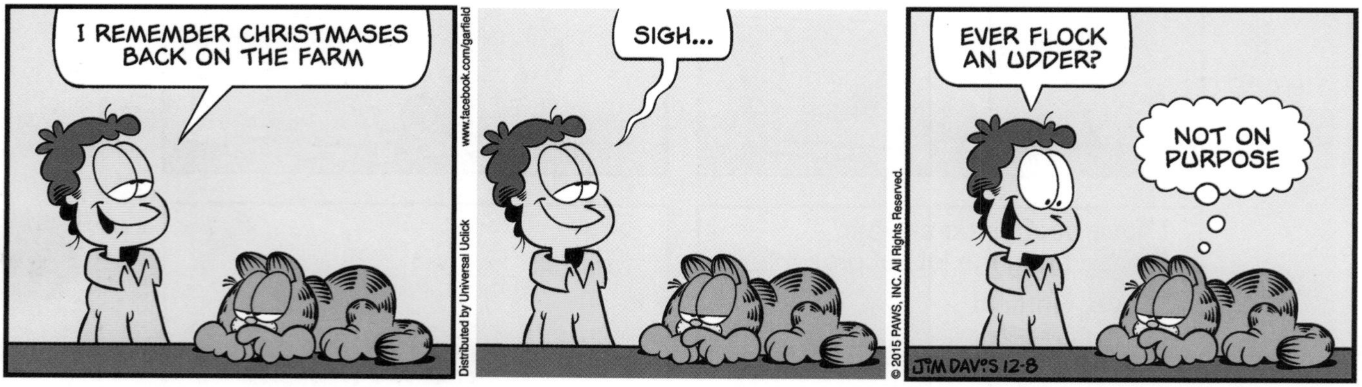
I REMEMBER CHRISTMASES BACK ON THE FARM
SIGH...
EVER FLOCK AN UDDER?
NOT ON PURPOSE
JIM DAVIS 12-8
www.facebook.com/garfield
Distributed by Universal Uclick
© 2015 PAWS, INC. All Rights Reserved.

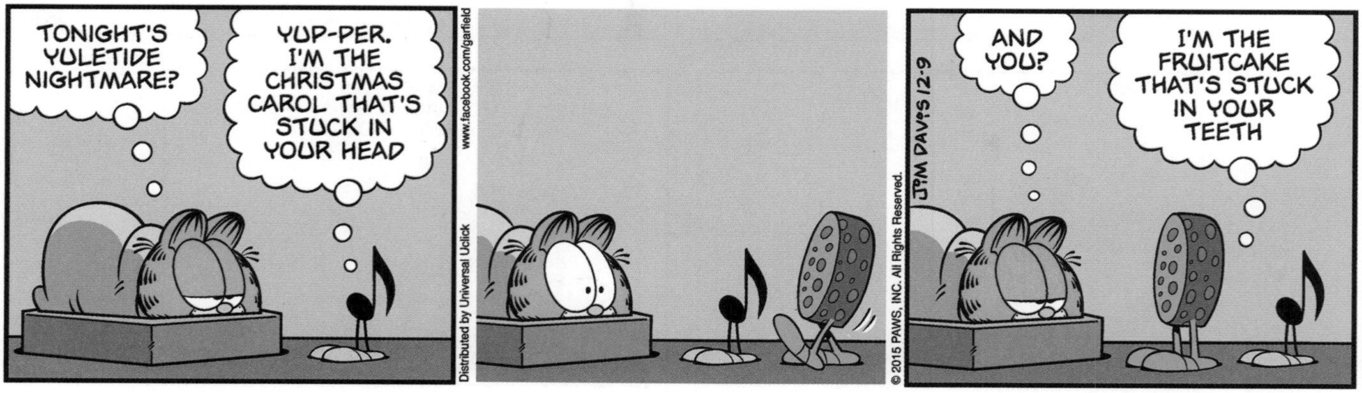
TONIGHT'S YULETIDE NIGHTMARE?
YUP-PER. I'M THE CHRISTMAS CAROL THAT'S STUCK IN YOUR HEAD
AND YOU?
I'M THE FRUITCAKE THAT'S STUCK IN YOUR TEETH
JIM DAVIS 12-9
www.facebook.com/garfield
Distributed by Universal Uclick
© 2015 PAWS, INC. All Rights Reserved.

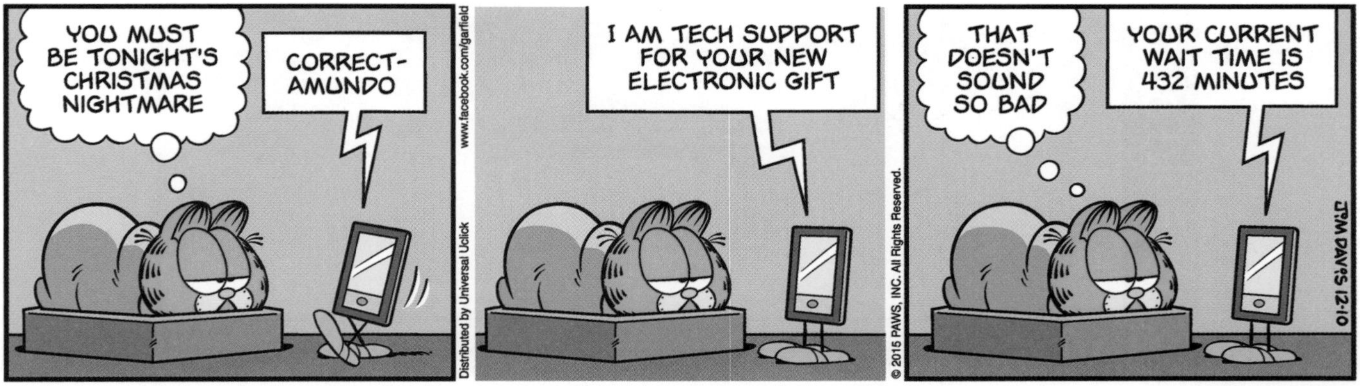
YOU MUST BE TONIGHT'S CHRISTMAS NIGHTMARE
CORRECT-AMUNDO
Distributed by Universal Uclick
www.facebook.com/garfield
I AM TECH SUPPORT FOR YOUR NEW ELECTRONIC GIFT
© 2015 PAWS, INC. All Rights Reserved.
THAT DOESN'T SOUND SO BAD
YOUR CURRENT WAIT TIME IS 432 MINUTES
JIM DAVIS 12-10

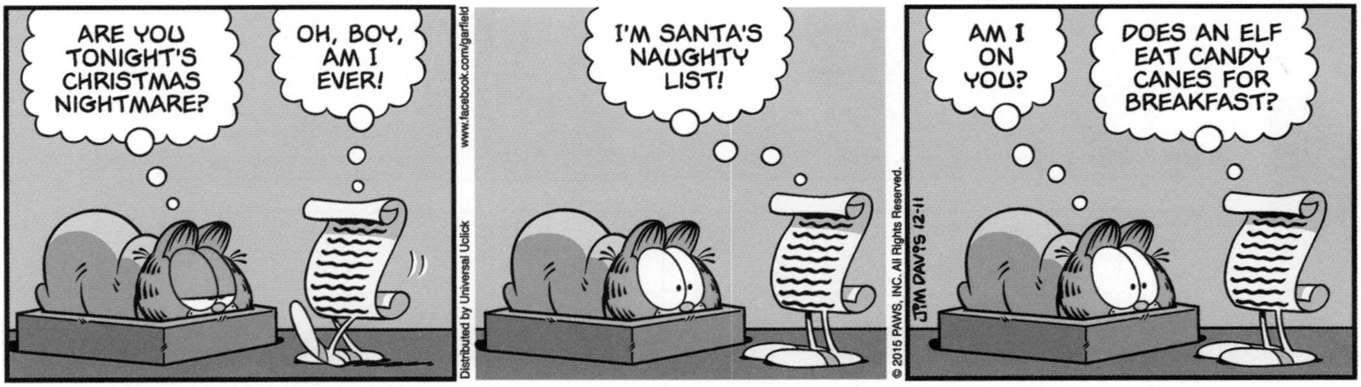
ARE YOU TONIGHT'S CHRISTMAS NIGHTMARE?
OH, BOY, AM I EVER!
Distributed by Universal Uclick
www.facebook.com/garfield
I'M SANTA'S NAUGHTY LIST!
© 2015 PAWS, INC. All Rights Reserved.
JIM DAVIS 12-11
AM I ON YOU?
DOES AN ELF EAT CANDY CANES FOR BREAKFAST?

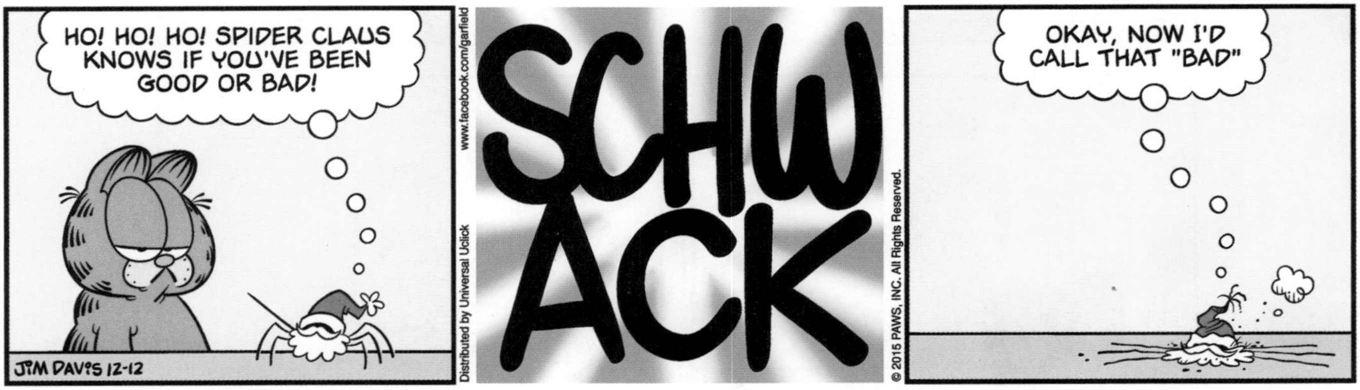
HO! HO! HO! SPIDER CLAUS KNOWS IF YOU'VE BEEN GOOD OR BAD!
JIM DAVIS 12-12
Distributed by Universal Uclick
www.facebook.com/garfield
SCHWACK
© 2015 PAWS, INC. All Rights Reserved.
OKAY, NOW I'D CALL THAT "BAD"

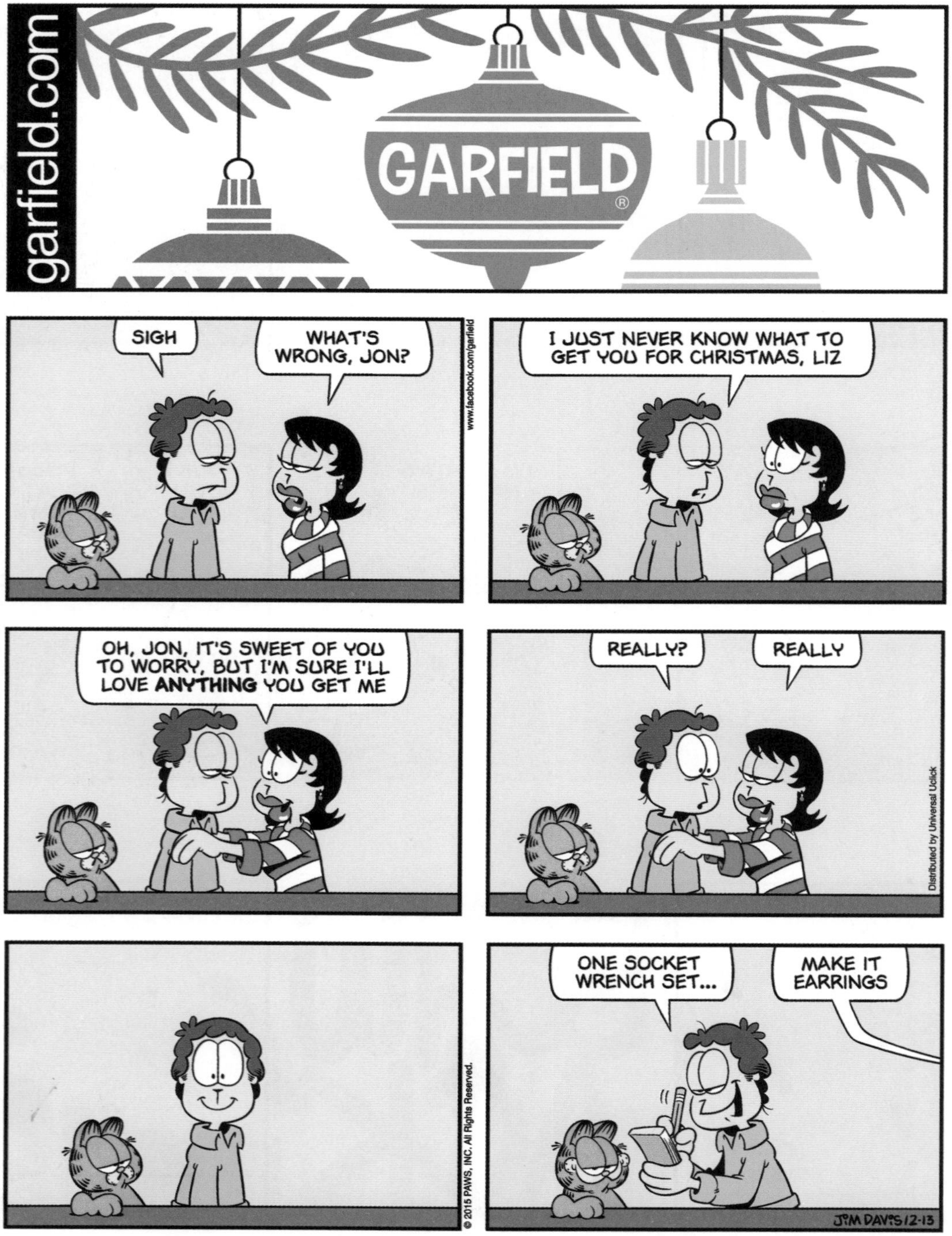
garfield.com
GARFIELD®
SIGH
WHAT'S WRONG, JON?
I JUST NEVER KNOW WHAT TO GET YOU FOR CHRISTMAS, LIZ
OH, JON, IT'S SWEET OF YOU TO WORRY, BUT I'M SURE I'LL LOVE **ANYTHING** YOU GET ME
REALLY?
REALLY
ONE SOCKET WRENCH SET...
MAKE IT EARRINGS
www.facebook.com/garfield
Distributed by Universal Uclick
© 2015 PAWS, INC. All Rights Reserved.
JIM DAVIS 12-13

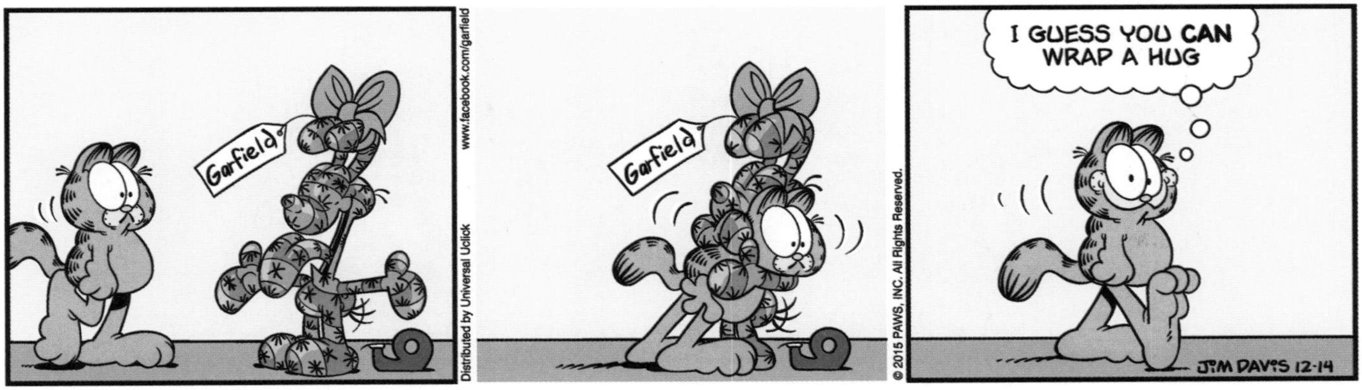
Garfield
Distributed by Universal Uclick www.facebook.com/garfield
Garfield
© 2015 PAWS, INC. All Rights Reserved.
I GUESS YOU CAN WRAP A HUG
JIM DAVIS 12-14

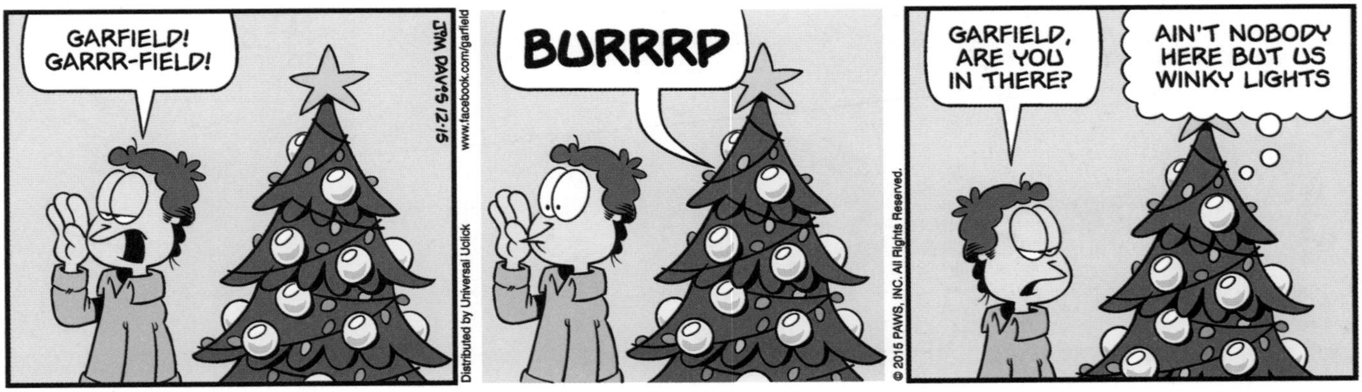
GARFIELD! GARRR-FIELD!
JIM DAVIS 12-15
Distributed by Universal Uclick www.facebook.com/garfield
BURRRP
© 2015 PAWS, INC. All Rights Reserved.
GARFIELD, ARE YOU IN THERE?
AIN'T NOBODY HERE BUT US WINKY LIGHTS

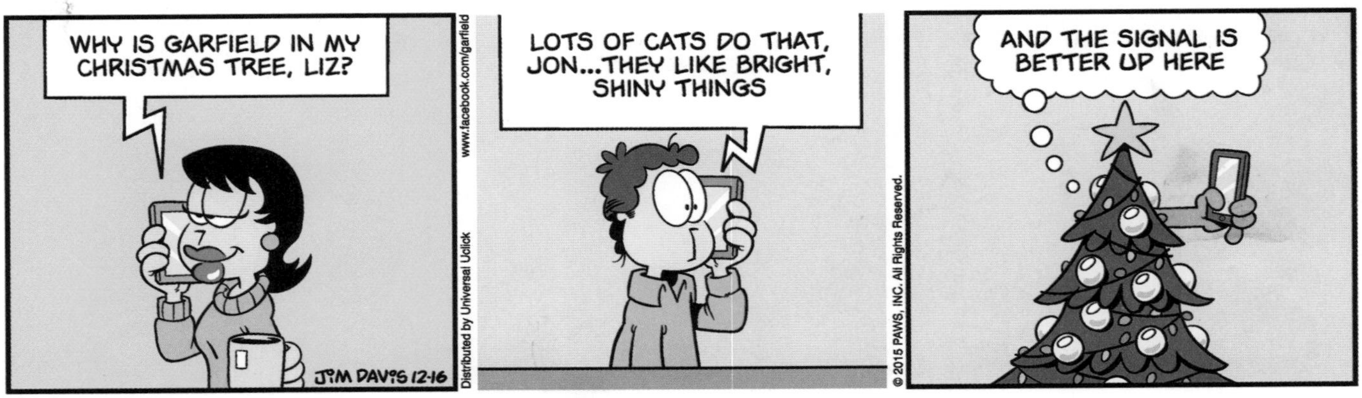
WHY IS GARFIELD IN MY CHRISTMAS TREE, LIZ?
JIM DAVIS 12-16
Distributed by Universal Uclick www.facebook.com/garfield
LOTS OF CATS DO THAT, JON...THEY LIKE BRIGHT, SHINY THINGS
© 2015 PAWS, INC. All Rights Reserved.
AND THE SIGNAL IS BETTER UP HERE

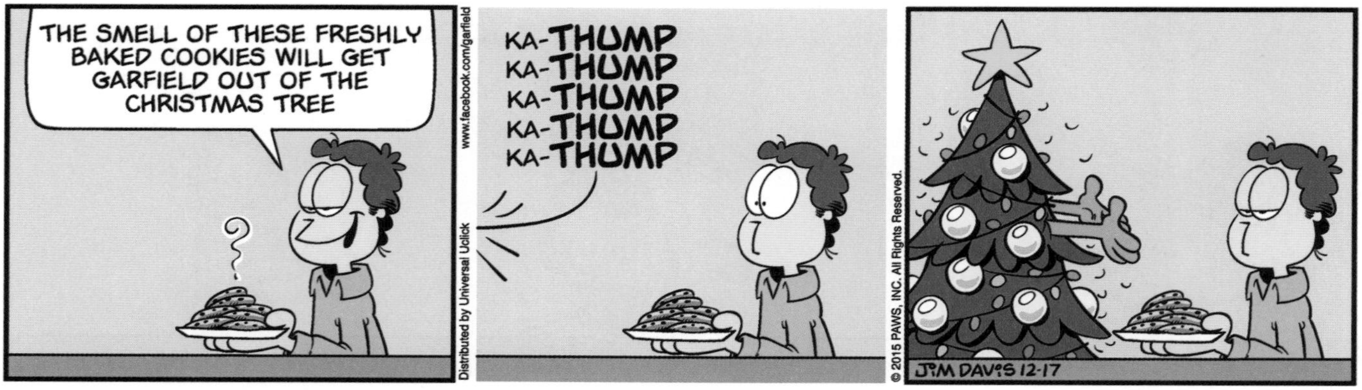
THE SMELL OF THESE FRESHLY BAKED COOKIES WILL GET GARFIELD OUT OF THE CHRISTMAS TREE
Distributed by Universal Uclick
www.facebook.com/garfield
KA-THUMP KA-THUMP KA-THUMP KA-THUMP KA-THUMP
© 2015 PAWS, INC. All Rights Reserved.
JIM DAVIS 12-17

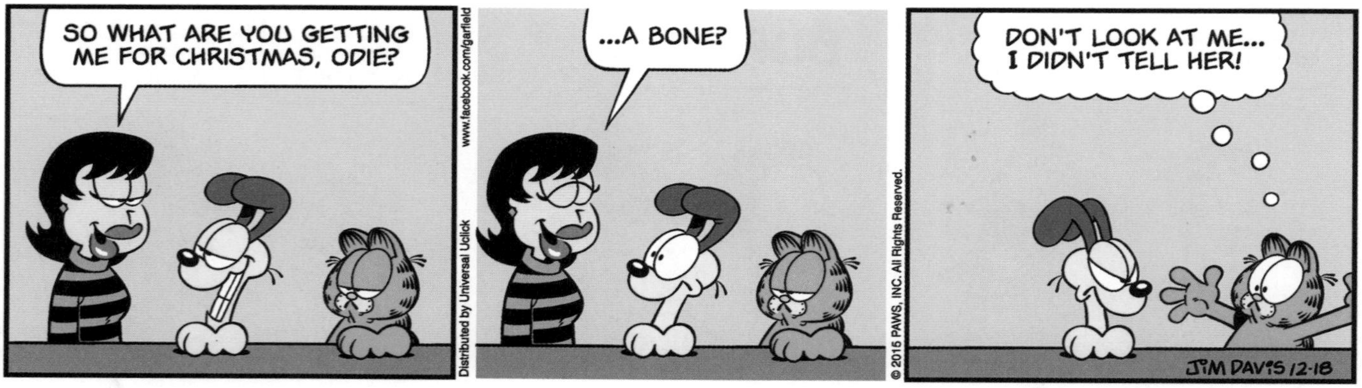
SO WHAT ARE YOU GETTING ME FOR CHRISTMAS, ODIE?
Distributed by Universal Uclick
www.facebook.com/garfield
...A BONE?
© 2015 PAWS, INC. All Rights Reserved.
DON'T LOOK AT ME... I DIDN'T TELL HER!
JIM DAVIS 12-18

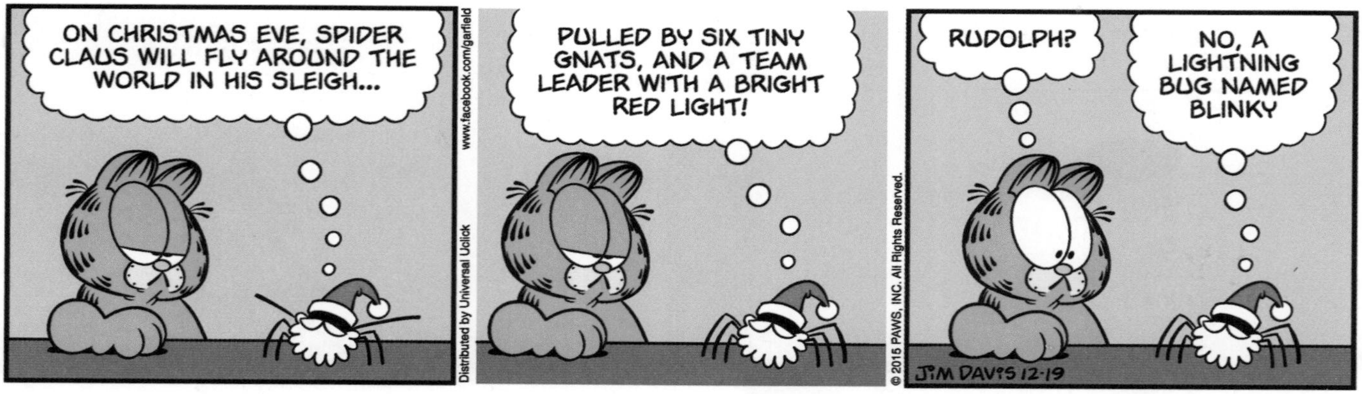
ON CHRISTMAS EVE, SPIDER CLAUS WILL FLY AROUND THE WORLD IN HIS SLEIGH...
Distributed by Universal Uclick
www.facebook.com/garfield
PULLED BY SIX TINY GNATS, AND A TEAM LEADER WITH A BRIGHT RED LIGHT!
© 2015 PAWS, INC. All Rights Reserved.
RUDOLPH?
NO, A LIGHTNING BUG NAMED BLINKY
JIM DAVIS 12-19

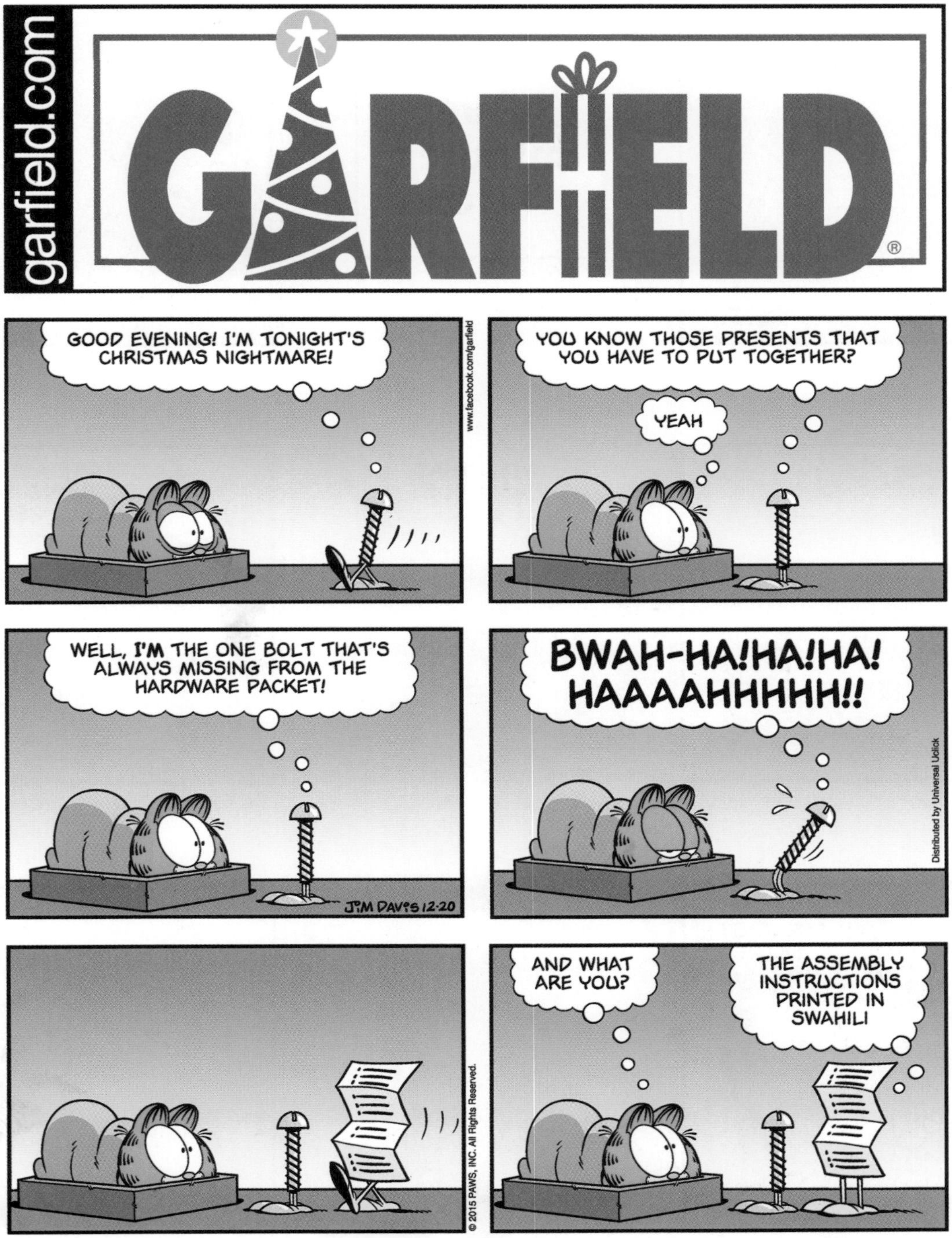
garfield.com
GARFIELD
GOOD EVENING! I'M TONIGHT'S CHRISTMAS NIGHTMARE!
YOU KNOW THOSE PRESENTS THAT YOU HAVE TO PUT TOGETHER?
YEAH
WELL, I'M THE ONE BOLT THAT'S ALWAYS MISSING FROM THE HARDWARE PACKET!
BWAH-HA!HA!HA! HAAAAHHHHH!!
AND WHAT ARE YOU?
THE ASSEMBLY INSTRUCTIONS PRINTED IN SWAHILI
JIM DAVIS 12-20
www.facebook.com/garfield
Distributed by Universal Uclick
© 2015 PAWS, INC. All Rights Reserved.

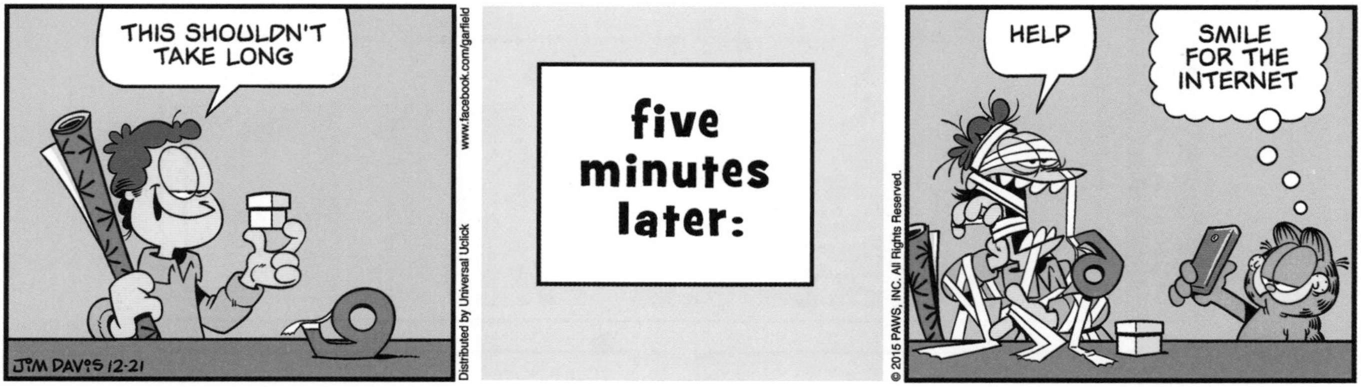
THIS SHOULDN'T TAKE LONG
JIM DAVIS 12-21
Distributed by Universal Uclick www.facebook.com/garfield
five minutes later:
© 2015 PAWS, INC. All Rights Reserved.
HELP
SMILE FOR THE INTERNET

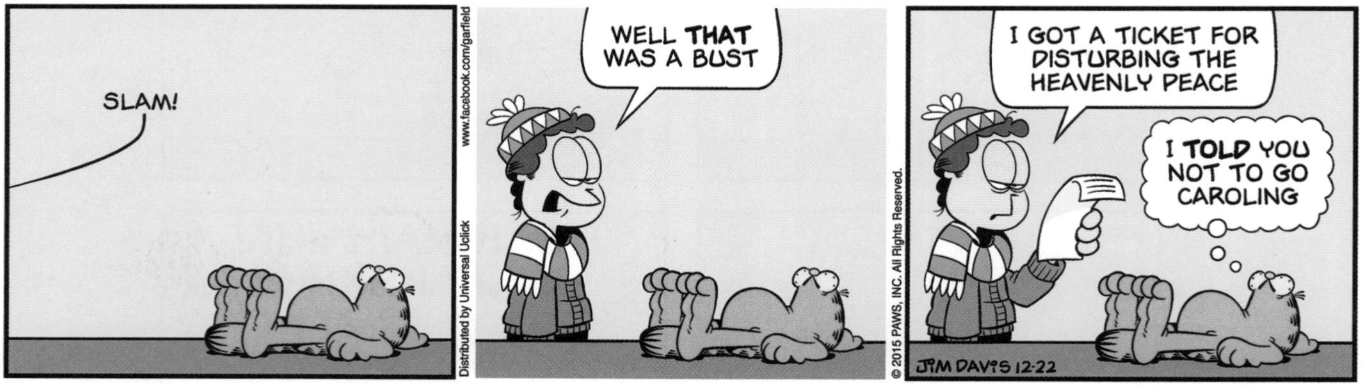
SLAM!
Distributed by Universal Uclick www.facebook.com/garfield
WELL THAT WAS A BUST
© 2015 PAWS, INC. All Rights Reserved.
I GOT A TICKET FOR DISTURBING THE HEAVENLY PEACE
I TOLD YOU NOT TO GO CAROLING
JIM DAVIS 12-22

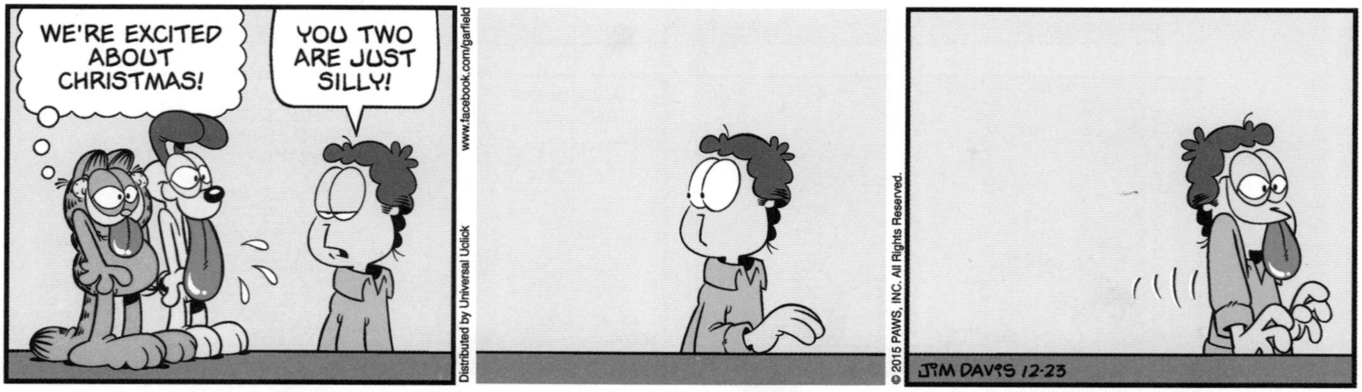
WE'RE EXCITED ABOUT CHRISTMAS!
YOU TWO ARE JUST SILLY!
Distributed by Universal Uclick www.facebook.com/garfield
© 2015 PAWS, INC. All Rights Reserved.
JIM DAVIS 12-23

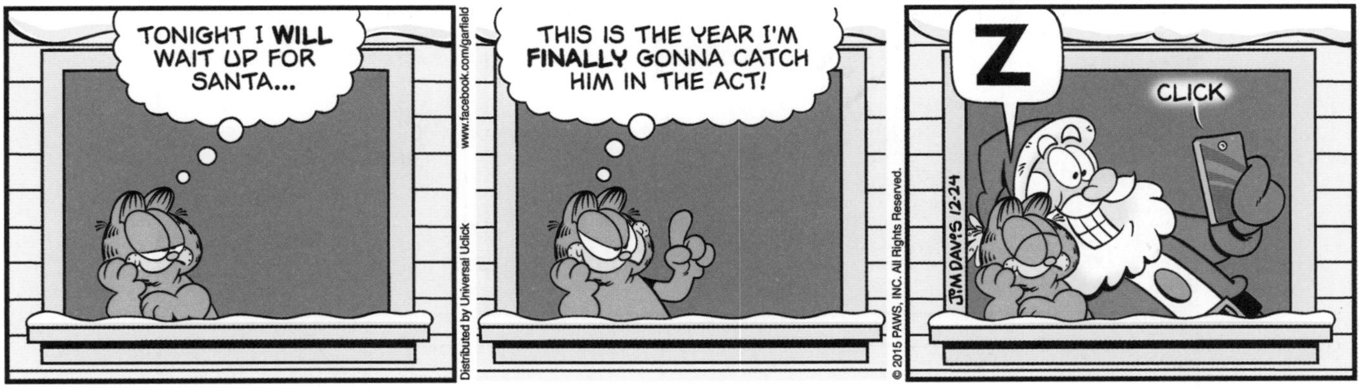
TONIGHT I WILL WAIT UP FOR SANTA...
THIS IS THE YEAR I'M FINALLY GONNA CATCH HIM IN THE ACT!
Z
CLICK
JIM DAVIS 12-24
Distributed by Universal Uclick www.facebook.com/garfield
© 2015 PAWS, INC. All Rights Reserved.

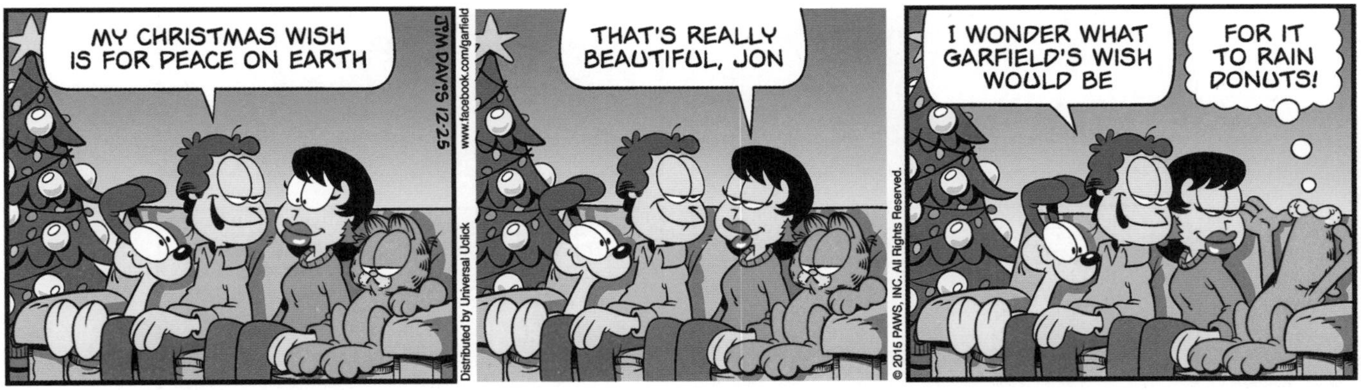
MY CHRISTMAS WISH IS FOR PEACE ON EARTH
JIM DAVIS 12-25
THAT'S REALLY BEAUTIFUL, JON
I WONDER WHAT GARFIELD'S WISH WOULD BE
FOR IT TO RAIN DONUTS!
Distributed by Universal Uclick www.facebook.com/garfield
© 2015 PAWS, INC. All Rights Reserved.

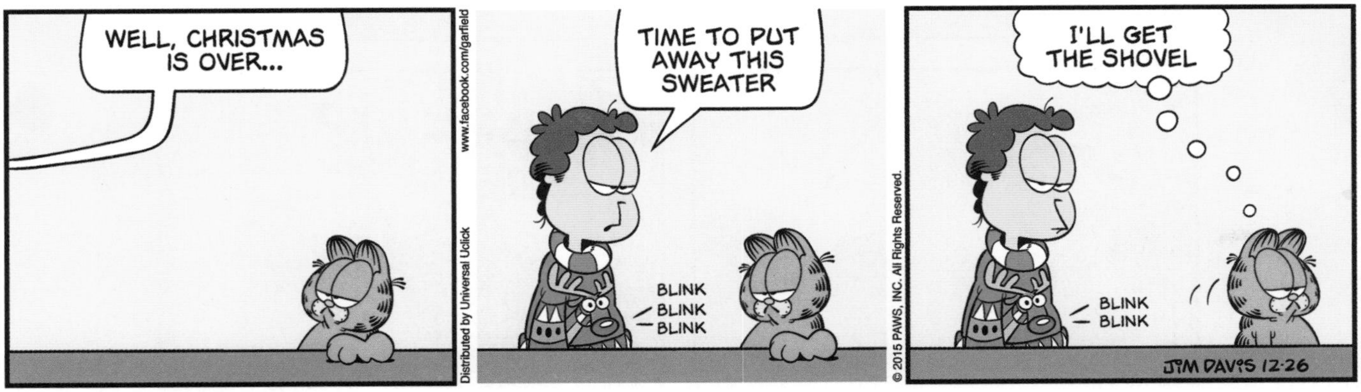
WELL, CHRISTMAS IS OVER...
TIME TO PUT AWAY THIS SWEATER
BLINK
BLINK
BLINK
I'LL GET THE SHOVEL
BLINK
BLINK
JIM DAVIS 12-26
Distributed by Universal Uclick www.facebook.com/garfield
© 2015 PAWS, INC. All Rights Reserved.

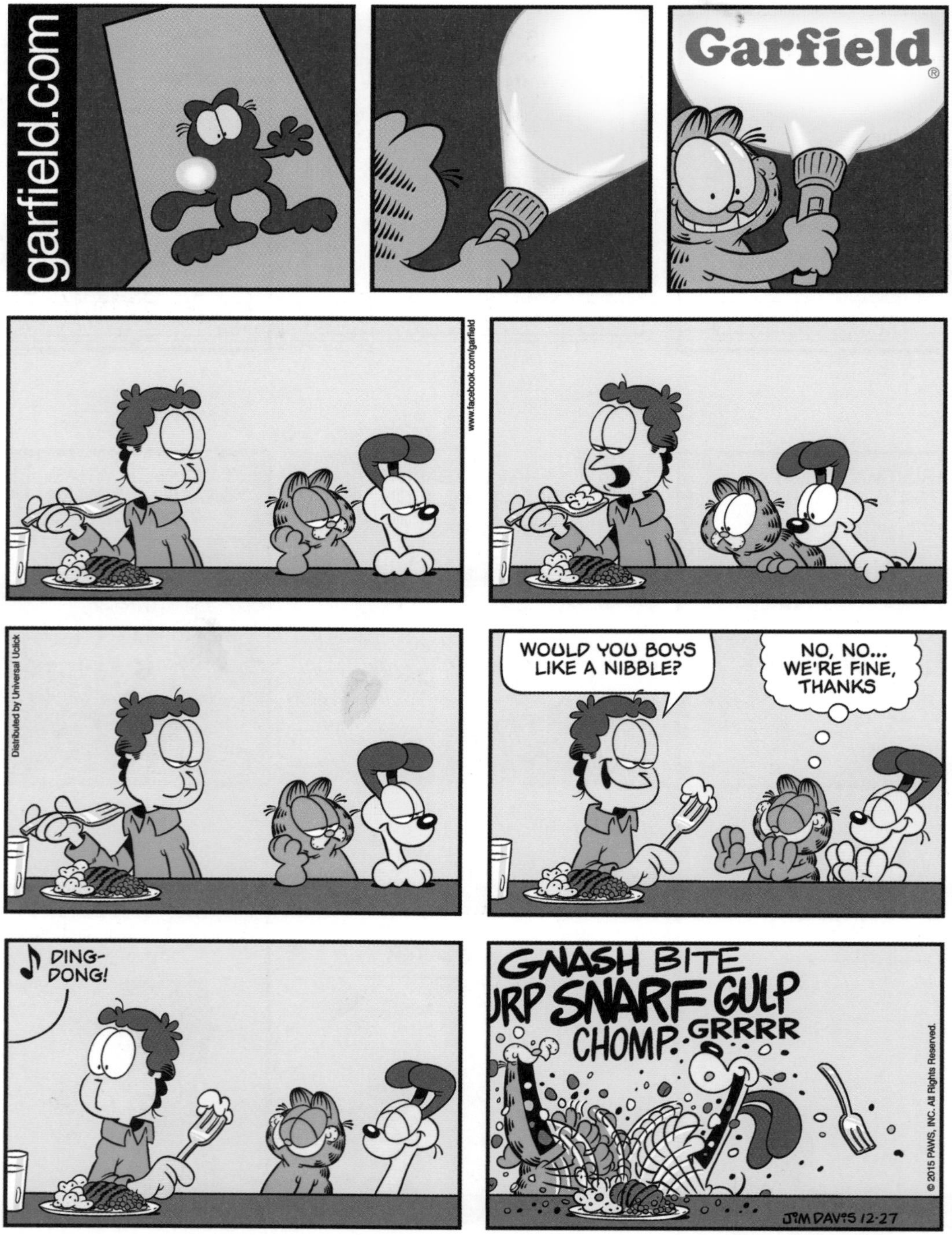
garfield.com
Garfield®
www.facebook.com/garfield
Distributed by Universal Uclick
WOULD YOU BOYS LIKE A NIBBLE?
NO, NO... WE'RE FINE, THANKS
DING-DONG!
GNASH BITE
RP SNARF GULP
CHOMP. GRRRR
© 2015 PAWS, INC. All Rights Reserved.
JIM DAVIS 12-27

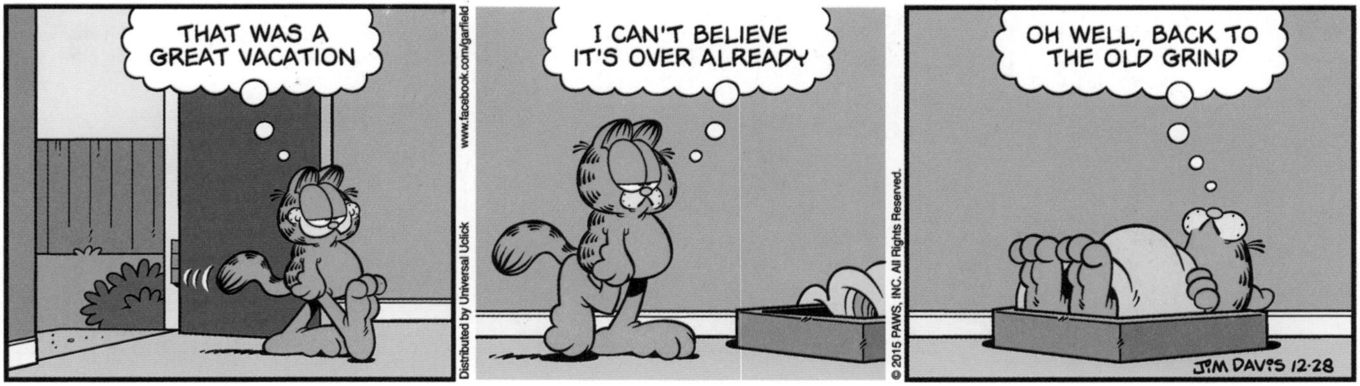
THAT WAS A GREAT VACATION
Distributed by Universal Uclick www.facebook.com/garfield
I CAN'T BELIEVE IT'S OVER ALREADY
© 2015 PAWS, INC. All Rights Reserved.
OH WELL, BACK TO THE OLD GRIND
JIM DAVIS 12-28

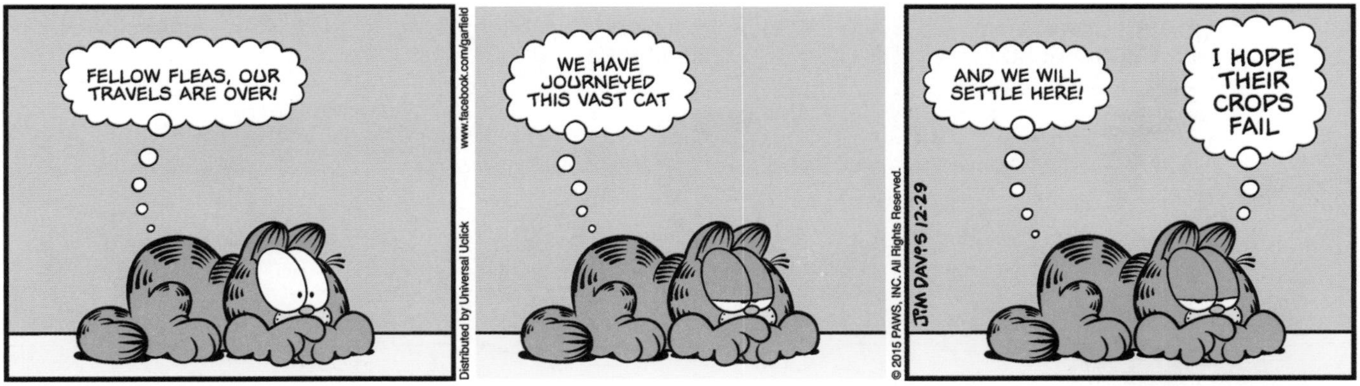
FELLOW FLEAS, OUR TRAVELS ARE OVER!
Distributed by Universal Uclick www.facebook.com/garfield
WE HAVE JOURNEYED THIS VAST CAT
© 2015 PAWS, INC. All Rights Reserved.
JIM DAVIS 12-29
AND WE WILL SETTLE HERE!
I HOPE THEIR CROPS FAIL

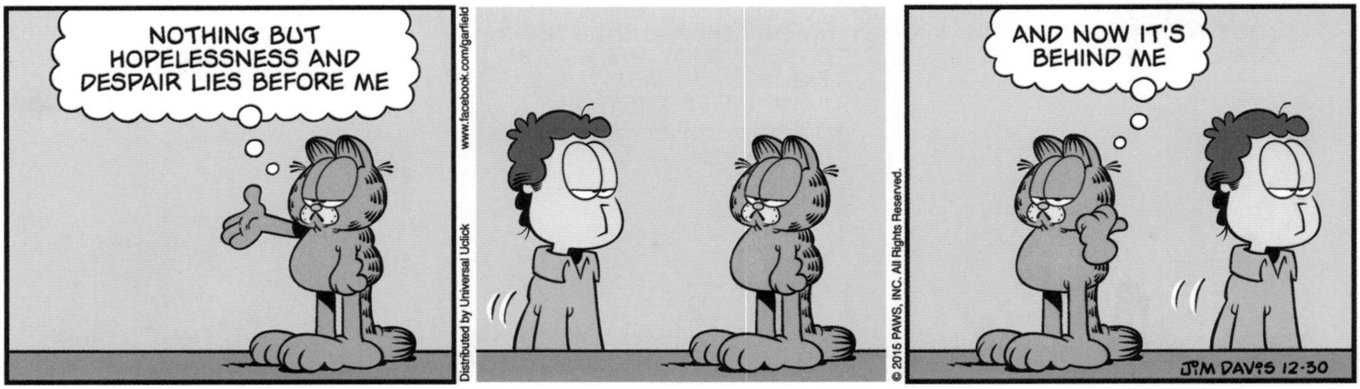
NOTHING BUT HOPELESSNESS AND DESPAIR LIES BEFORE ME
Distributed by Universal Uclick www.facebook.com/garfield
© 2015 PAWS, INC. All Rights Reserved.
AND NOW IT'S BEHIND ME
JIM DAVIS 12-30

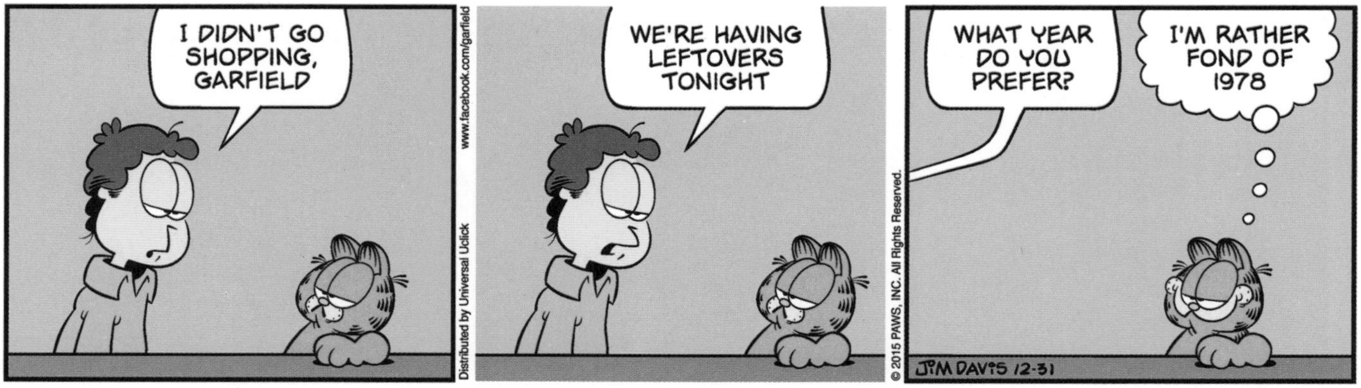
I DIDN'T GO SHOPPING, GARFIELD
www.facebook.com/garfield
Distributed by Universal Uclick
WE'RE HAVING LEFTOVERS TONIGHT
© 2015 PAWS, INC. All Rights Reserved.
WHAT YEAR DO YOU PREFER?
I'M RATHER FOND OF 1978
JIM DAVIS 12-31

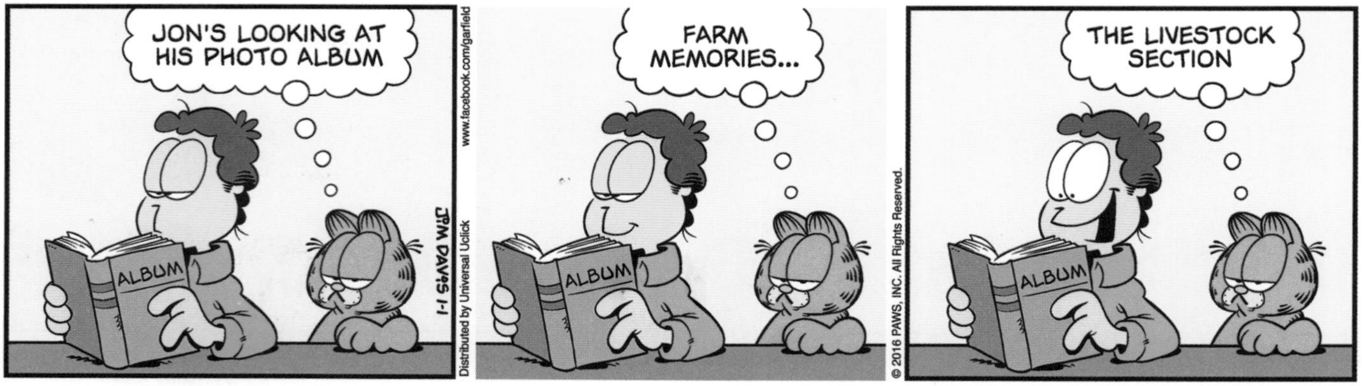
JON'S LOOKING AT HIS PHOTO ALBUM
ALBUM
JIM DAVIS 1-1
www.facebook.com/garfield
Distributed by Universal Uclick
FARM MEMORIES...
ALBUM
© 2016 PAWS, INC. All Rights Reserved.
THE LIVESTOCK SECTION
ALBUM

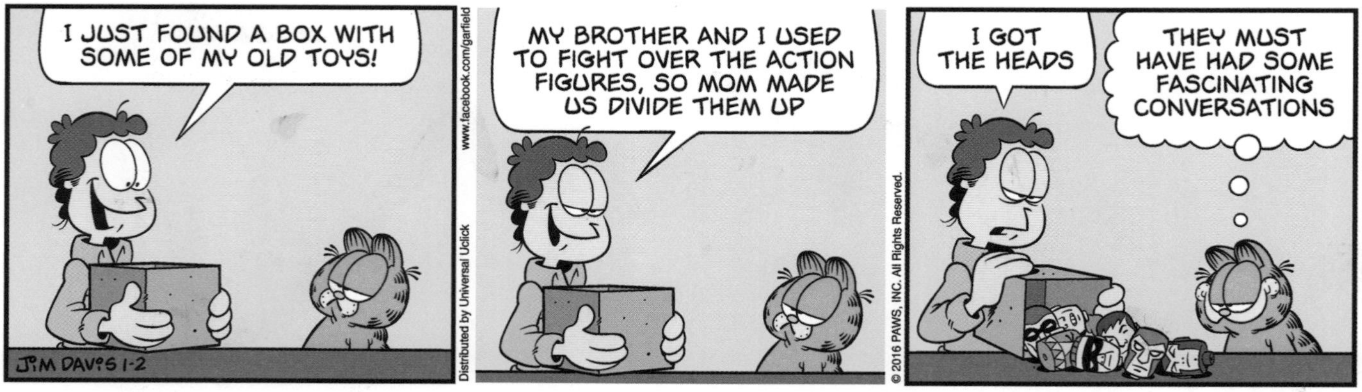
I JUST FOUND A BOX WITH SOME OF MY OLD TOYS!
JIM DAVIS 1-2
www.facebook.com/garfield
Distributed by Universal Uclick
MY BROTHER AND I USED TO FIGHT OVER THE ACTION FIGURES, SO MOM MADE US DIVIDE THEM UP
© 2016 PAWS, INC. All Rights Reserved.
I GOT THE HEADS
THEY MUST HAVE HAD SOME FASCINATING CONVERSATIONS

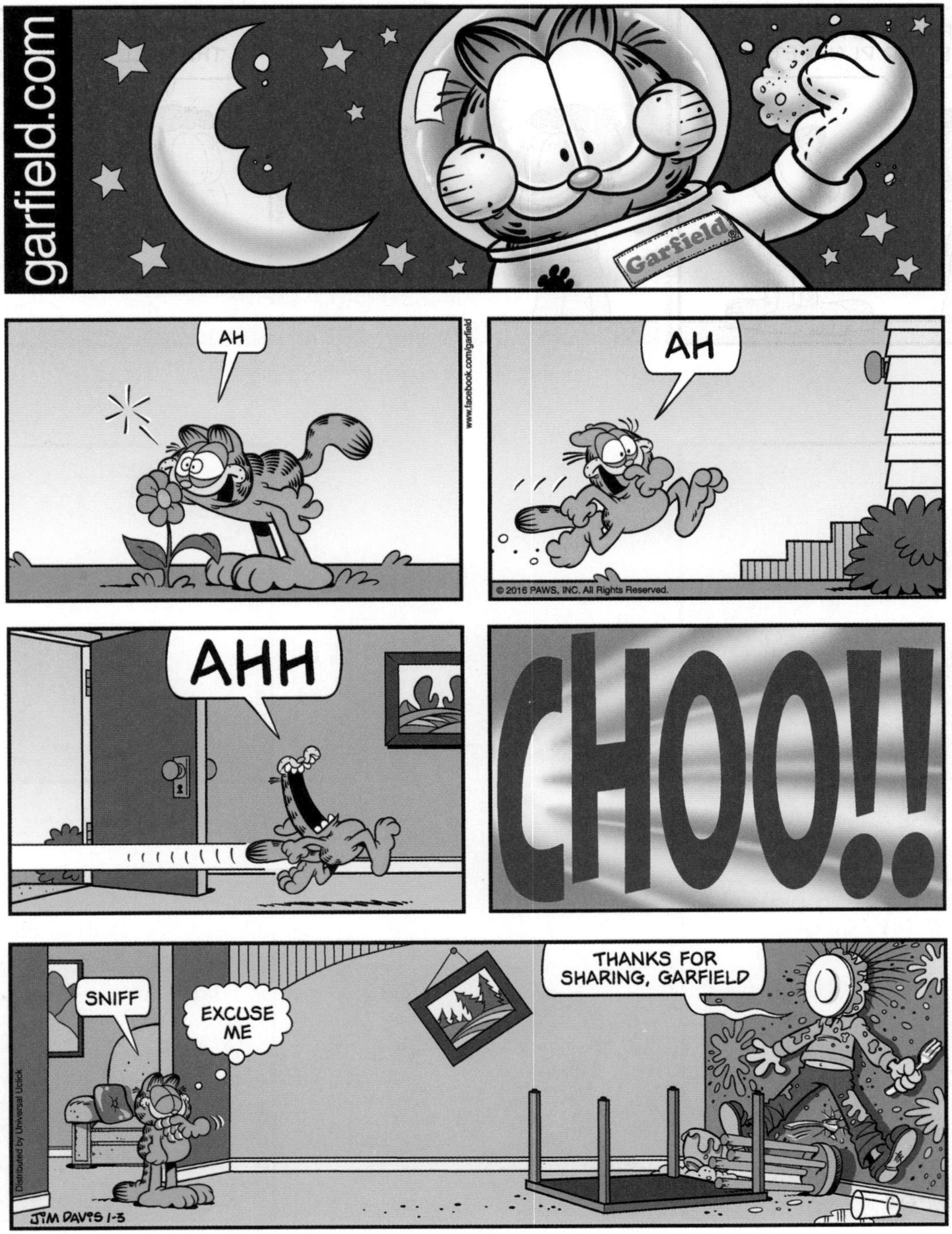
garfield.com
Garfield
AH
www.facebook.com/garfield
AH
© 2016 PAWS, INC. All Rights Reserved.
AHH
CHOO!!
SNIFF
EXCUSE ME
THANKS FOR SHARING, GARFIELD
Distributed by Universal Uclick
JIM DAVIS 1-3

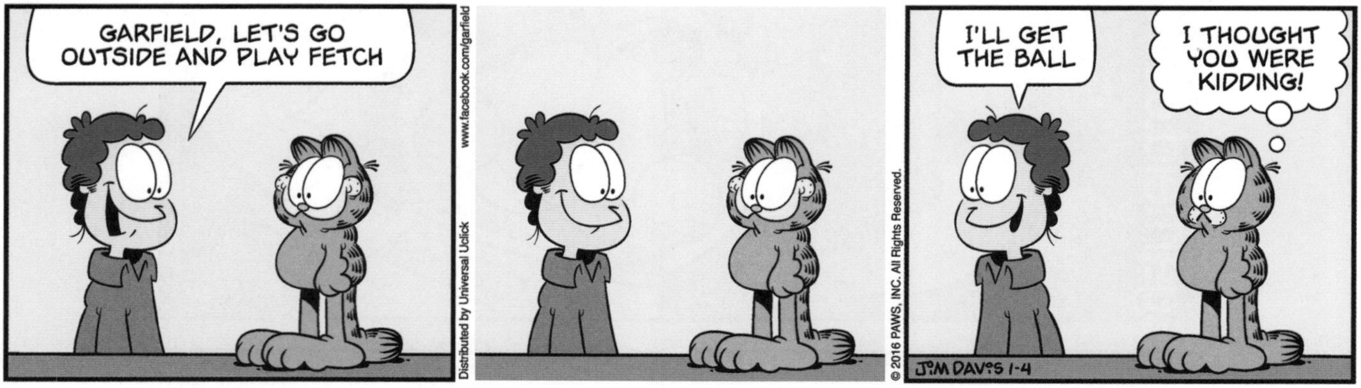
GARFIELD, LET'S GO OUTSIDE AND PLAY FETCH
I'LL GET THE BALL
I THOUGHT YOU WERE KIDDING!
Distributed by Universal Uclick www.facebook.com/garfield
© 2016 PAWS, INC. All Rights Reserved.
JIM DAVIS 1-4

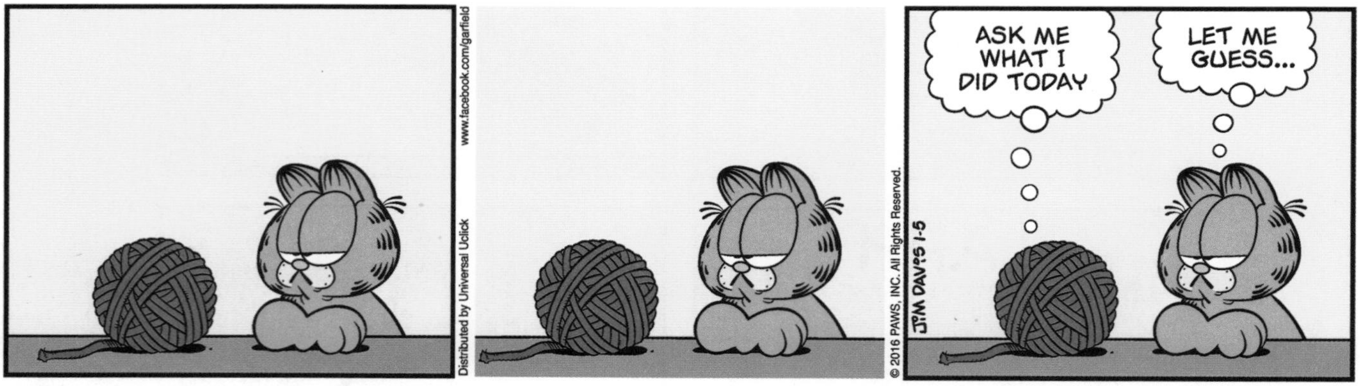
ASK ME WHAT I DID TODAY
LET ME GUESS...
Distributed by Universal Uclick www.facebook.com/garfield
© 2016 PAWS, INC. All Rights Reserved.
JIM DAVIS 1-5

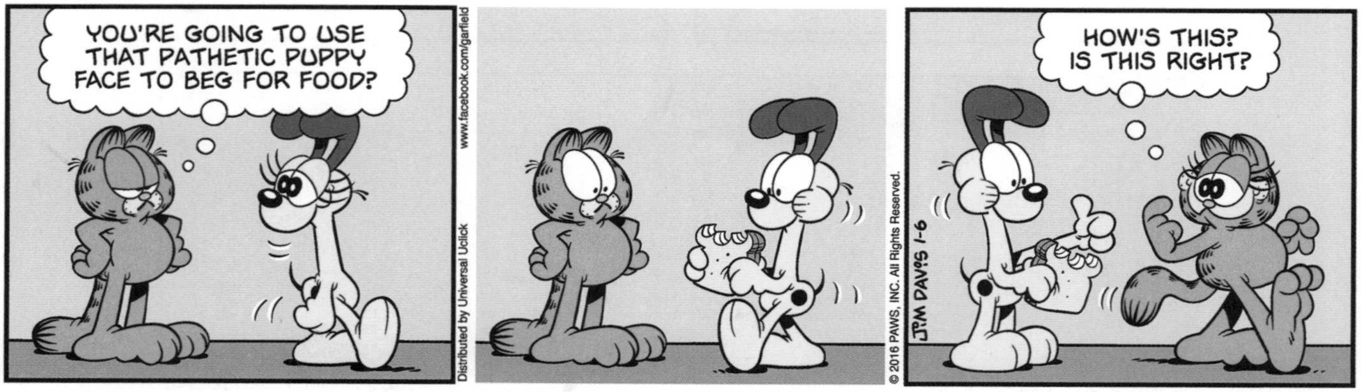
YOU'RE GOING TO USE THAT PATHETIC PUPPY FACE TO BEG FOR FOOD?
HOW'S THIS? IS THIS RIGHT?
Distributed by Universal Uclick www.facebook.com/garfield
© 2016 PAWS, INC. All Rights Reserved.
JIM DAVIS 1-6

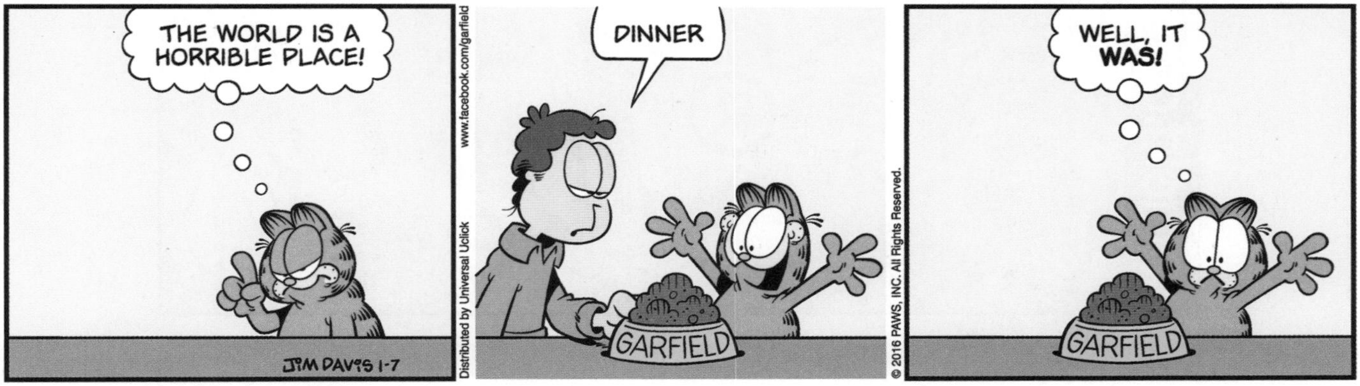
THE WORLD IS A HORRIBLE PLACE!
JIM DAVIS 1-7
Distributed by Universal Uclick www.facebook.com/garfield
DINNER
GARFIELD
© 2016 PAWS, INC. All Rights Reserved.
WELL, IT **WAS!**
GARFIELD

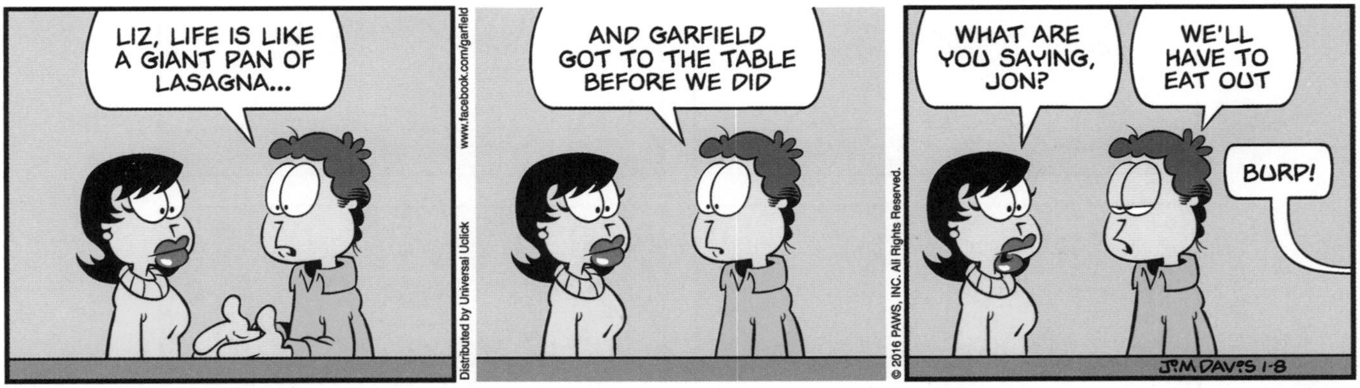
LIZ, LIFE IS LIKE A GIANT PAN OF LASAGNA...
Distributed by Universal Uclick www.facebook.com/garfield
AND GARFIELD GOT TO THE TABLE BEFORE WE DID
© 2016 PAWS, INC. All Rights Reserved.
WHAT ARE YOU SAYING, JON?
WE'LL HAVE TO EAT OUT
BURP!
JIM DAVIS 1-8

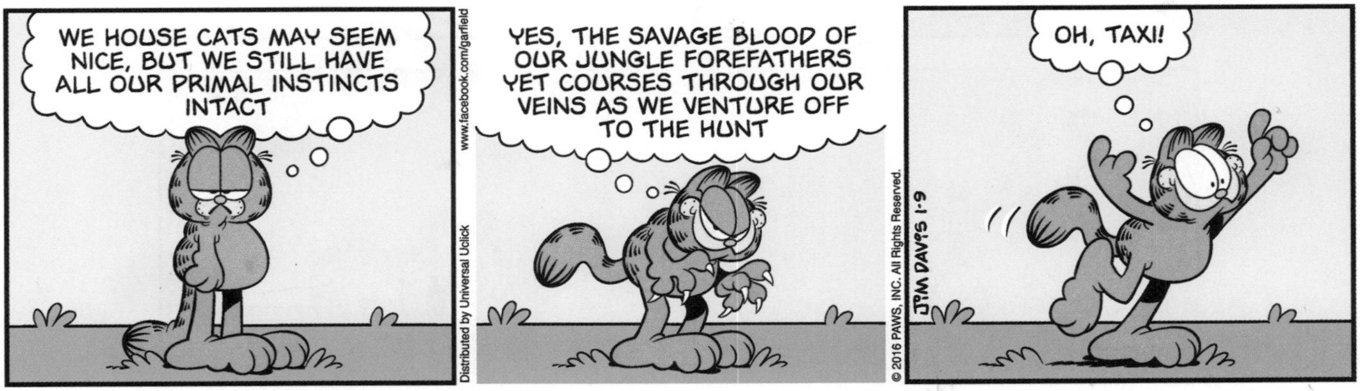
WE HOUSE CATS MAY SEEM NICE, BUT WE STILL HAVE ALL OUR PRIMAL INSTINCTS INTACT
Distributed by Universal Uclick www.facebook.com/garfield
YES, THE SAVAGE BLOOD OF OUR JUNGLE FOREFATHERS YET COURSES THROUGH OUR VEINS AS WE VENTURE OFF TO THE HUNT
© 2016 PAWS, INC. All Rights Reserved.
JIM DAVIS 1-9
OH, TAXI!

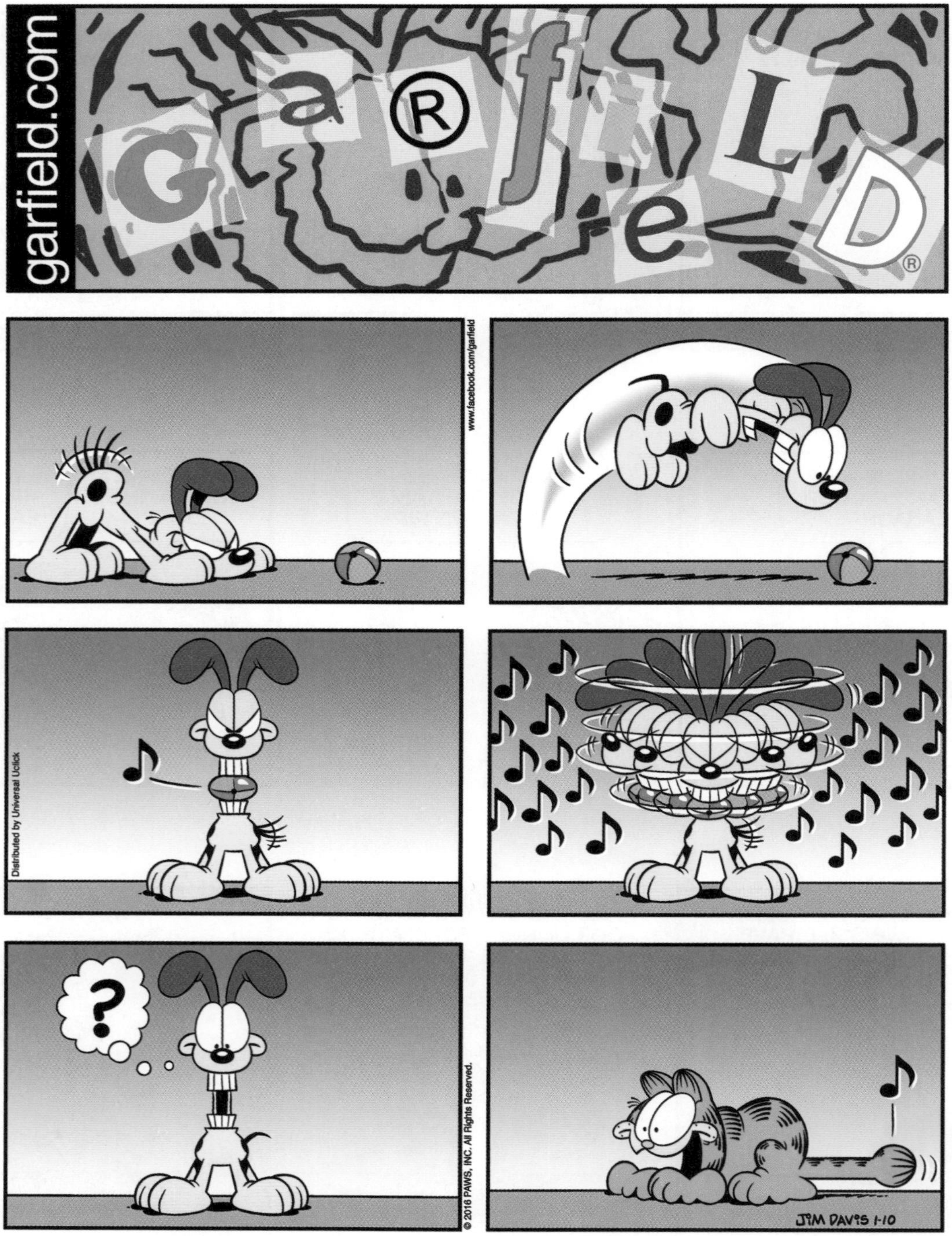
garfield.com
GARFIELD
www.facebook.com/garfield
Distributed by Universal Uclick
?
© 2016 PAWS, INC. All Rights Reserved.
JIM DAVIS 1-10

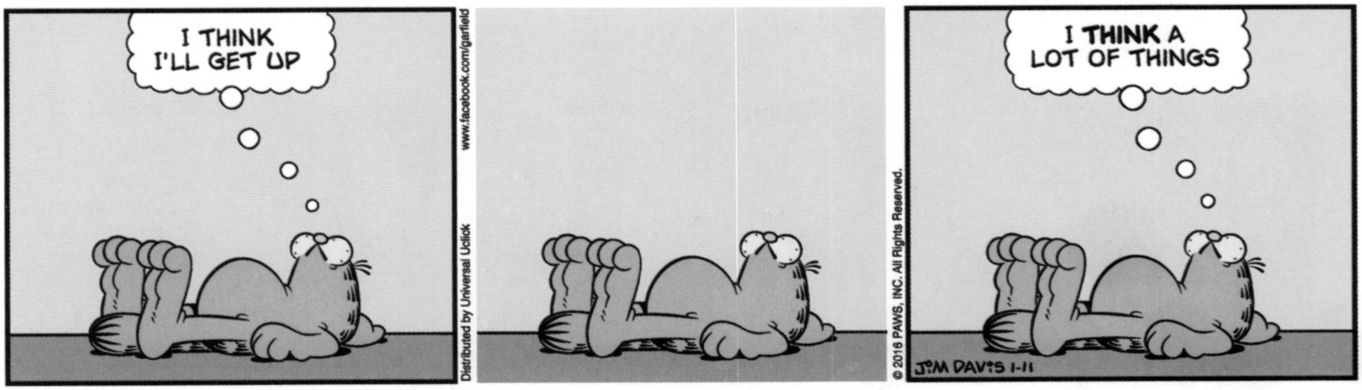
I THINK
I'LL GET UP
I **THINK** A
LOT OF THINGS
JIM DAVIS 1-11
Distributed by Universal Uclick www.facebook.com/garfield
© 2016 PAWS, INC. All Rights Reserved.

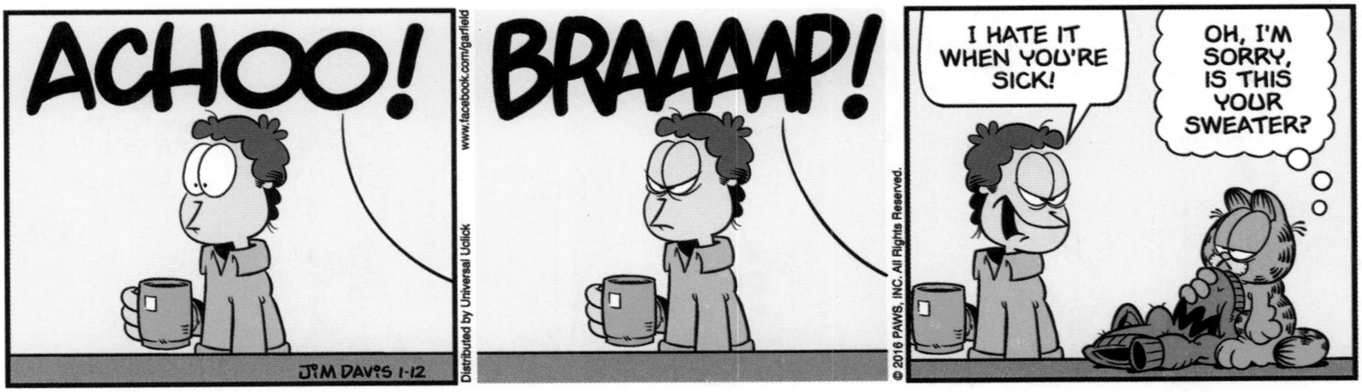
ACHOO!
BRAAAAP!
I HATE IT
WHEN YOU'RE
SICK!
OH, I'M
SORRY,
IS THIS
YOUR
SWEATER?
JIM DAVIS 1-12
Distributed by Universal Uclick www.facebook.com/garfield
© 2016 PAWS, INC. All Rights Reserved.

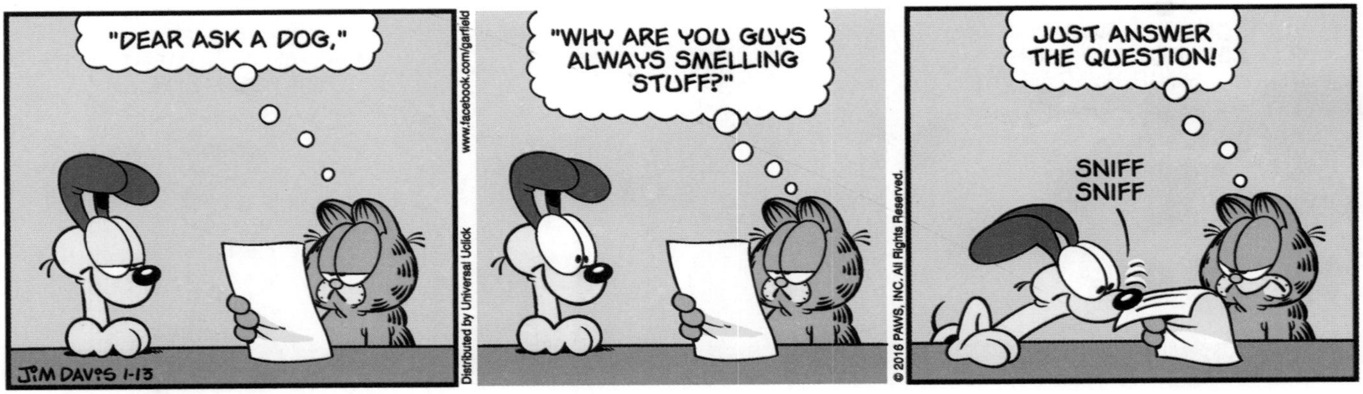
"DEAR ASK A DOG,"
"WHY ARE YOU GUYS
ALWAYS SMELLING
STUFF?"
JUST ANSWER
THE QUESTION!
SNIFF
SNIFF
JIM DAVIS 1-13
Distributed by Universal Uclick www.facebook.com/garfield
© 2016 PAWS, INC. All Rights Reserved.

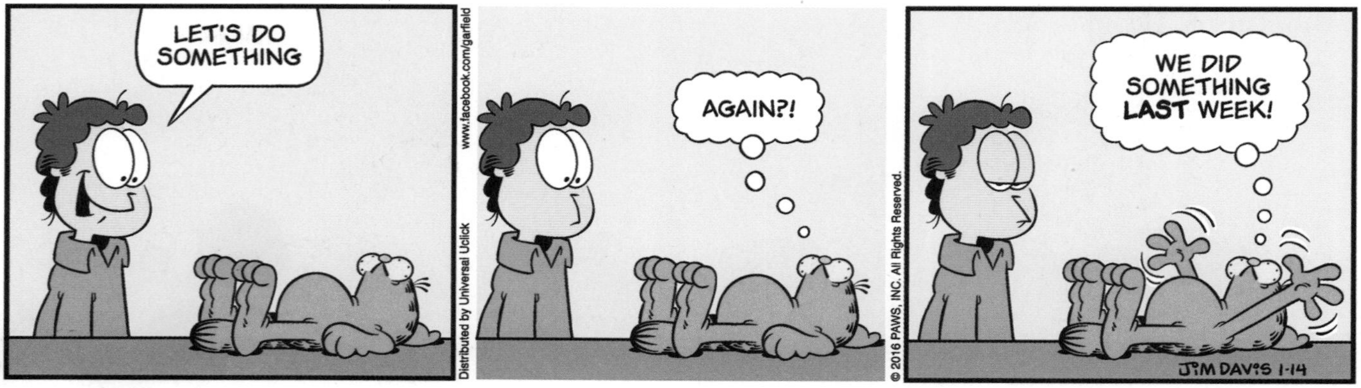
LET'S DO SOMETHING
AGAIN?!
WE DID SOMETHING LAST WEEK!
JIM DAVIS 1-14
Distributed by Universal Uclick www.facebook.com/garfield
© 2016 PAWS, INC. All Rights Reserved.

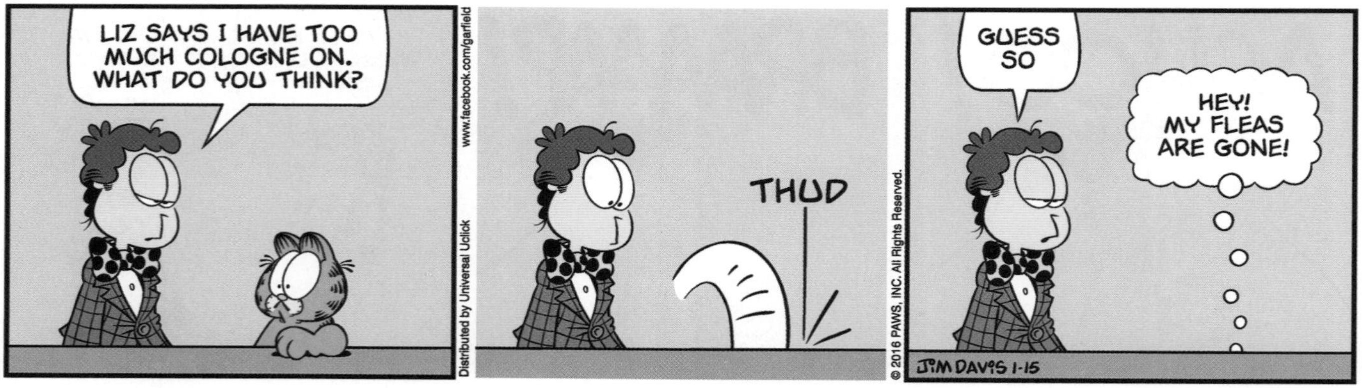
LIZ SAYS I HAVE TOO MUCH COLOGNE ON. WHAT DO YOU THINK?
THUD
GUESS SO
HEY! MY FLEAS ARE GONE!
JIM DAVIS 1-15
Distributed by Universal Uclick www.facebook.com/garfield
© 2016 PAWS, INC. All Rights Reserved.

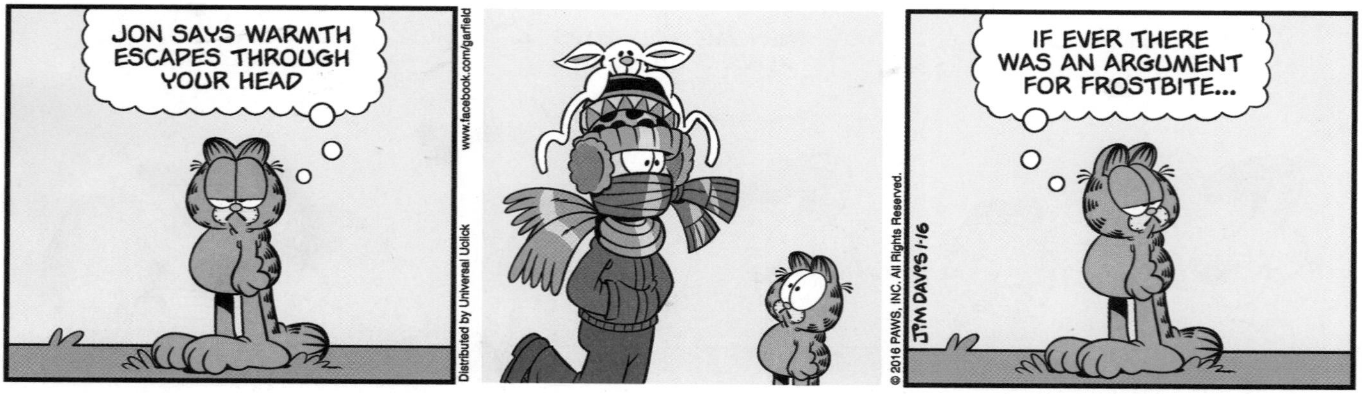
JON SAYS WARMTH ESCAPES THROUGH YOUR HEAD
IF EVER THERE WAS AN ARGUMENT FOR FROSTBITE...
JIM DAVIS 1-16
Distributed by Universal Uclick www.facebook.com/garfield
© 2016 PAWS, INC. All Rights Reserved.

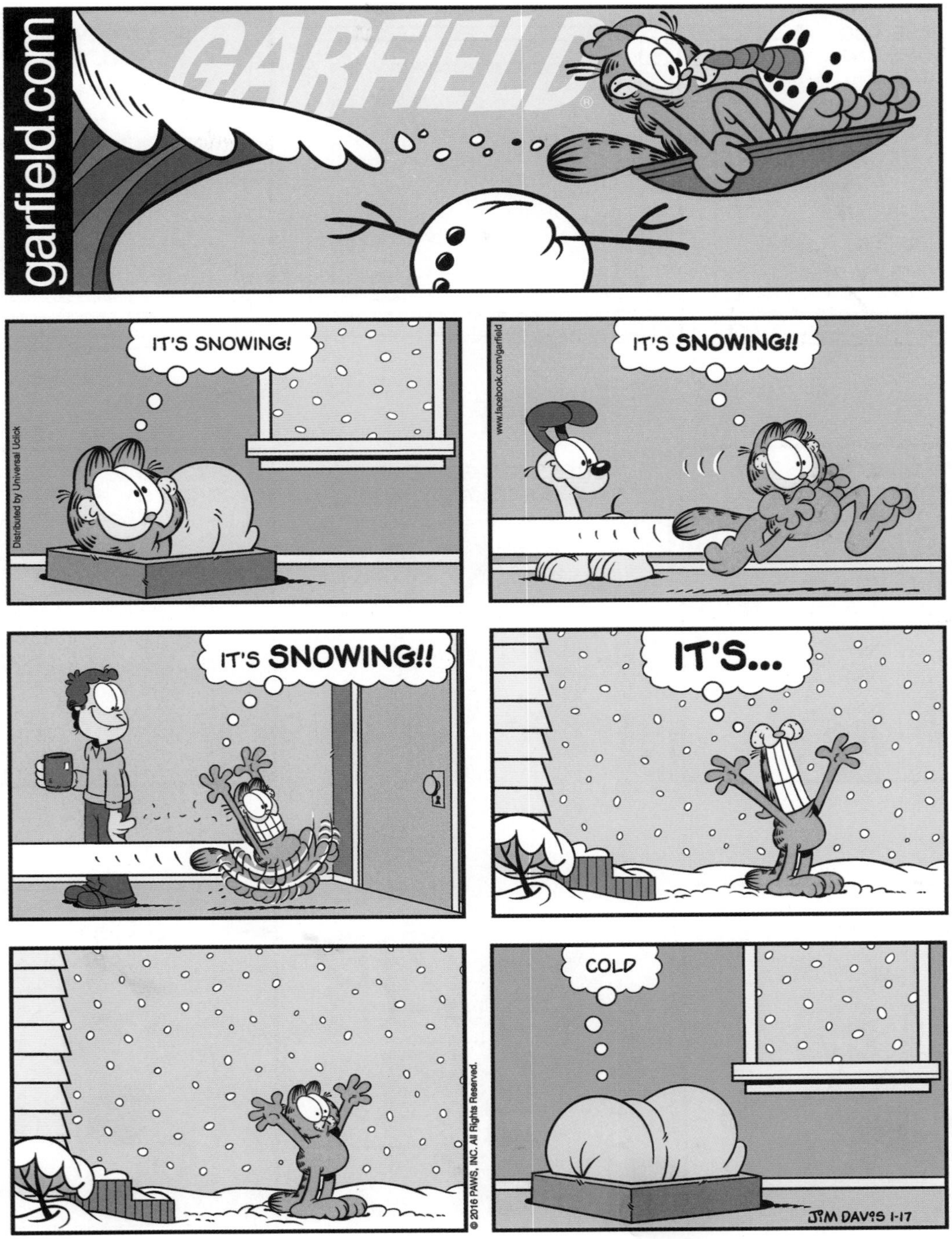
garfield.com
GARFIELD
Distributed by Universal Uclick
IT'S SNOWING!
www.facebook.com/garfield
IT'S SNOWING!!
IT'S SNOWING!!
IT'S...
© 2016 PAWS, INC. All Rights Reserved.
COLD
JIM DAVIS 1-17

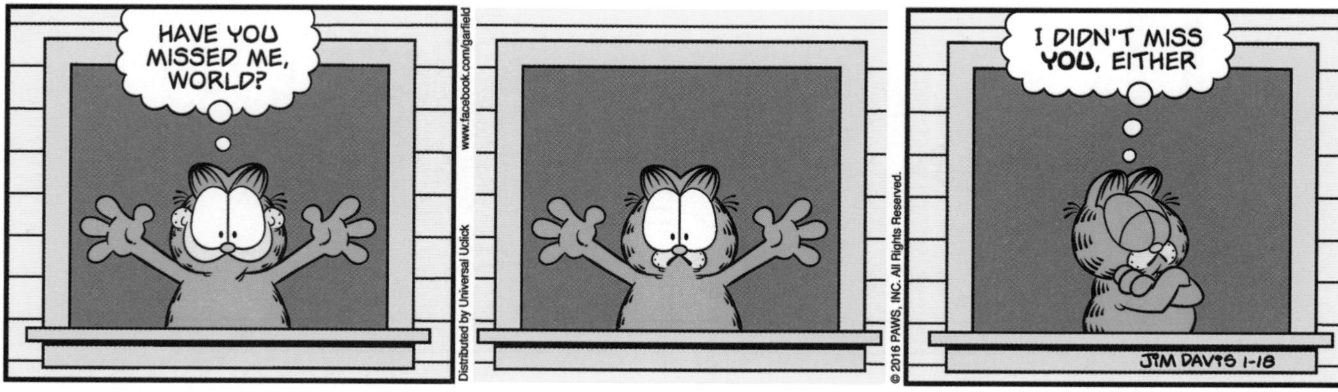
HAVE YOU MISSED ME, WORLD?
Distributed by Universal Uclick www.facebook.com/garfield
I DIDN'T MISS **YOU**, EITHER
© 2016 PAWS, INC. All Rights Reserved.
JIM DAVIS 1-18

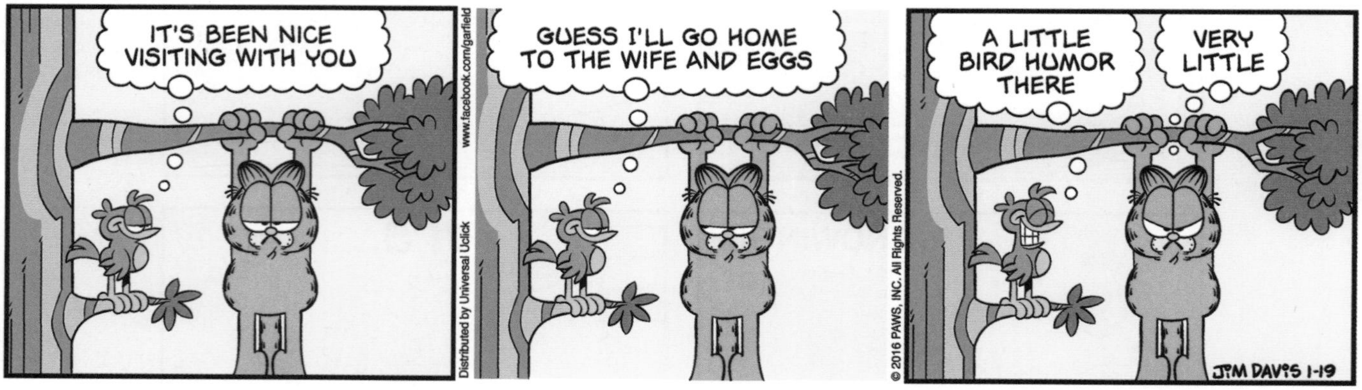
IT'S BEEN NICE VISITING WITH YOU
Distributed by Universal Uclick www.facebook.com/garfield
GUESS I'LL GO HOME TO THE WIFE AND EGGS
© 2016 PAWS, INC. All Rights Reserved.
A LITTLE BIRD HUMOR THERE
VERY LITTLE
JIM DAVIS 1-19

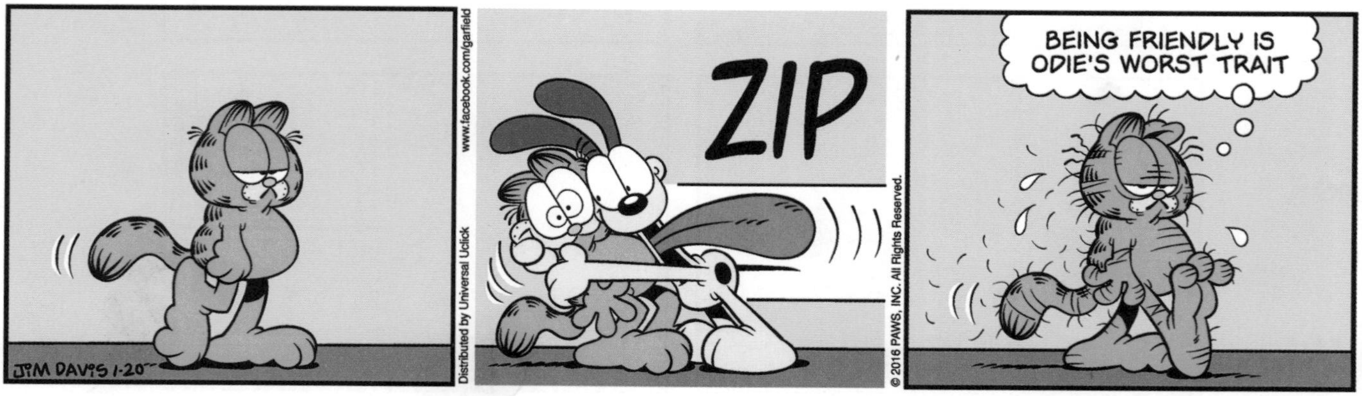
JIM DAVIS 1-20
Distributed by Universal Uclick www.facebook.com/garfield
ZIP
© 2016 PAWS, INC. All Rights Reserved.
BEING FRIENDLY IS ODIE'S WORST TRAIT

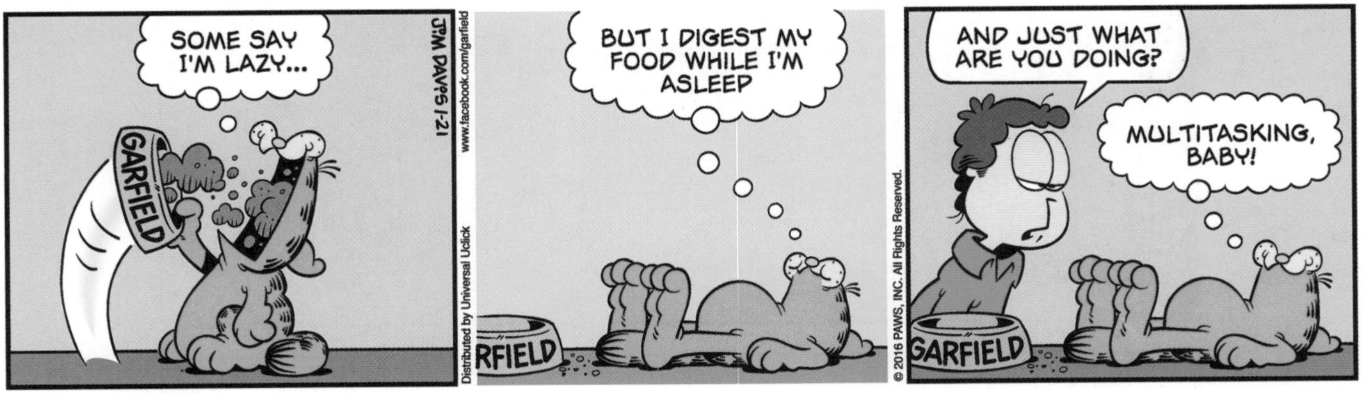
SOME SAY I'M LAZY...
JIM DAVIS 1-21
www.facebook.com/garfield
Distributed by Universal Uclick
GARFIELD
BUT I DIGEST MY FOOD WHILE I'M ASLEEP
RFIELD
© 2016 PAWS, INC. All Rights Reserved.
AND JUST WHAT ARE YOU DOING?
MULTITASKING, BABY!
GARFIELD

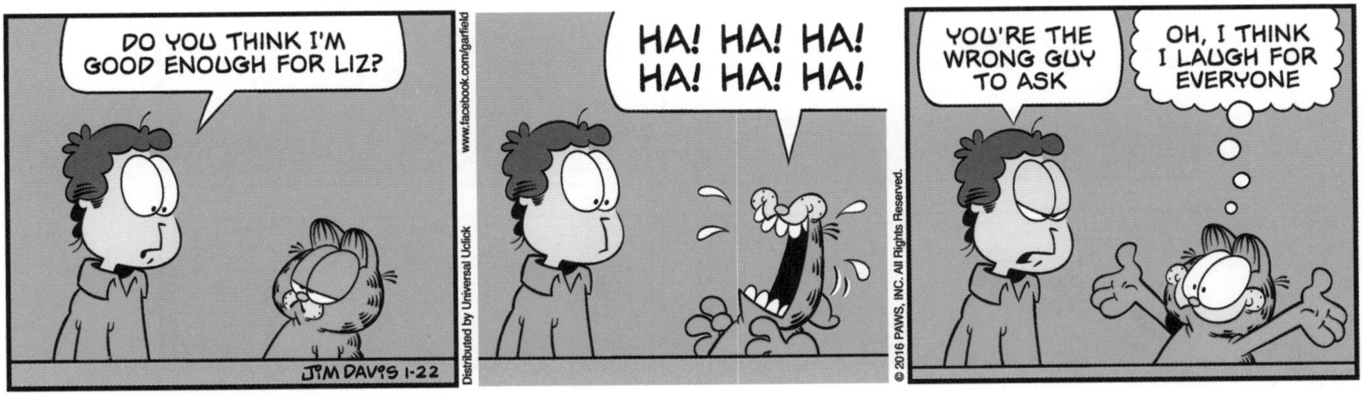
DO YOU THINK I'M GOOD ENOUGH FOR LIZ?
JIM DAVIS 1-22
www.facebook.com/garfield
Distributed by Universal Uclick
HA! HA! HA! HA! HA! HA!
© 2016 PAWS, INC. All Rights Reserved.
YOU'RE THE WRONG GUY TO ASK
OH, I THINK I LAUGH FOR EVERYONE

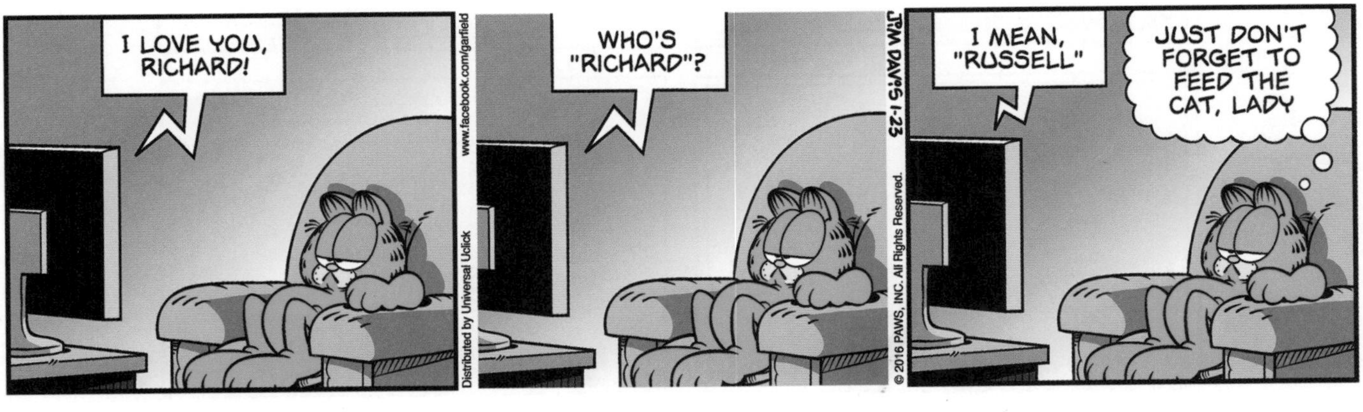
I LOVE YOU, RICHARD!
www.facebook.com/garfield
Distributed by Universal Uclick
WHO'S "RICHARD"?
JIM DAVIS 1-23
© 2016 PAWS, INC. All Rights Reserved.
I MEAN, "RUSSELL"
JUST DON'T FORGET TO FEED THE CAT, LADY

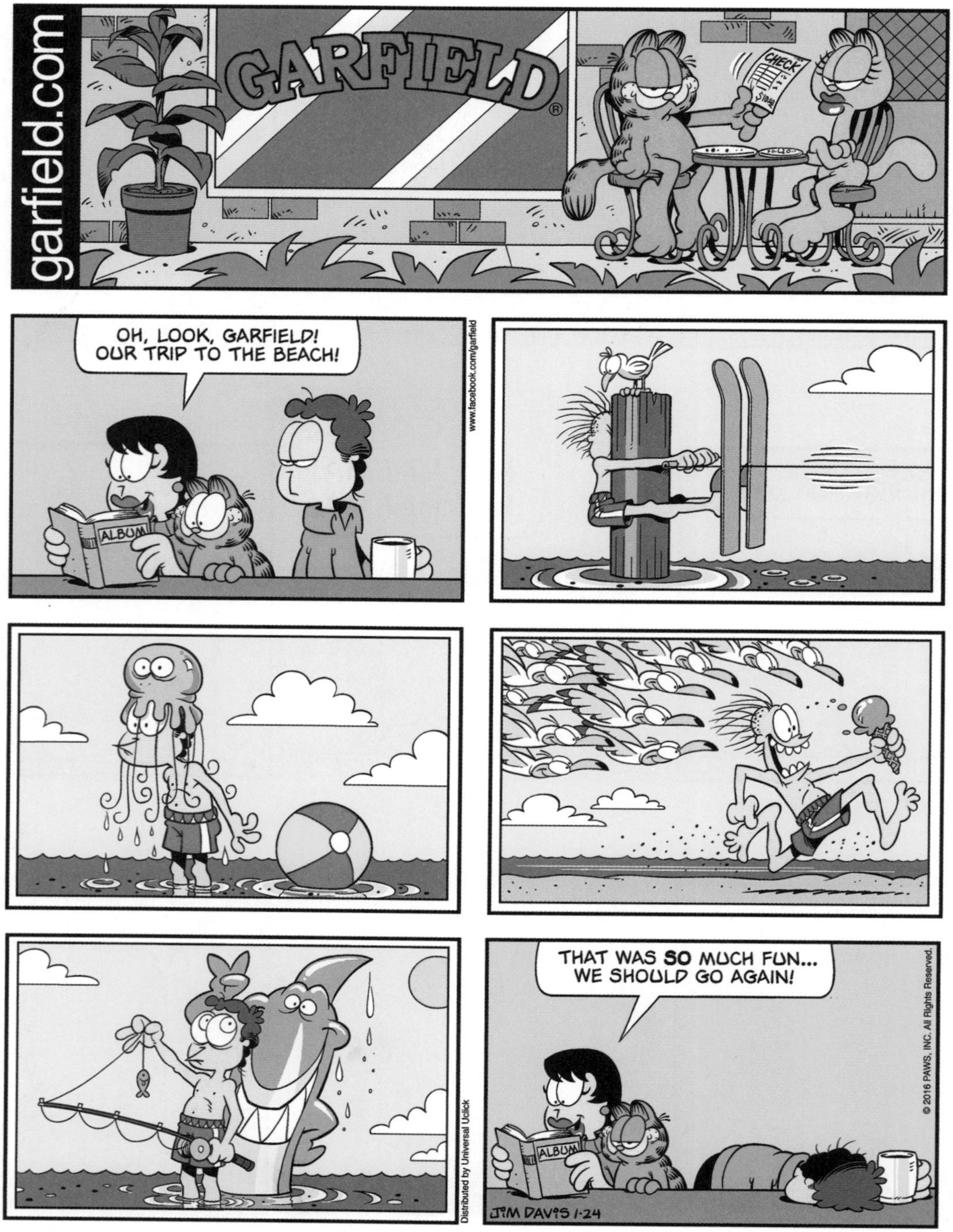
garfield.com
GARFIELD®
CHECK
www.facebook.com/garfield
OH, LOOK, GARFIELD! OUR TRIP TO THE BEACH!
ALBUM
Distributed by Universal Uclick
THAT WAS SO MUCH FUN... WE SHOULD GO AGAIN!
ALBUM
JIM DAVIS 1-24
© 2016 PAWS, INC. All Rights Reserved.

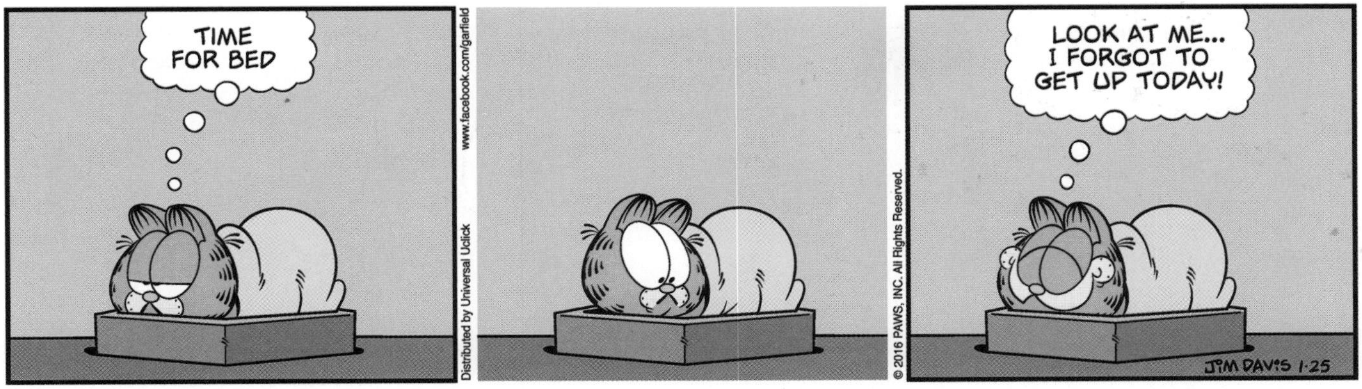
TIME FOR BED
Distributed by Universal Uclick www.facebook.com/garfield
© 2016 PAWS, INC. All Rights Reserved.
LOOK AT ME... I FORGOT TO GET UP TODAY!
JIM DAVIS 1-25

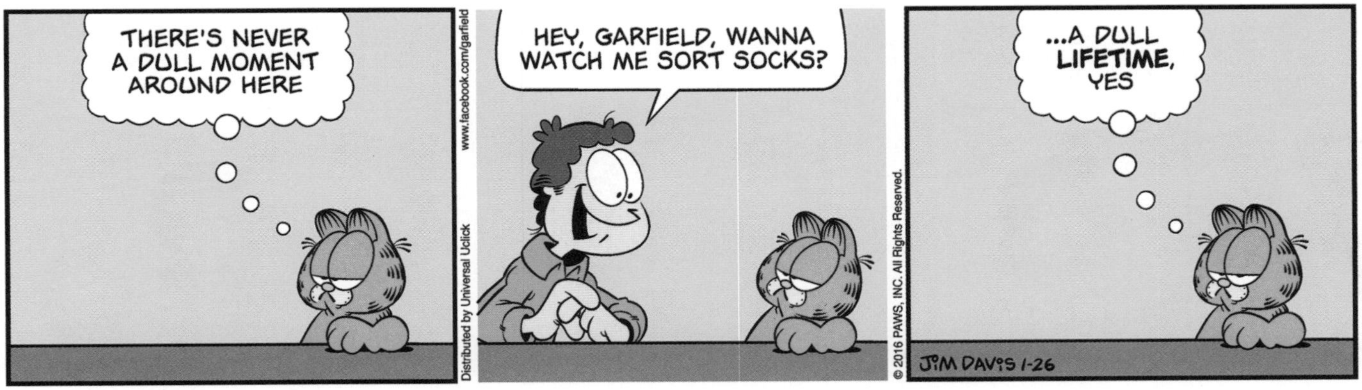
THERE'S NEVER A DULL MOMENT AROUND HERE
Distributed by Universal Uclick www.facebook.com/garfield
HEY, GARFIELD, WANNA WATCH ME SORT SOCKS?
© 2016 PAWS, INC. All Rights Reserved.
...A DULL **LIFETIME**, YES
JIM DAVIS 1-26

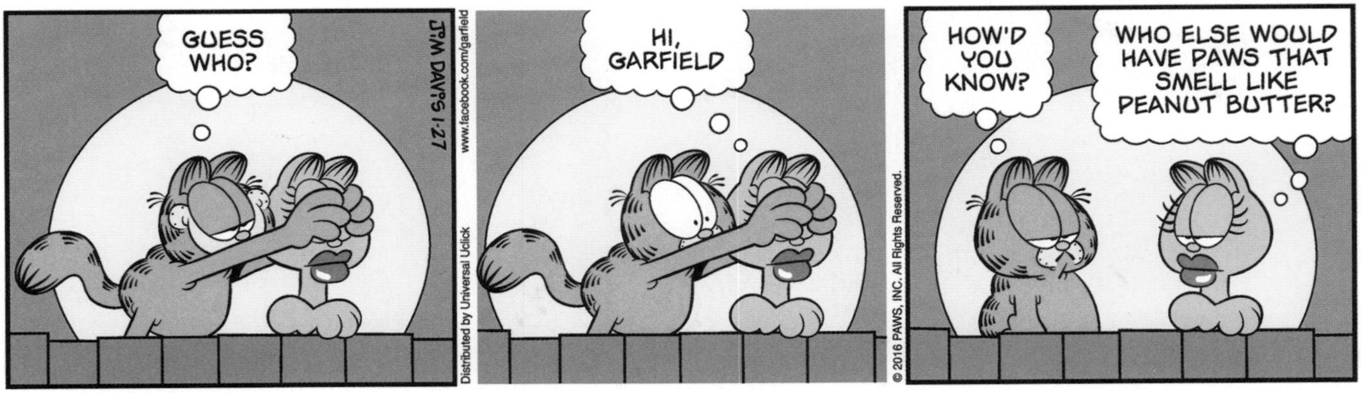
GUESS WHO?
JIM DAVIS 1-27
Distributed by Universal Uclick www.facebook.com/garfield
HI, GARFIELD
© 2016 PAWS, INC. All Rights Reserved.
HOW'D YOU KNOW?
WHO ELSE WOULD HAVE PAWS THAT SMELL LIKE PEANUT BUTTER?

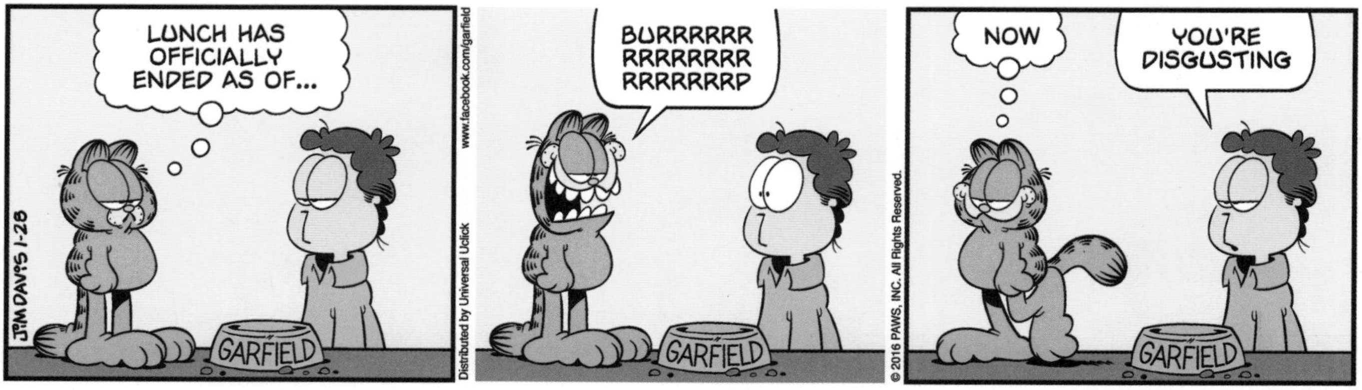
LUNCH HAS OFFICIALLY ENDED AS OF...
JIM DAVIS 1-28
GARFIELD
Distributed by Universal Uclick www.facebook.com/garfield
BURRRRRR RRRRRRRR RRRRRRRP
GARFIELD
© 2016 PAWS, INC. All Rights Reserved.
NOW
YOU'RE DISGUSTING
GARFIELD

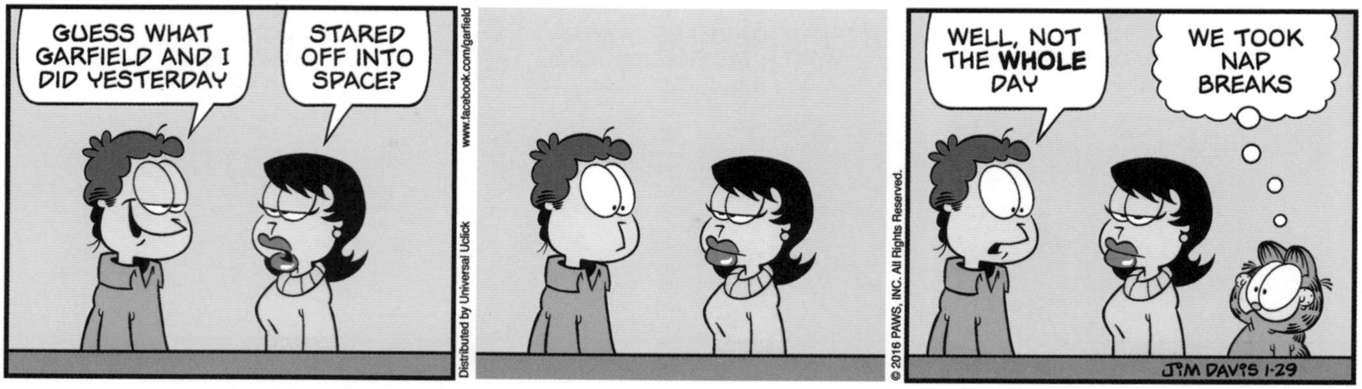
GUESS WHAT GARFIELD AND I DID YESTERDAY
STARED OFF INTO SPACE?
Distributed by Universal Uclick www.facebook.com/garfield
© 2016 PAWS, INC. All Rights Reserved.
WELL, NOT THE **WHOLE** DAY
WE TOOK NAP BREAKS
JIM DAVIS 1-29

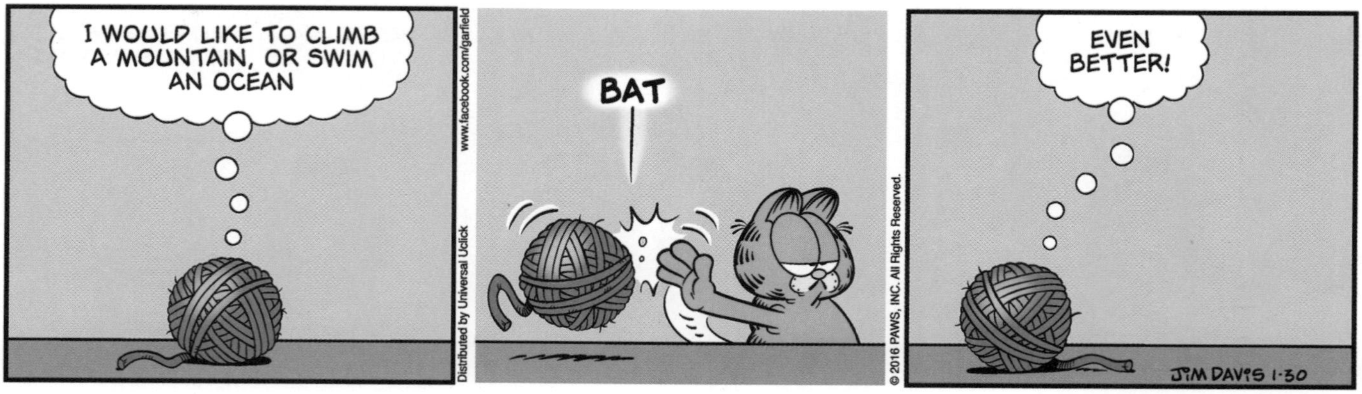
I WOULD LIKE TO CLIMB A MOUNTAIN, OR SWIM AN OCEAN
Distributed by Universal Uclick www.facebook.com/garfield
BAT
© 2016 PAWS, INC. All Rights Reserved.
EVEN BETTER!
JIM DAVIS 1-30

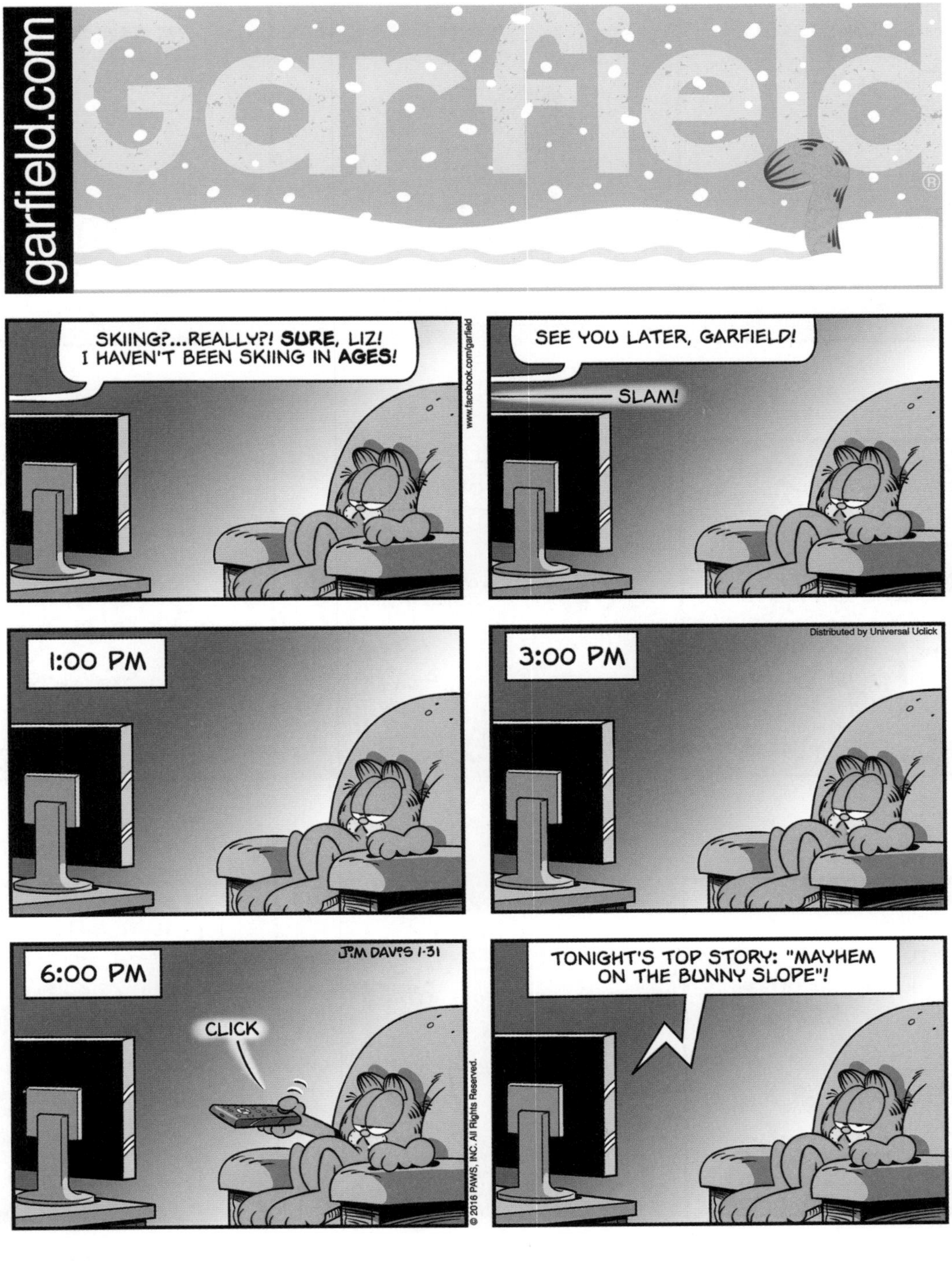
garfield.com
Garfield®
SKIING?...REALLY?! SURE, LIZ! I HAVEN'T BEEN SKIING IN AGES!
www.facebook.com/garfield
SEE YOU LATER, GARFIELD!
SLAM!
1:00 PM
3:00 PM
Distributed by Universal Uclick
6:00 PM
JPM DAVPS 1-31
CLICK
© 2016 PAWS, INC. All Rights Reserved.
TONIGHT'S TOP STORY: "MAYHEM ON THE BUNNY SLOPE"!

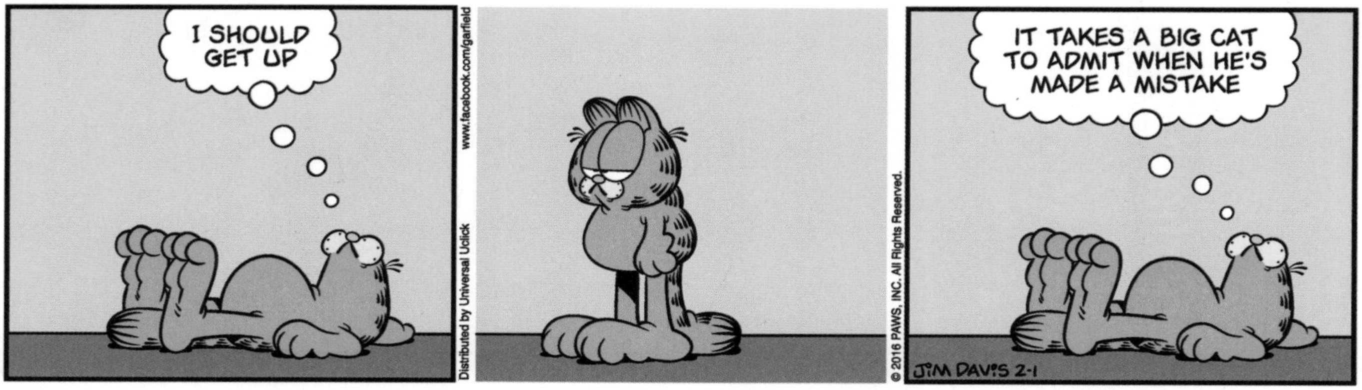
I SHOULD GET UP
www.facebook.com/garfield
Distributed by Universal Uclick
IT TAKES A BIG CAT TO ADMIT WHEN HE'S MADE A MISTAKE
© 2016 PAWS, INC. All Rights Reserved.
JIM DAVIS 2-1

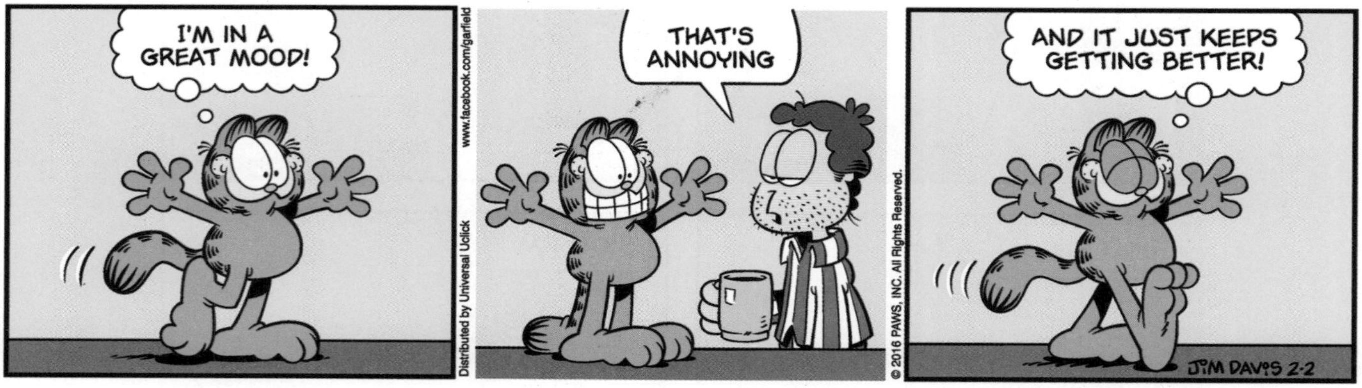
I'M IN A GREAT MOOD!
Distributed by Universal Uclick
www.facebook.com/garfield
THAT'S ANNOYING
© 2016 PAWS, INC. All Rights Reserved.
AND IT JUST KEEPS GETTING BETTER!
JIM DAVIS 2-2

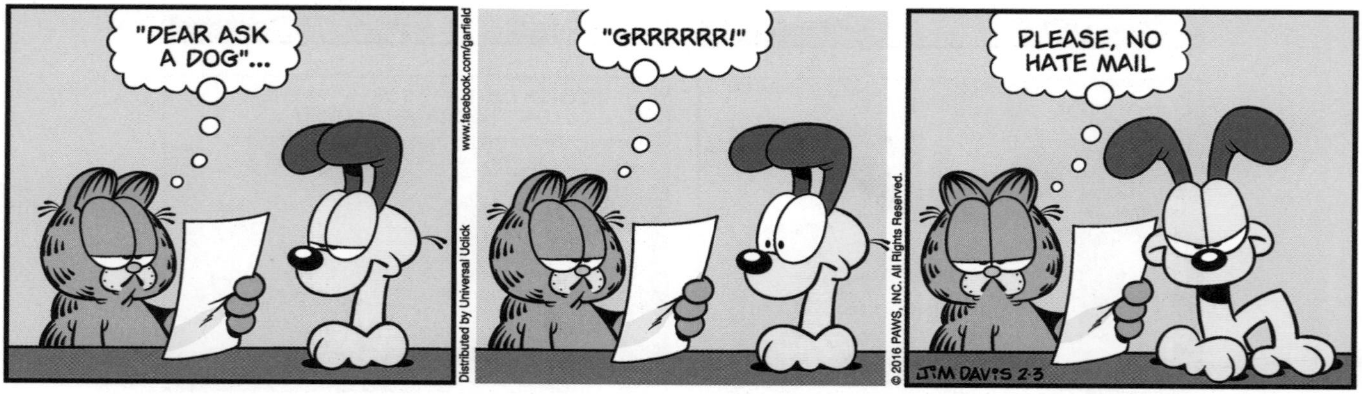
"DEAR ASK A DOG"...
www.facebook.com/garfield
Distributed by Universal Uclick
"GRRRRRR!"
© 2016 PAWS, INC. All Rights Reserved.
PLEASE, NO HATE MAIL
JIM DAVIS 2-3

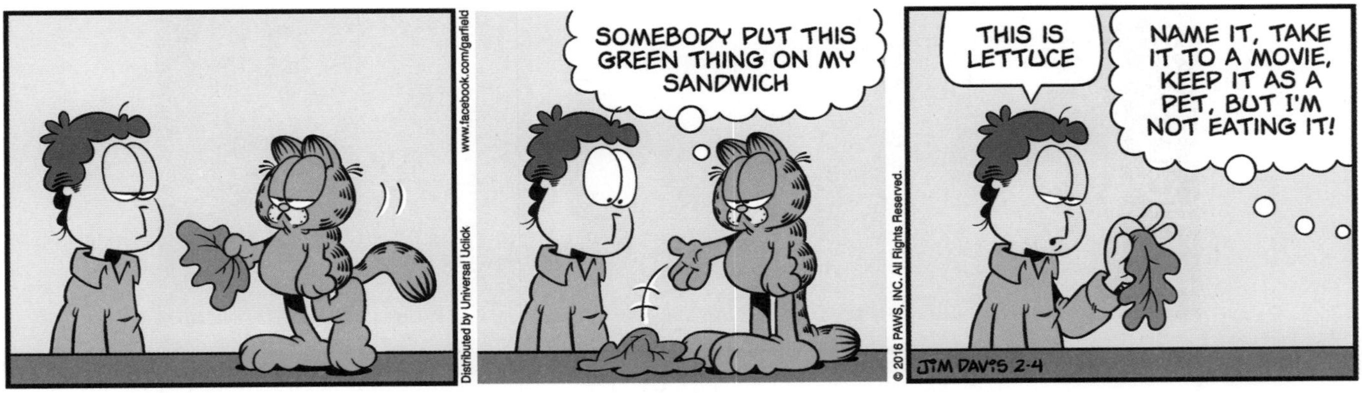
Distributed by Universal Uclick www.facebook.com/garfield
SOMEBODY PUT THIS GREEN THING ON MY SANDWICH
© 2016 PAWS, INC. All Rights Reserved.
THIS IS LETTUCE
NAME IT, TAKE IT TO A MOVIE, KEEP IT AS A PET, BUT I'M NOT EATING IT!
JIM DAVIS 2-4

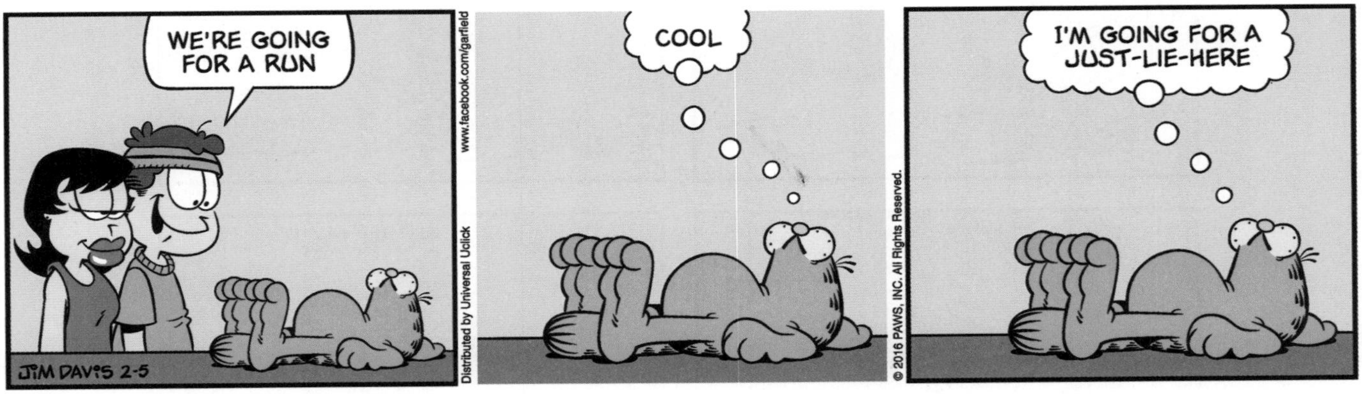
WE'RE GOING FOR A RUN
JIM DAVIS 2-5
Distributed by Universal Uclick www.facebook.com/garfield
COOL
© 2016 PAWS, INC. All Rights Reserved.
I'M GOING FOR A JUST-LIE-HERE

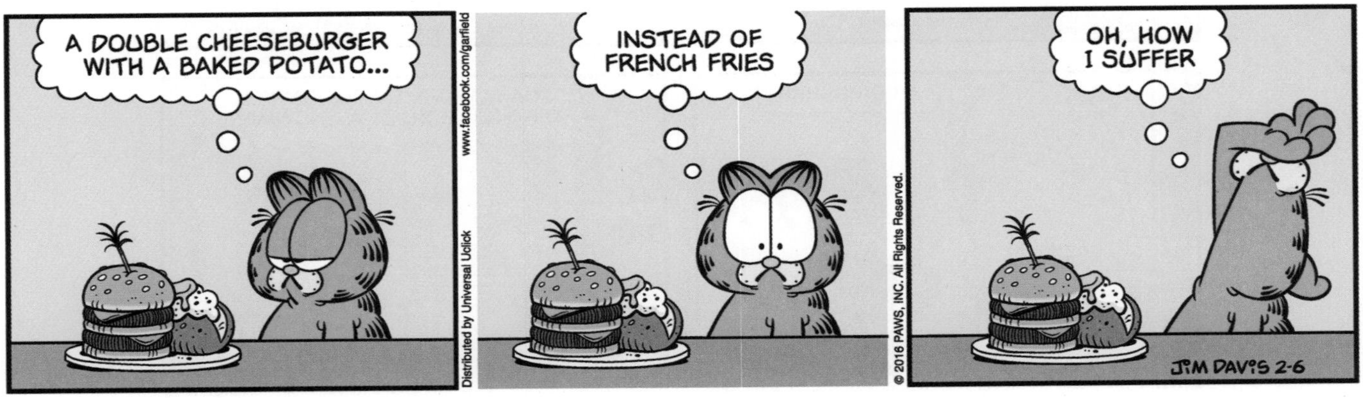
A DOUBLE CHEESEBURGER WITH A BAKED POTATO...
Distributed by Universal Uclick www.facebook.com/garfield
INSTEAD OF FRENCH FRIES
© 2016 PAWS, INC. All Rights Reserved.
OH, HOW I SUFFER
JIM DAVIS 2-6

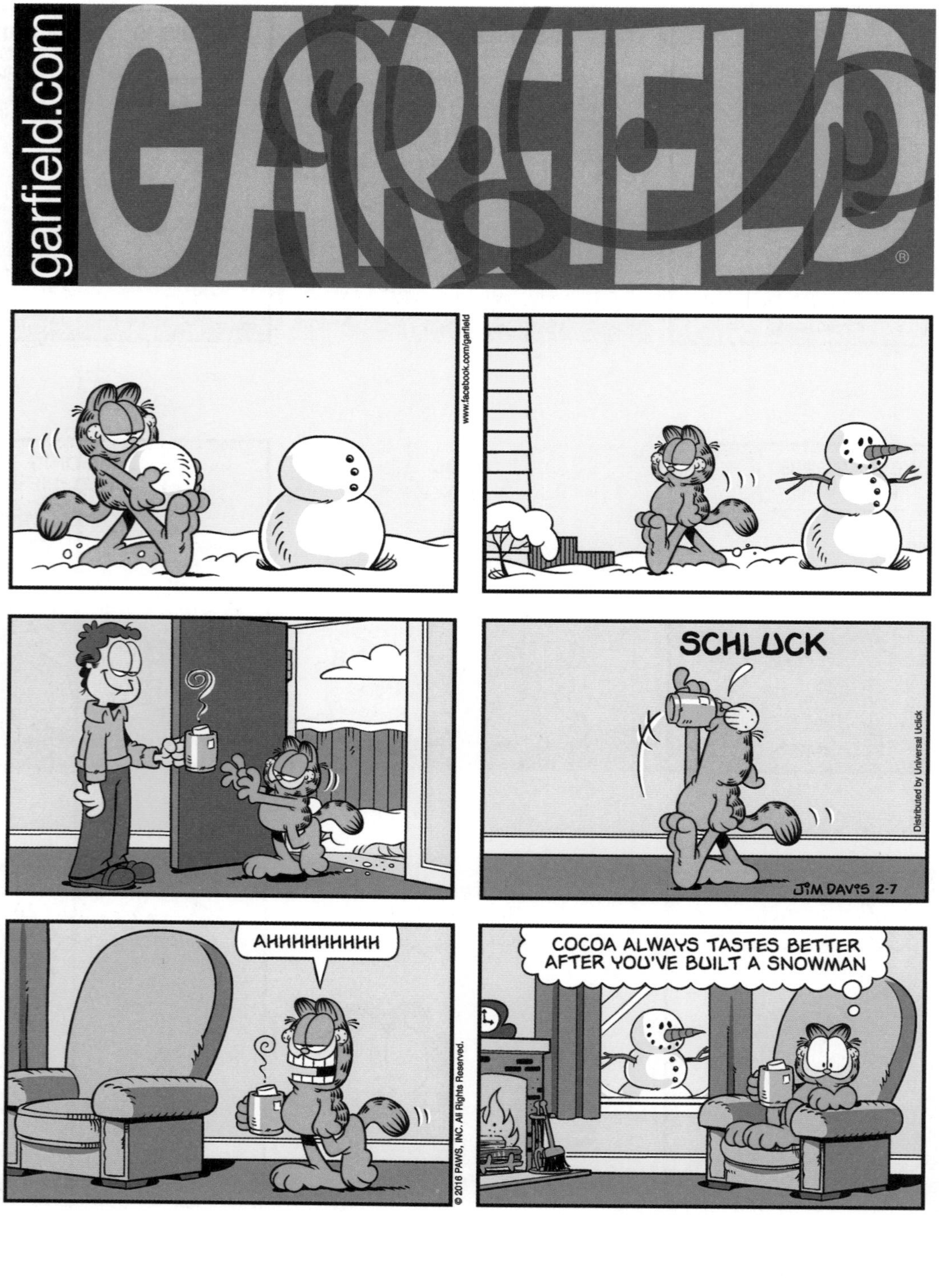
garfield.com
GARFIELD
www.facebook.com/garfield
SCHLUCK
Distributed by Universal Uclick
JIM DAVIS 2-7
AHHHHHHHHH
© 2016 PAWS, INC. All Rights Reserved.
COCOA ALWAYS TASTES BETTER AFTER YOU'VE BUILT A SNOWMAN

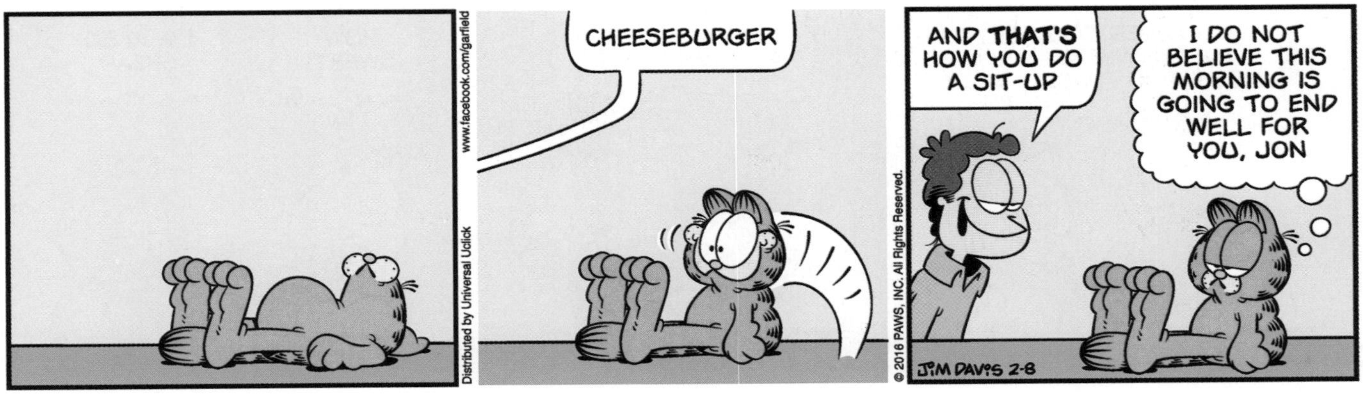
www.facebook.com/garfield
Distributed by Universal Uclick
CHEESEBURGER
© 2016 PAWS, INC. All Rights Reserved.
AND THAT'S HOW YOU DO A SIT-UP
I DO NOT BELIEVE THIS MORNING IS GOING TO END WELL FOR YOU, JON
JIM DAVIS 2-8

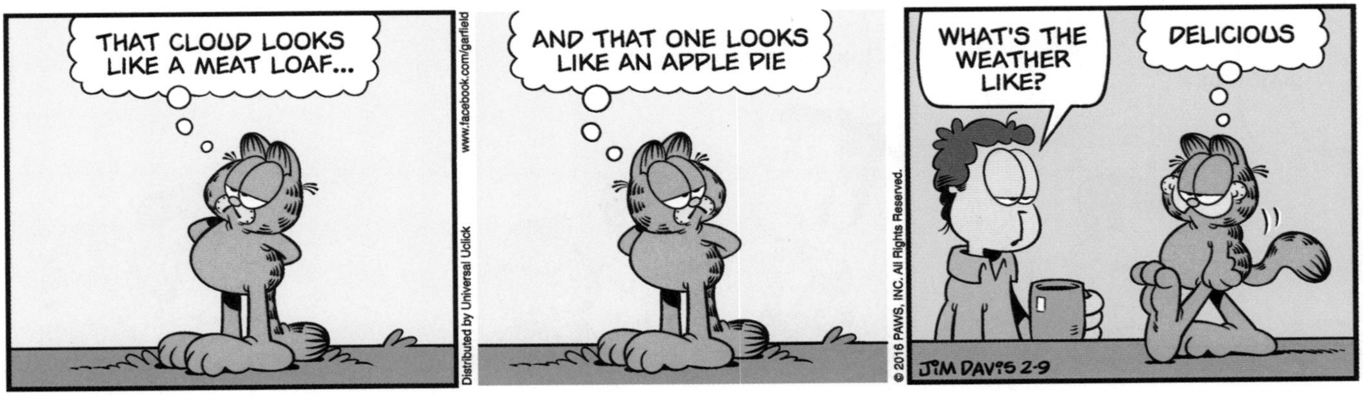
THAT CLOUD LOOKS LIKE A MEAT LOAF...
www.facebook.com/garfield
Distributed by Universal Uclick
AND THAT ONE LOOKS LIKE AN APPLE PIE
© 2016 PAWS, INC. All Rights Reserved.
WHAT'S THE WEATHER LIKE?
DELICIOUS
JIM DAVIS 2-9

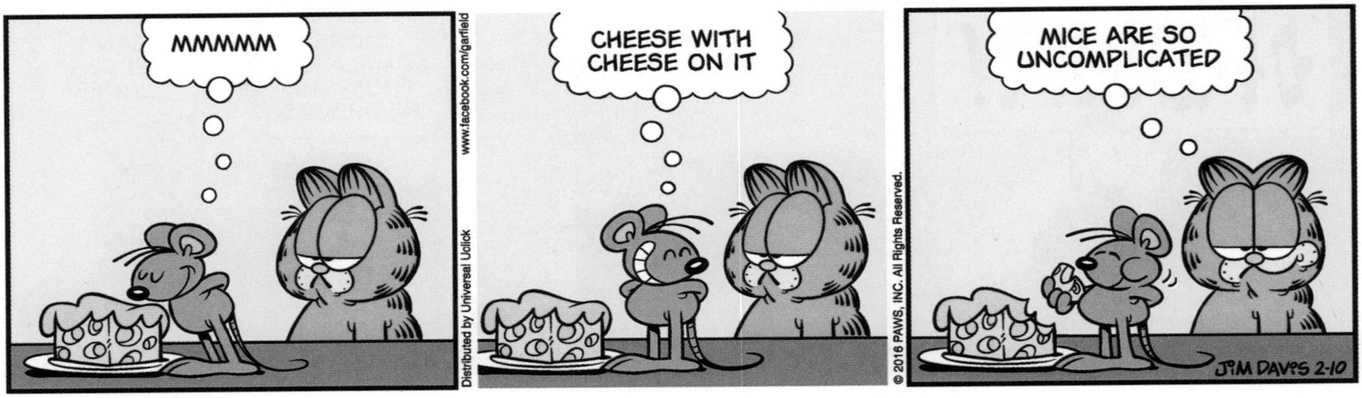
MMMMM
www.facebook.com/garfield
Distributed by Universal Uclick
CHEESE WITH CHEESE ON IT
© 2016 PAWS, INC. All Rights Reserved.
MICE ARE SO UNCOMPLICATED
JIM DAVIS 2-10

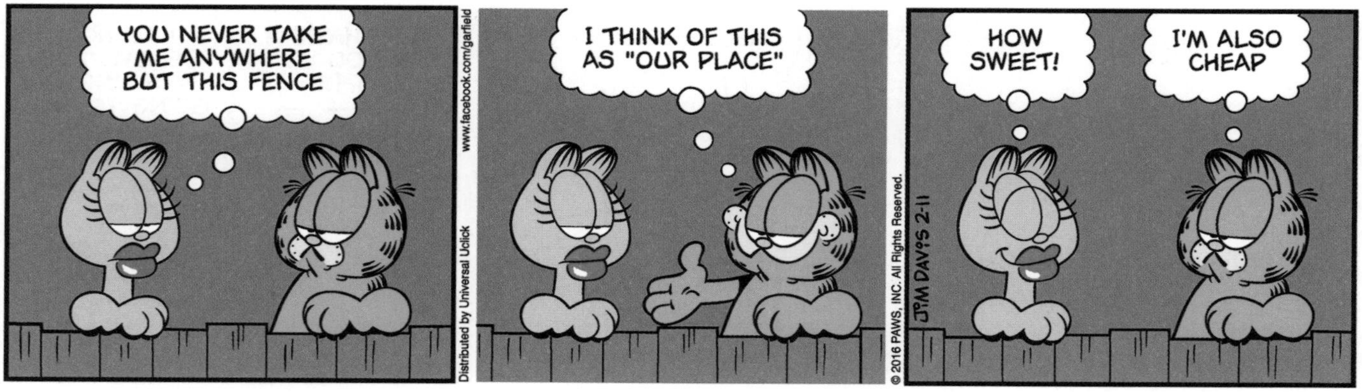
YOU NEVER TAKE ME ANYWHERE BUT THIS FENCE
Distributed by Universal Uclick www.facebook.com/garfield
I THINK OF THIS AS "OUR PLACE"
© 2016 PAWS, INC. All Rights Reserved.
HOW SWEET!
I'M ALSO CHEAP
JIM DAVIS 2-11

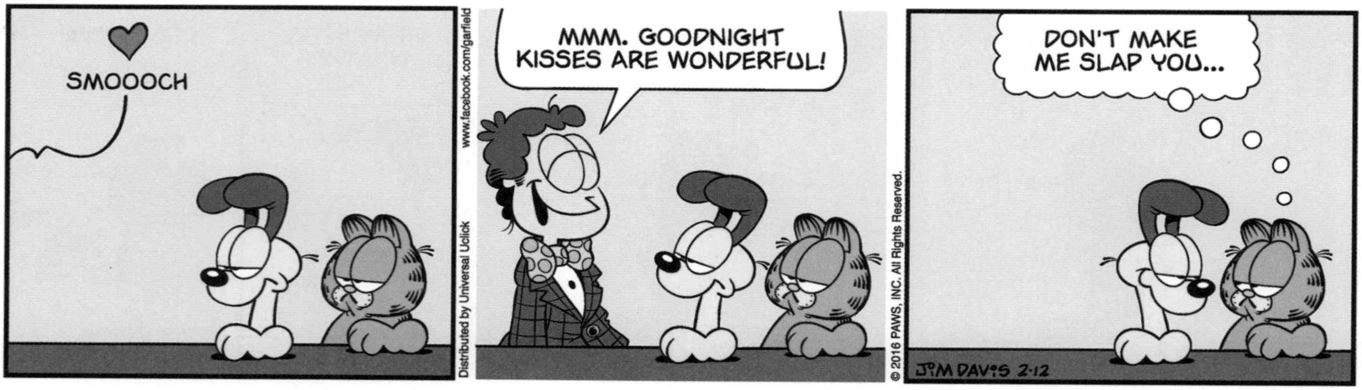
SMOOOCH
Distributed by Universal Uclick www.facebook.com/garfield
MMM. GOODNIGHT KISSES ARE WONDERFUL!
© 2016 PAWS, INC. All Rights Reserved.
DON'T MAKE ME SLAP YOU...
JIM DAVIS 2-12

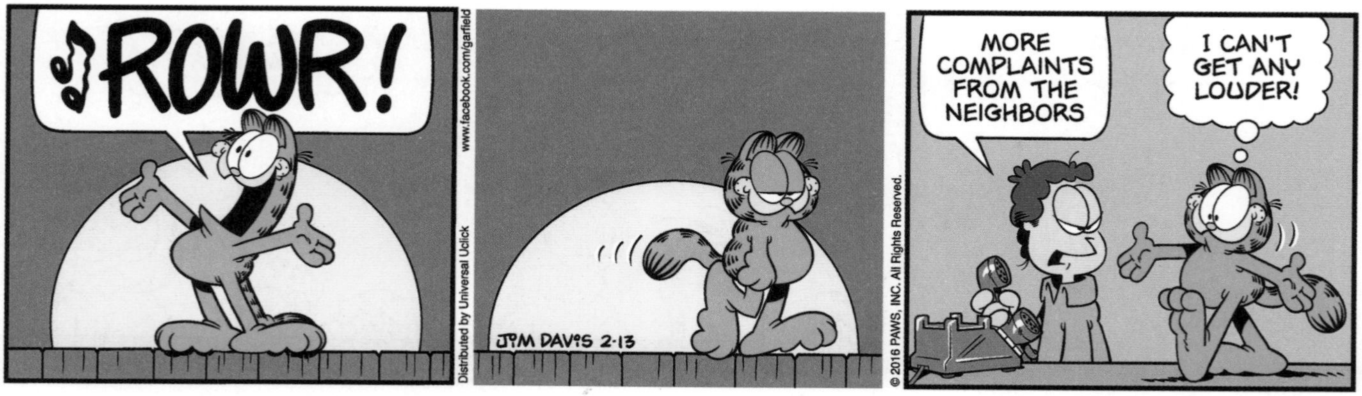
ROWR!
Distributed by Universal Uclick www.facebook.com/garfield
JIM DAVIS 2-13
© 2016 PAWS, INC. All Rights Reserved.
MORE COMPLAINTS FROM THE NEIGHBORS
I CAN'T GET ANY LOUDER!

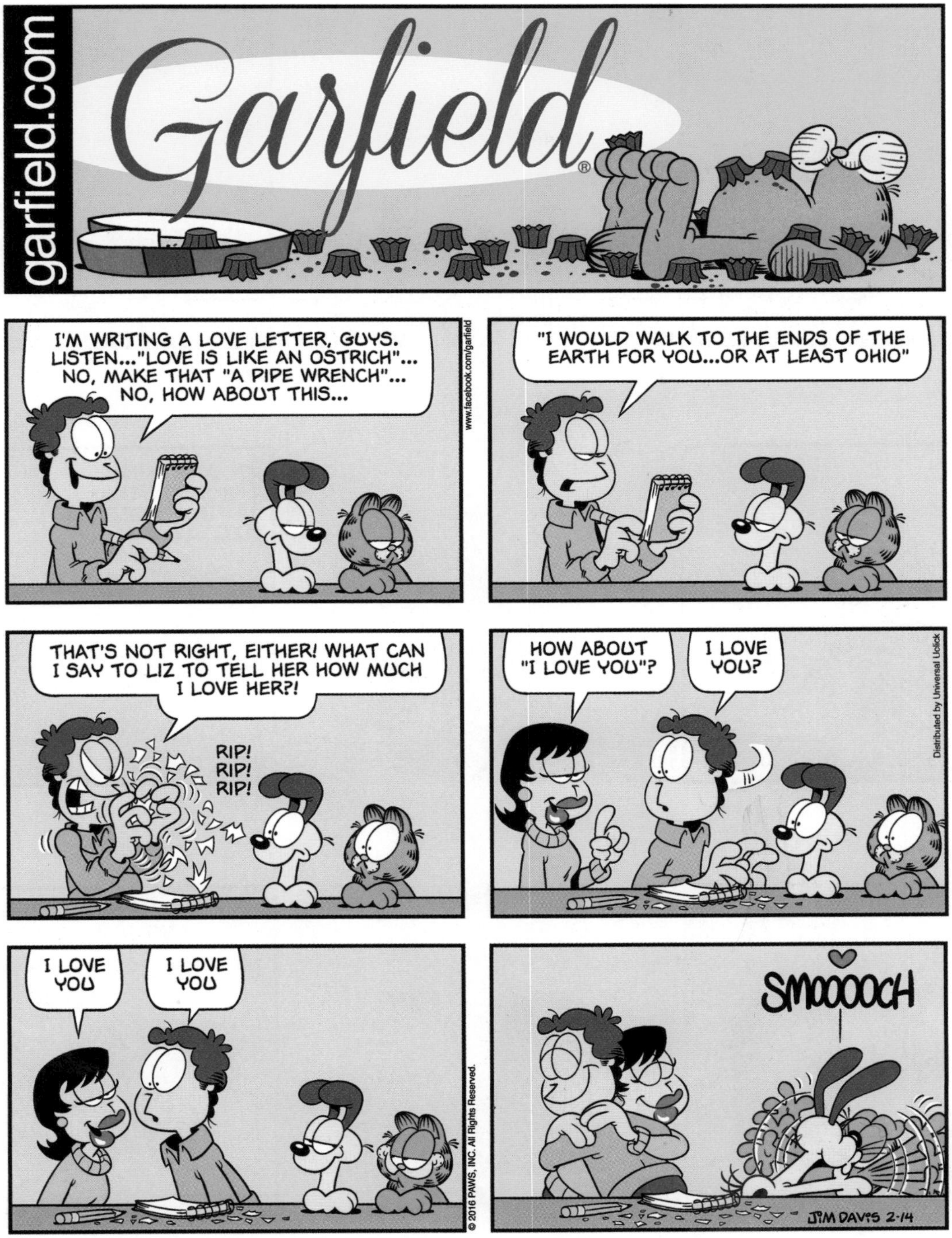
garfield.com
Garfield
I'M WRITING A LOVE LETTER, GUYS. LISTEN..."LOVE IS LIKE AN OSTRICH"... NO, MAKE THAT "A PIPE WRENCH"... NO, HOW ABOUT THIS...
www.facebook.com/garfield
"I WOULD WALK TO THE ENDS OF THE EARTH FOR YOU...OR AT LEAST OHIO"
THAT'S NOT RIGHT, EITHER! WHAT CAN I SAY TO LIZ TO TELL HER HOW MUCH I LOVE HER?!
RIP! RIP! RIP!
HOW ABOUT "I LOVE YOU"?
I LOVE YOU?
Distributed by Universal Uclick
I LOVE YOU
I LOVE YOU
© 2016 PAWS, INC. All Rights Reserved.
SMOOOOCH
JIM DAVIS 2-14

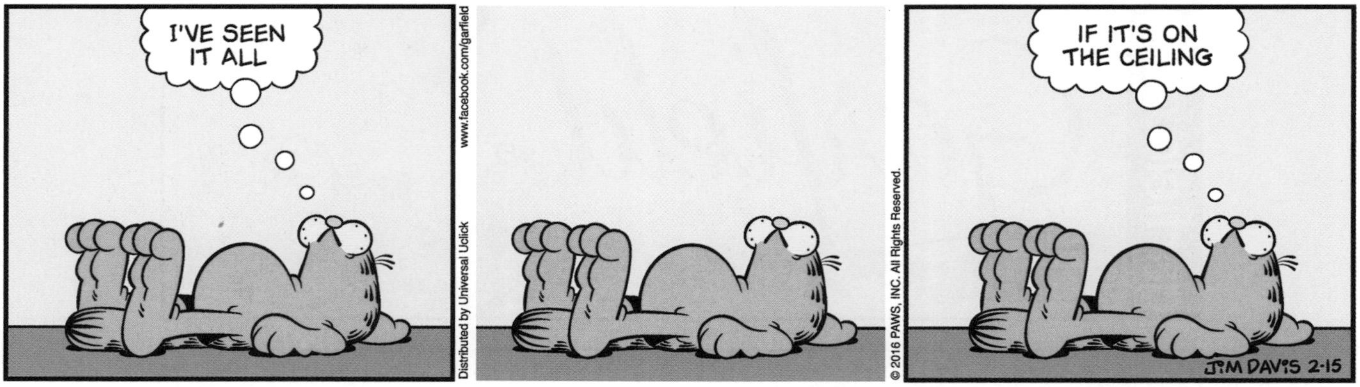
I'VE SEEN IT ALL
Distributed by Universal Uclick www.facebook.com/garfield
© 2016 PAWS, INC. All Rights Reserved.
IF IT'S ON THE CEILING
JIM DAVIS 2-15

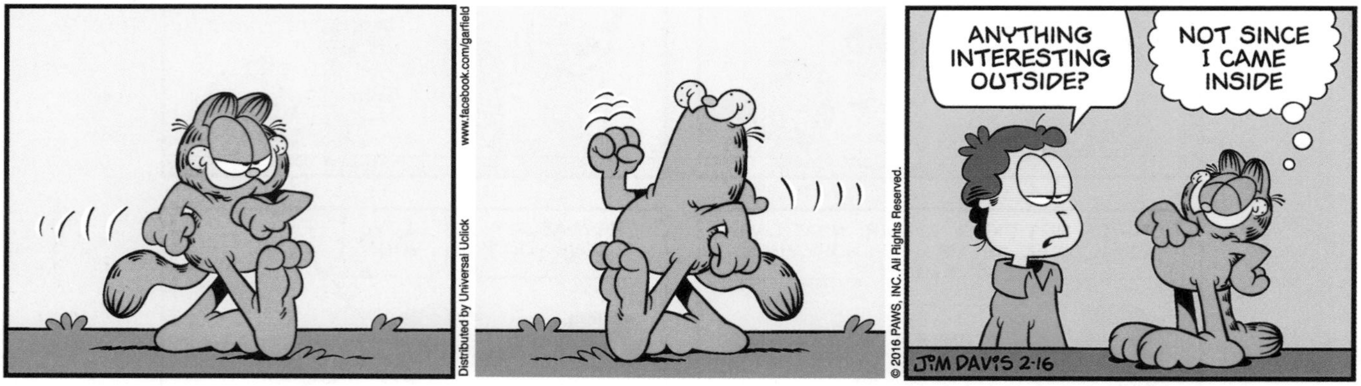
Distributed by Universal Uclick www.facebook.com/garfield
© 2016 PAWS, INC. All Rights Reserved.
ANYTHING INTERESTING OUTSIDE?
NOT SINCE I CAME INSIDE
JIM DAVIS 2-16

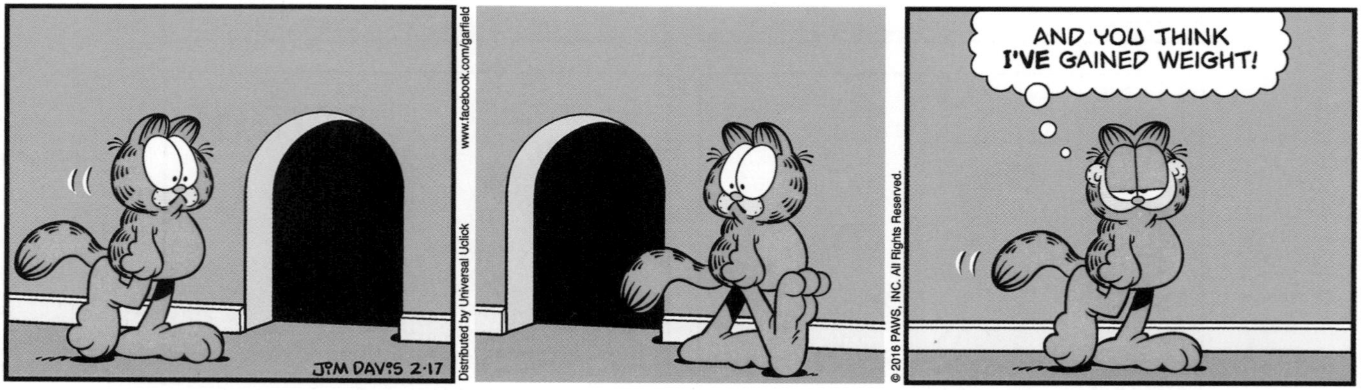
JIM DAVIS 2-17
Distributed by Universal Uclick www.facebook.com/garfield
© 2016 PAWS, INC. All Rights Reserved.
AND YOU THINK **I'VE** GAINED WEIGHT!

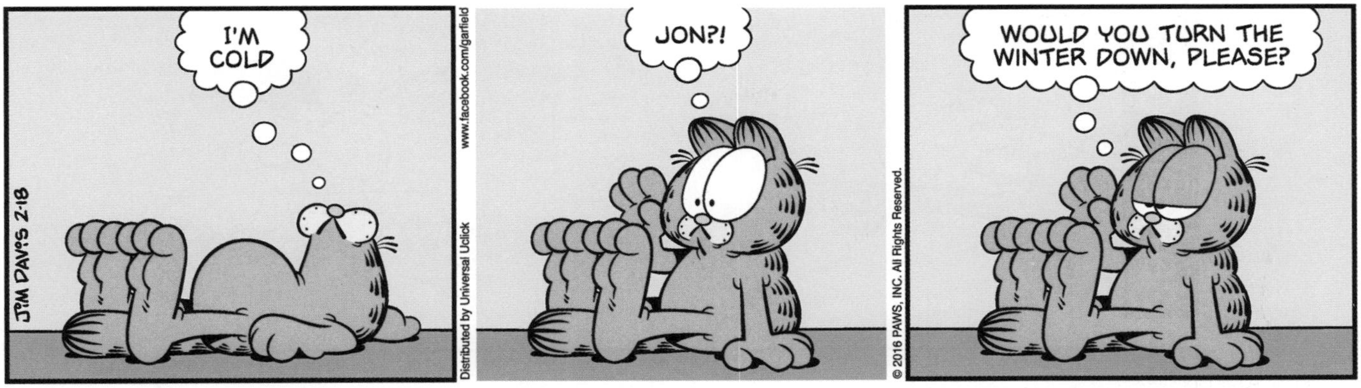
JIM DAVIS 2·18
I'M COLD
Distributed by Universal Uclick www.facebook.com/garfield
JON?!
© 2016 PAWS, INC. All Rights Reserved.
WOULD YOU TURN THE WINTER DOWN, PLEASE?

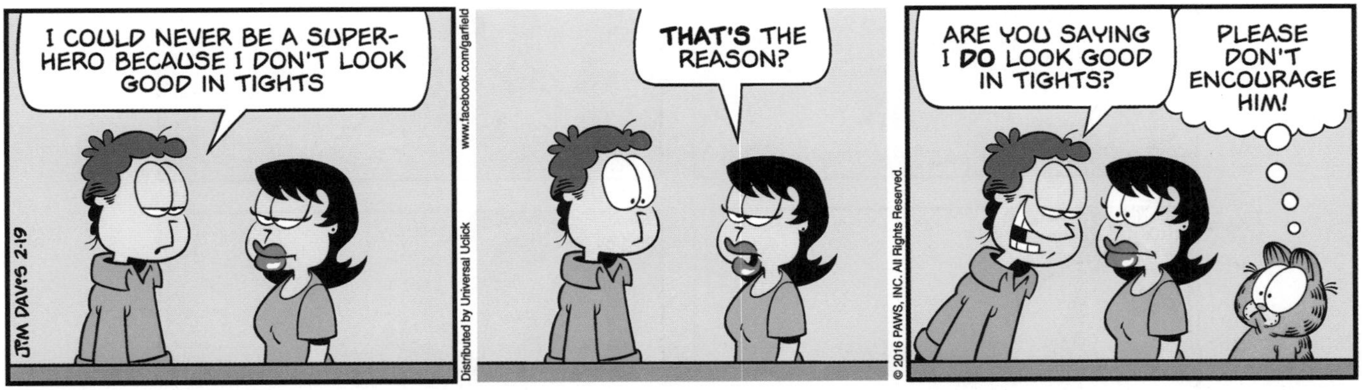
JIM DAVIS 2·19
I COULD NEVER BE A SUPER-HERO BECAUSE I DON'T LOOK GOOD IN TIGHTS
Distributed by Universal Uclick www.facebook.com/garfield
THAT'S THE REASON?
© 2016 PAWS, INC. All Rights Reserved.
ARE YOU SAYING I **DO** LOOK GOOD IN TIGHTS?
PLEASE DON'T ENCOURAGE HIM!

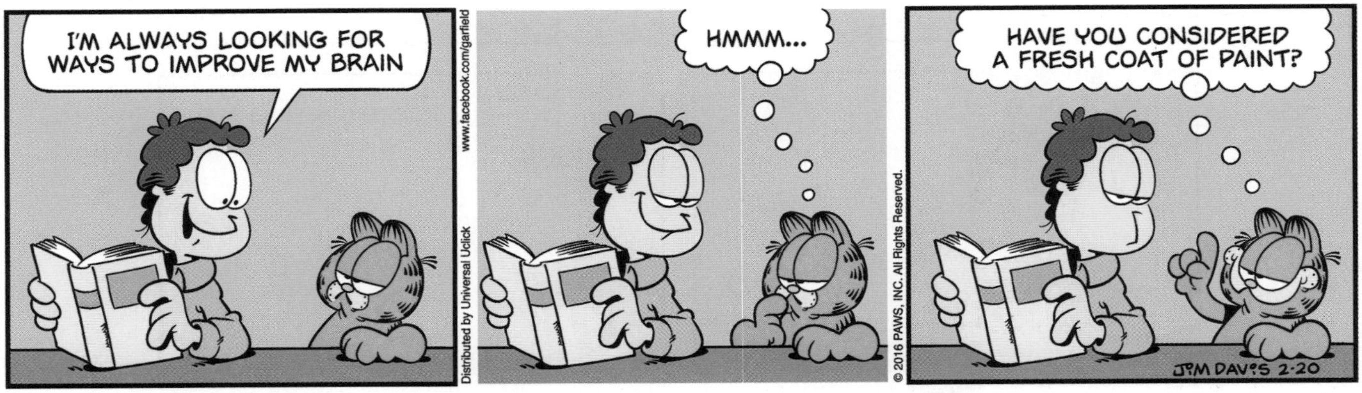
I'M ALWAYS LOOKING FOR WAYS TO IMPROVE MY BRAIN
Distributed by Universal Uclick www.facebook.com/garfield
HMMM...
© 2016 PAWS, INC. All Rights Reserved.
HAVE YOU CONSIDERED A FRESH COAT OF PAINT?
JIM DAVIS 2·20

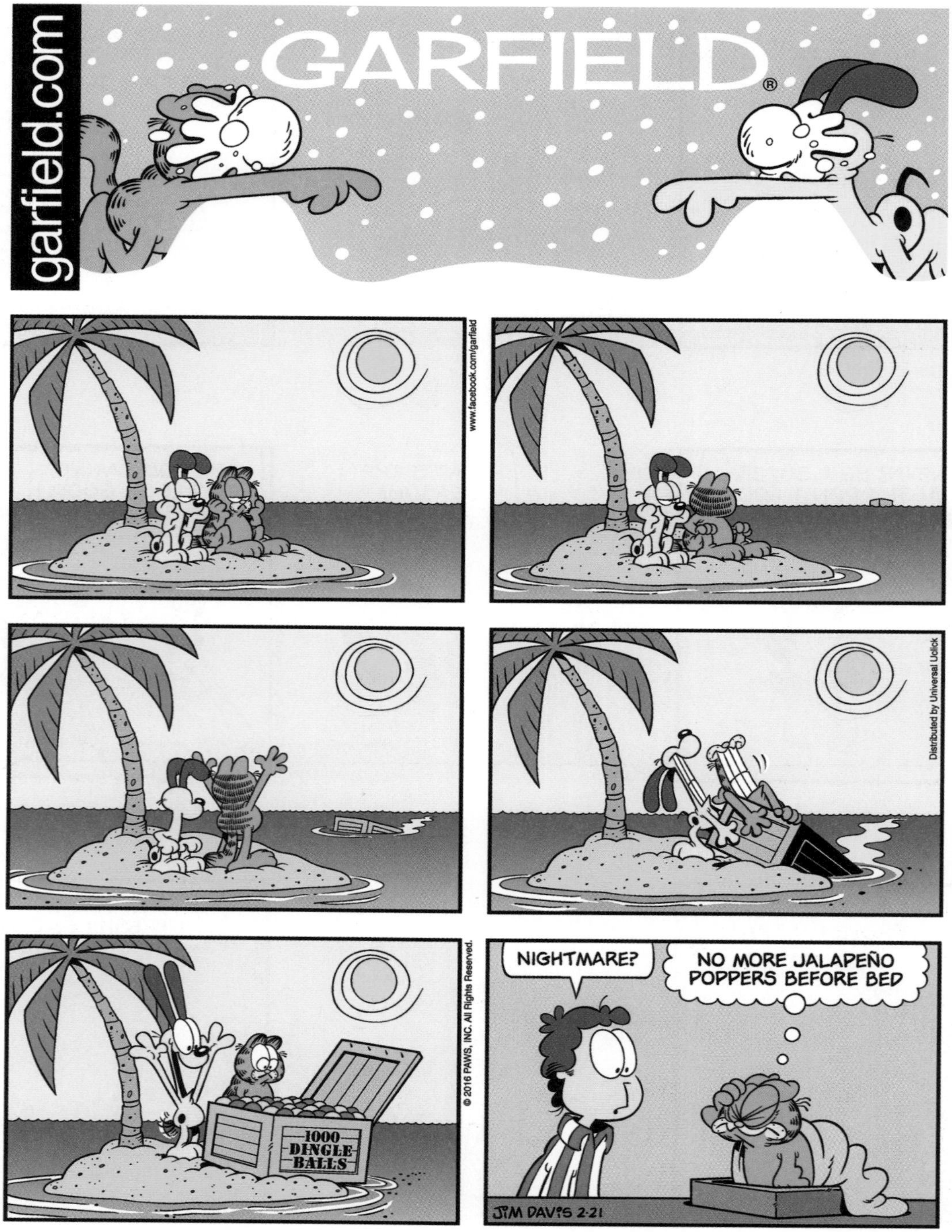
garfield.com
GARFIELD®
www.facebook.com/garfield
Distributed by Universal Uclick
© 2016 PAWS, INC. All Rights Reserved.
1000 DINGLE BALLS
NIGHTMARE?
NO MORE JALAPEÑO POPPERS BEFORE BED
JIM DAVIS 2-21

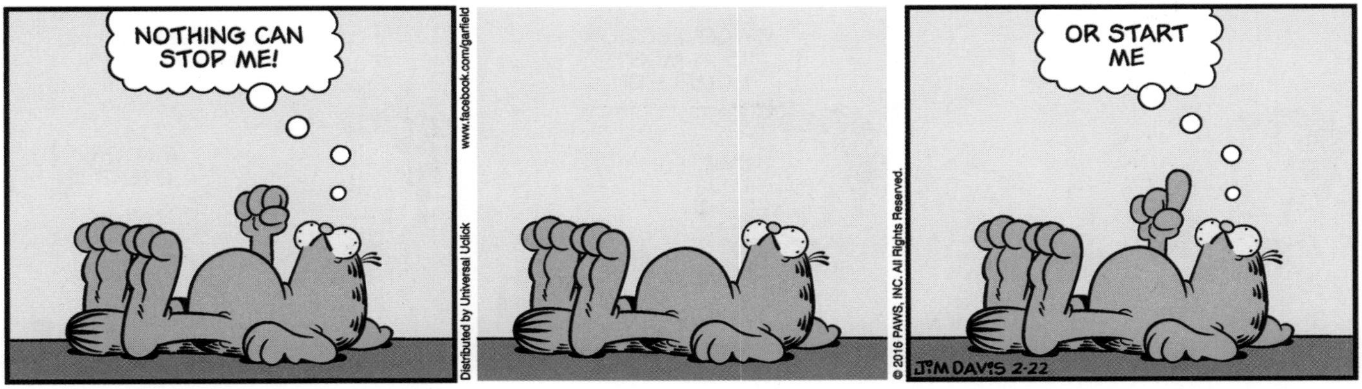
NOTHING CAN STOP ME!
OR START ME
Distributed by Universal Uclick www.facebook.com/garfield
© 2016 PAWS, INC. All Rights Reserved.
JIM DAVIS 2-22

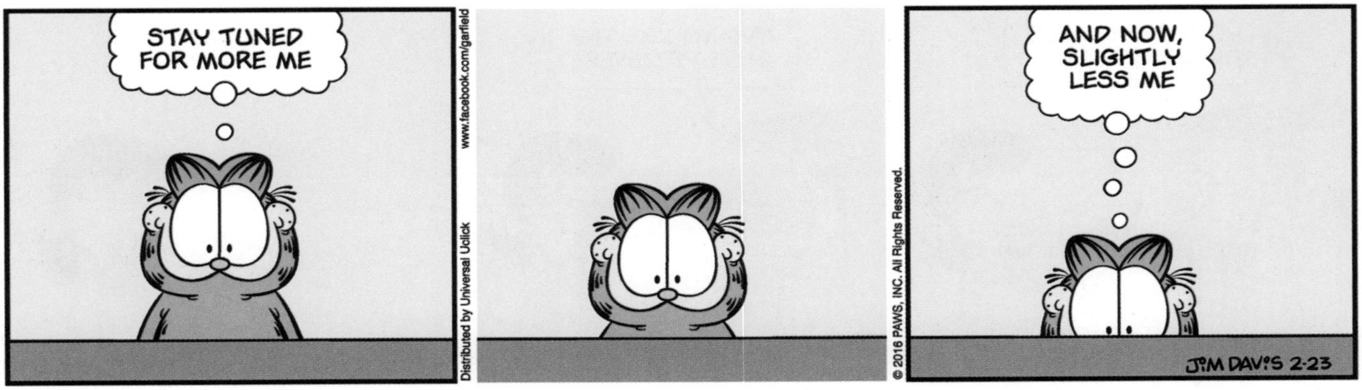
STAY TUNED FOR MORE ME
AND NOW, SLIGHTLY LESS ME
Distributed by Universal Uclick www.facebook.com/garfield
© 2016 PAWS, INC. All Rights Reserved.
JIM DAVIS 2-23

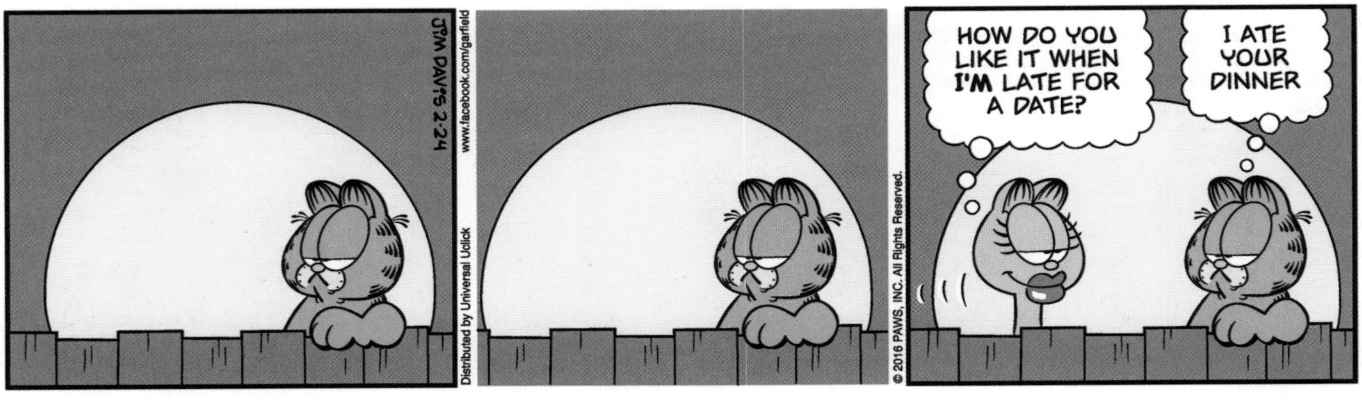
JIM DAVIS 2-24
Distributed by Universal Uclick www.facebook.com/garfield
© 2016 PAWS, INC. All Rights Reserved.
HOW DO YOU LIKE IT WHEN I'M LATE FOR A DATE?
I ATE YOUR DINNER

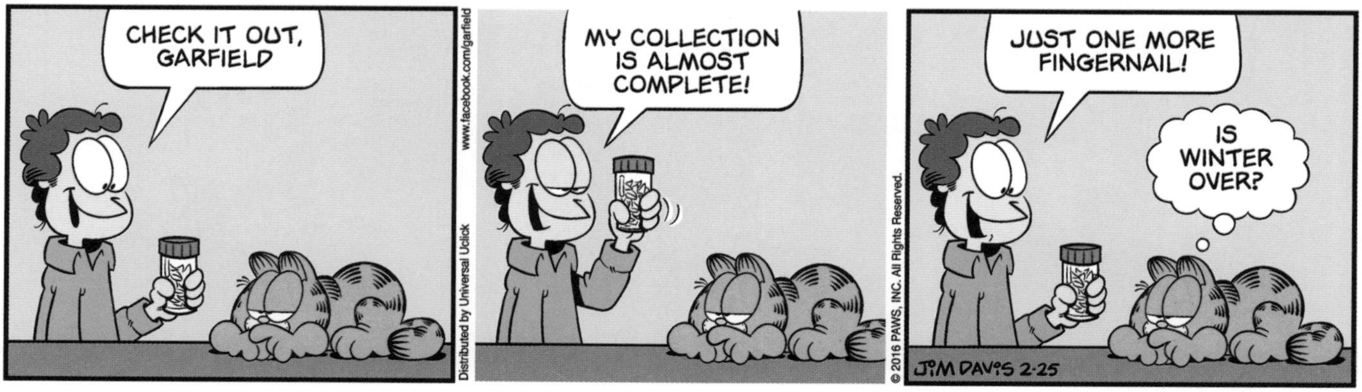
CHECK IT OUT, GARFIELD
MY COLLECTION IS ALMOST COMPLETE!
JUST ONE MORE FINGERNAIL!
IS WINTER OVER?
JIM DAVIS 2-25
Distributed by Universal Uclick
www.facebook.com/garfield
© 2016 PAWS, INC. All Rights Reserved.

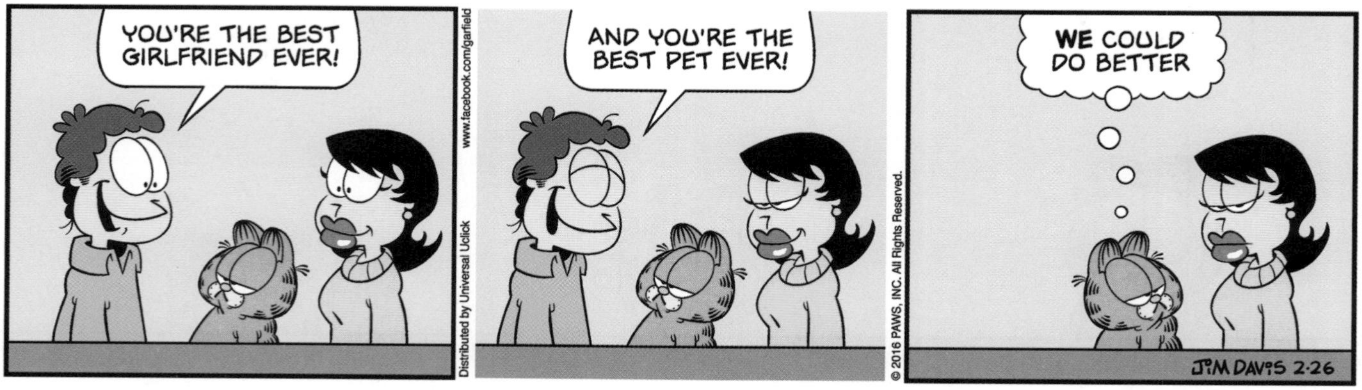
YOU'RE THE BEST GIRLFRIEND EVER!
AND YOU'RE THE BEST PET EVER!
WE COULD DO BETTER
JIM DAVIS 2-26
Distributed by Universal Uclick
www.facebook.com/garfield
© 2016 PAWS, INC. All Rights Reserved.

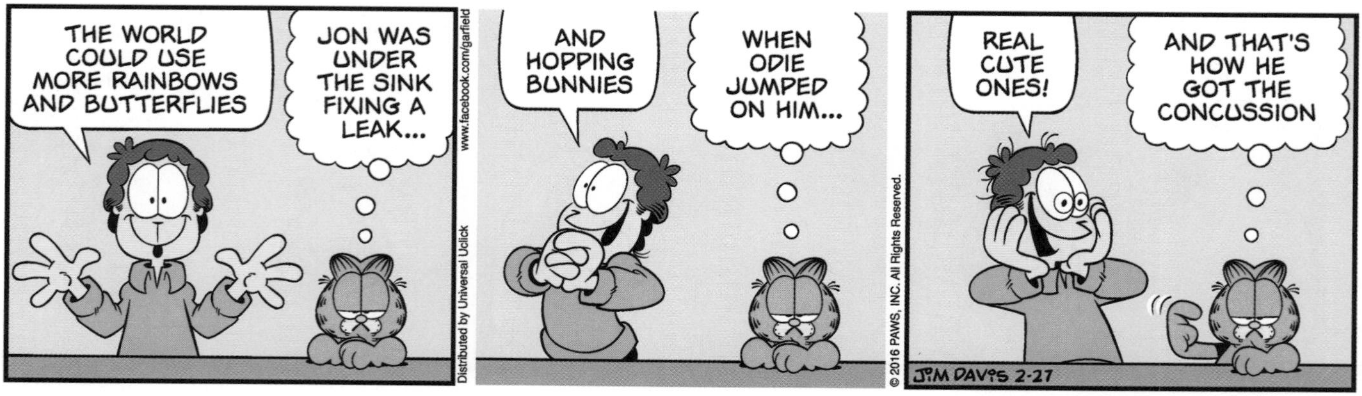
THE WORLD COULD USE MORE RAINBOWS AND BUTTERFLIES
JON WAS UNDER THE SINK FIXING A LEAK...
AND HOPPING BUNNIES
WHEN ODIE JUMPED ON HIM...
REAL CUTE ONES!
AND THAT'S HOW HE GOT THE CONCUSSION
JIM DAVIS 2-27
Distributed by Universal Uclick
www.facebook.com/garfield
© 2016 PAWS, INC. All Rights Reserved.

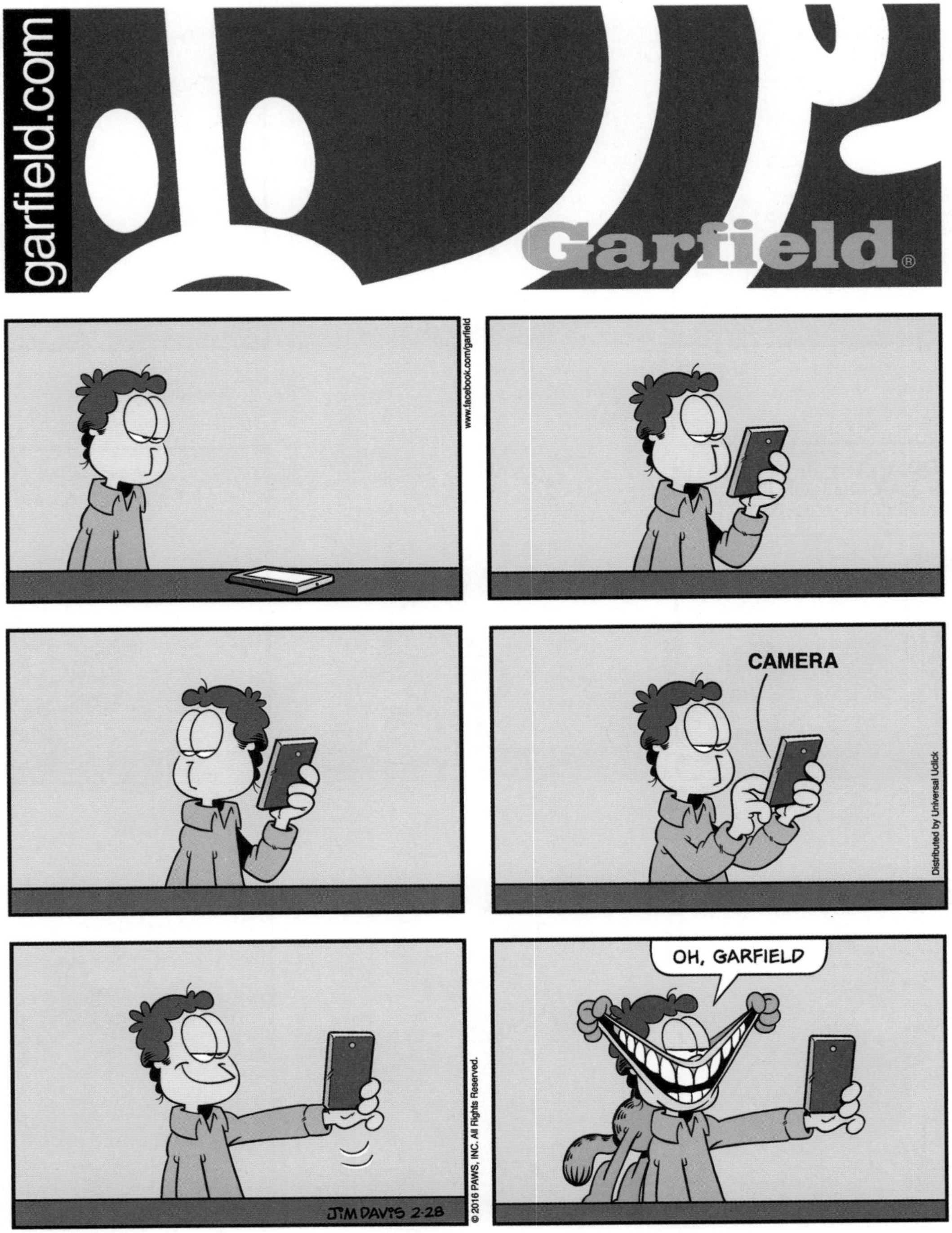
garfield.com
Garfield®
www.facebook.com/garfield
CAMERA
Distributed by Universal Uclick
© 2016 PAWS, INC. All Rights Reserved.
JIM DAVIS 2-28
OH, GARFIELD

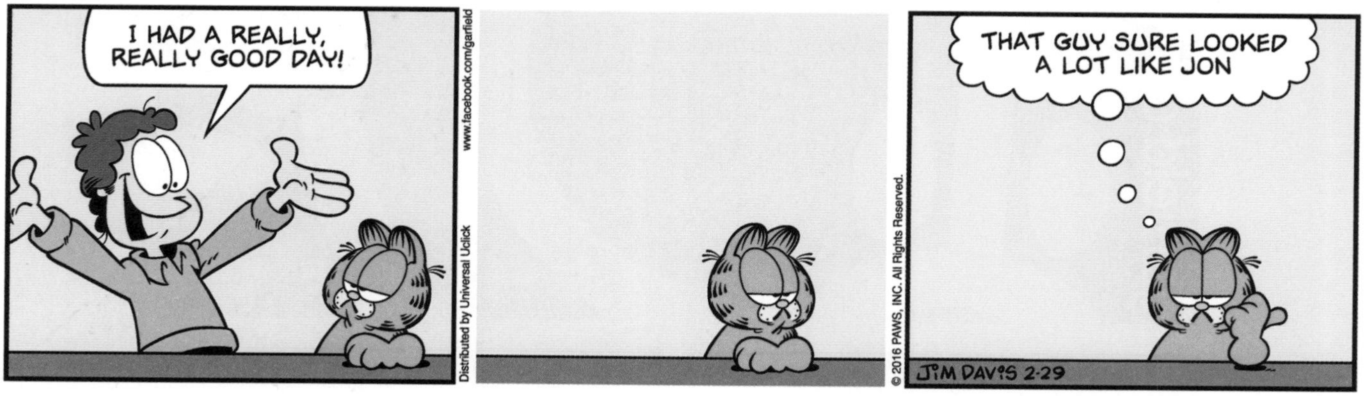
I HAD A REALLY, REALLY GOOD DAY!
THAT GUY SURE LOOKED A LOT LIKE JON
JIM DAVIS 2-29

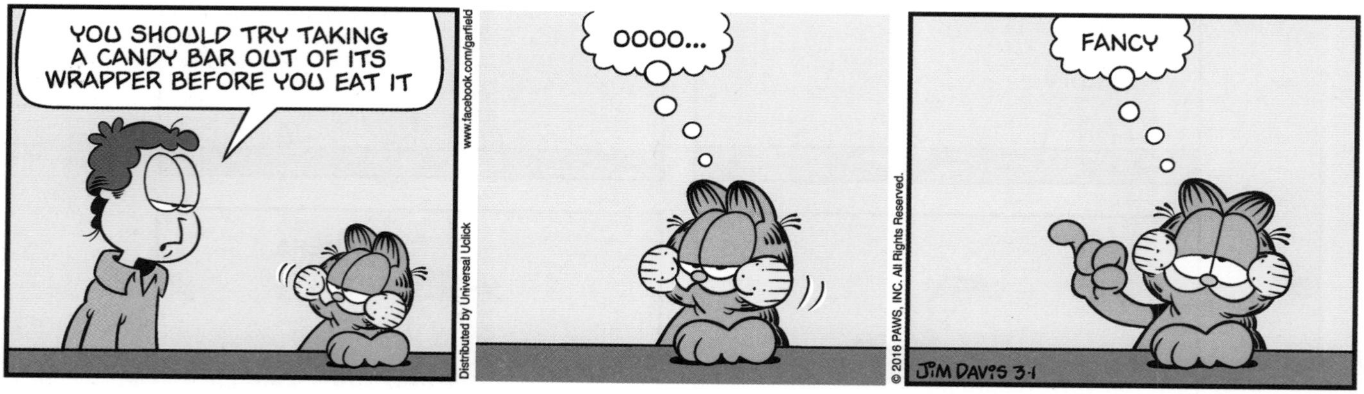
YOU SHOULD TRY TAKING A CANDY BAR OUT OF ITS WRAPPER BEFORE YOU EAT IT
OOOO...
FANCY
JIM DAVIS 3-1

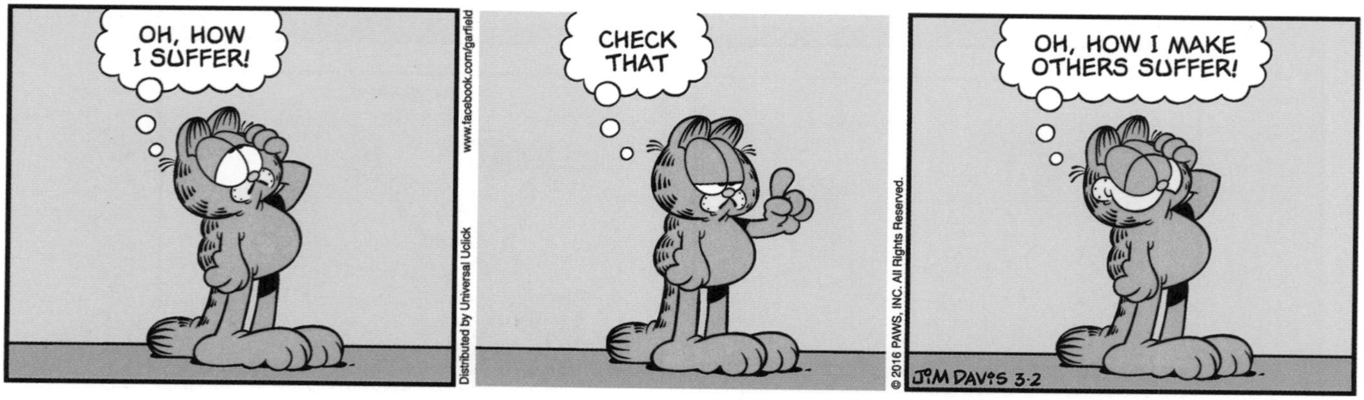
OH, HOW I SUFFER!
CHECK THAT
OH, HOW I MAKE OTHERS SUFFER!
JIM DAVIS 3-2

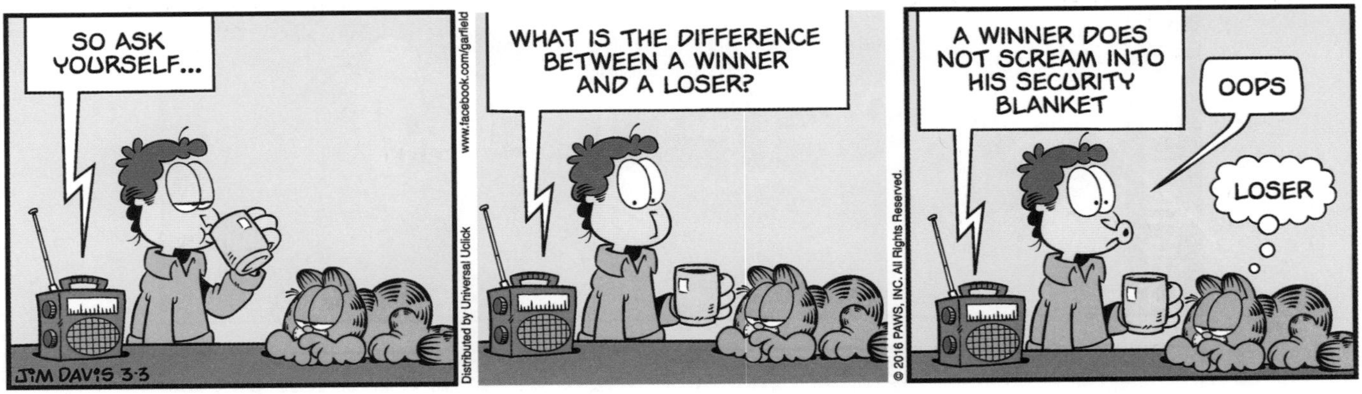
SO ASK YOURSELF...
JIM DAVIS 3-3
Distributed by Universal Uclick
www.facebook.com/garfield
WHAT IS THE DIFFERENCE BETWEEN A WINNER AND A LOSER?
© 2016 PAWS, INC. All Rights Reserved.
A WINNER DOES NOT SCREAM INTO HIS SECURITY BLANKET
OOPS
LOSER

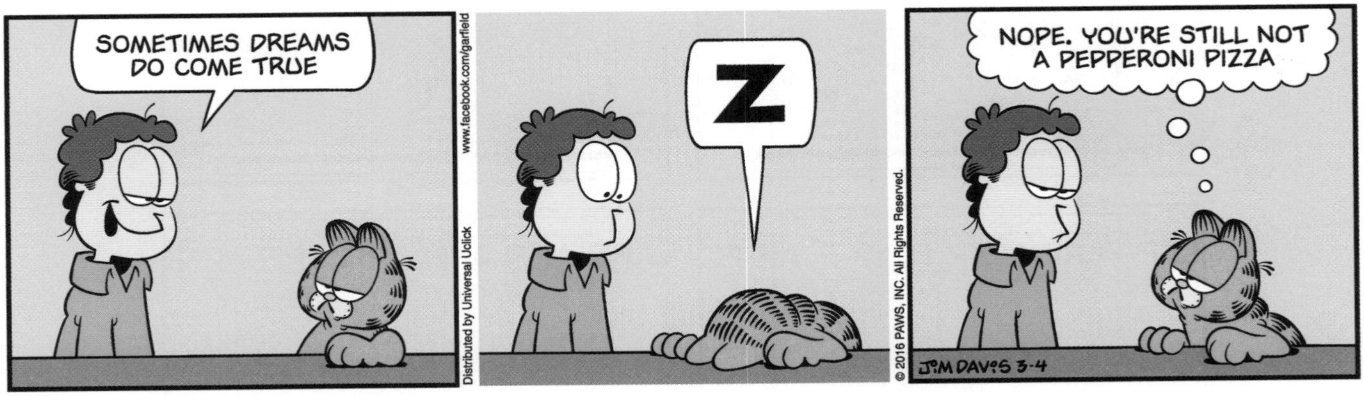
SOMETIMES DREAMS DO COME TRUE
Distributed by Universal Uclick
www.facebook.com/garfield
Z
© 2016 PAWS, INC. All Rights Reserved.
NOPE. YOU'RE STILL NOT A PEPPERONI PIZZA
JIM DAVIS 3-4

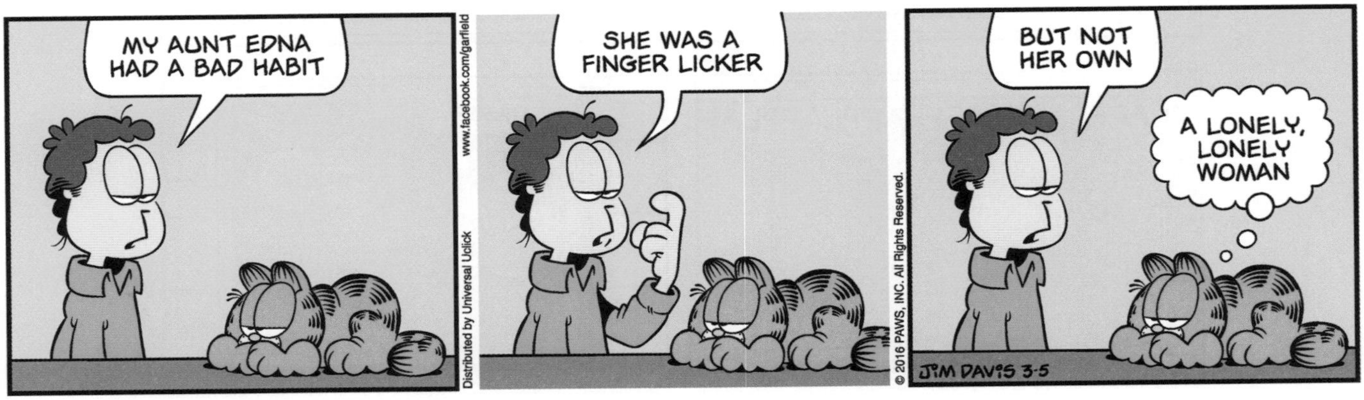
MY AUNT EDNA HAD A BAD HABIT
Distributed by Universal Uclick
www.facebook.com/garfield
SHE WAS A FINGER LICKER
© 2016 PAWS, INC. All Rights Reserved.
BUT NOT HER OWN
A LONELY, LONELY WOMAN
JIM DAVIS 3-5

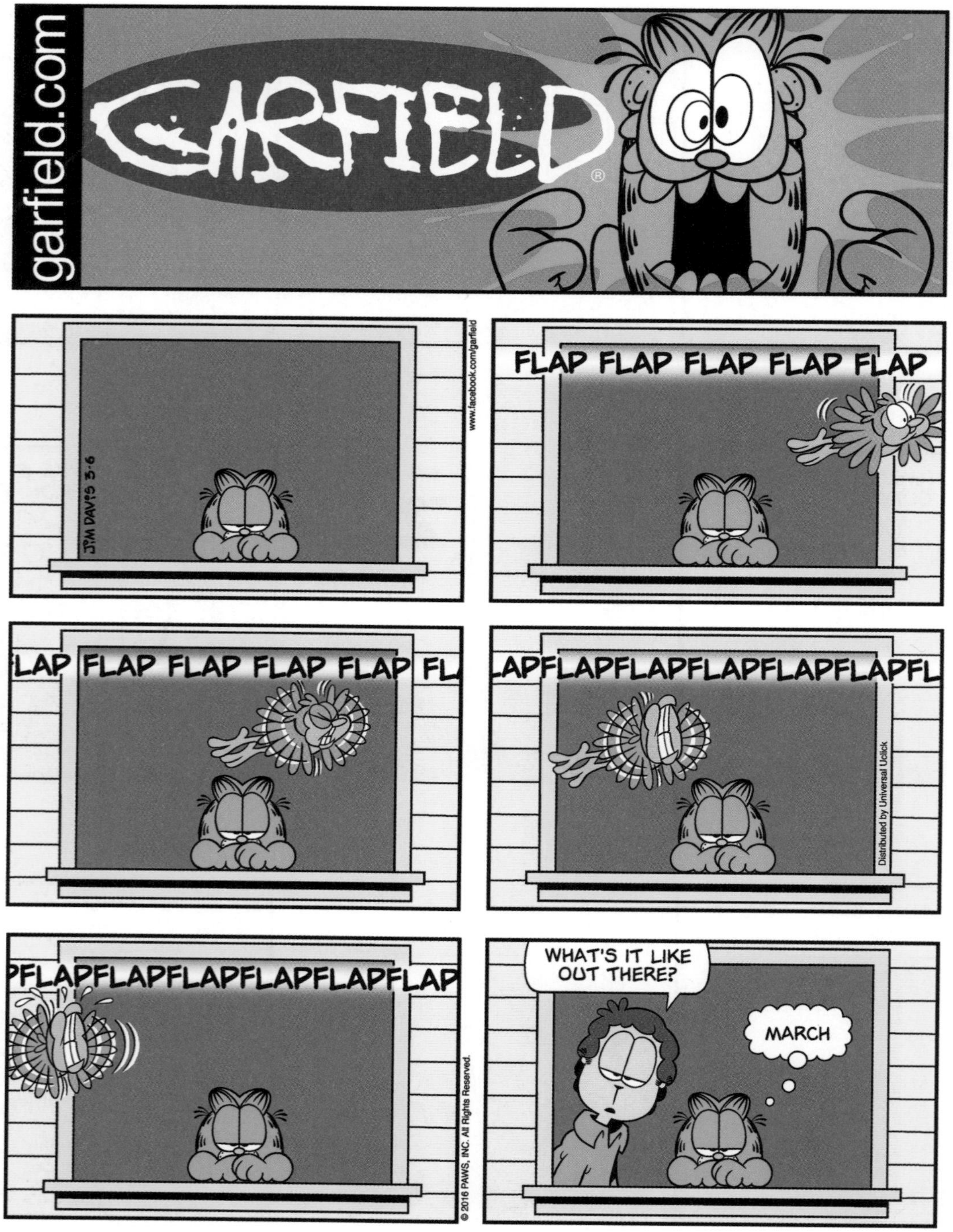
garfield.com
GARFIELD®
JIM DAVIS 3-6
www.facebook.com/garfield
FLAP FLAP FLAP FLAP FLAP
FLAP FLAP FLAP FLAP FLAP FL
LAPFLAPFLAPFLAPFLAPFLAPFL
Distributed by Universal Uclick
PFLAPFLAPFLAPFLAPFLAPFLAP
© 2016 PAWS, INC. All Rights Reserved.
WHAT'S IT LIKE OUT THERE?
MARCH

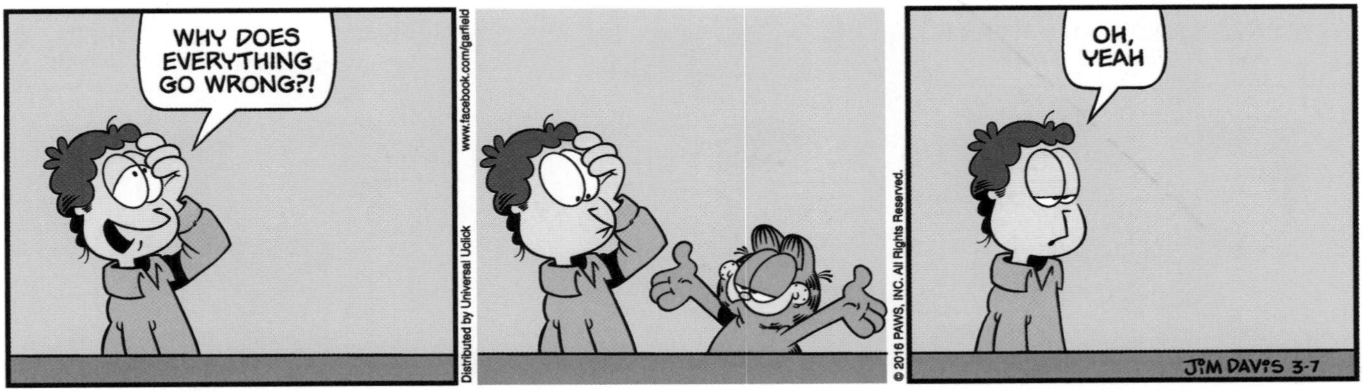
WHY DOES EVERYTHING GO WRONG?!
Distributed by Universal Uclick www.facebook.com/garfield
© 2016 PAWS, INC. All Rights Reserved.
OH, YEAH
JIM DAVIS 3-7

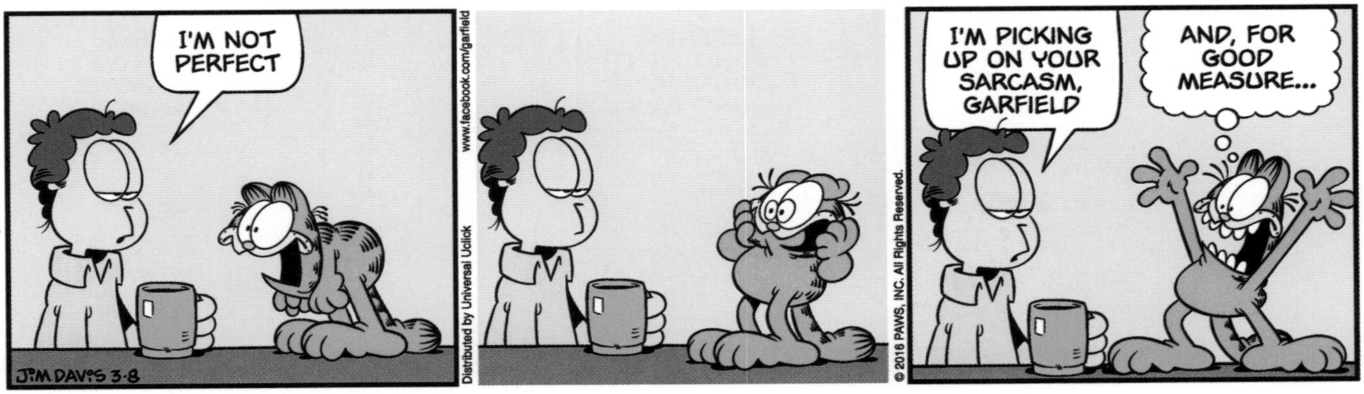
I'M NOT PERFECT
JIM DAVIS 3-8
Distributed by Universal Uclick www.facebook.com/garfield
© 2016 PAWS, INC. All Rights Reserved.
I'M PICKING UP ON YOUR SARCASM, GARFIELD
AND, FOR GOOD MEASURE...

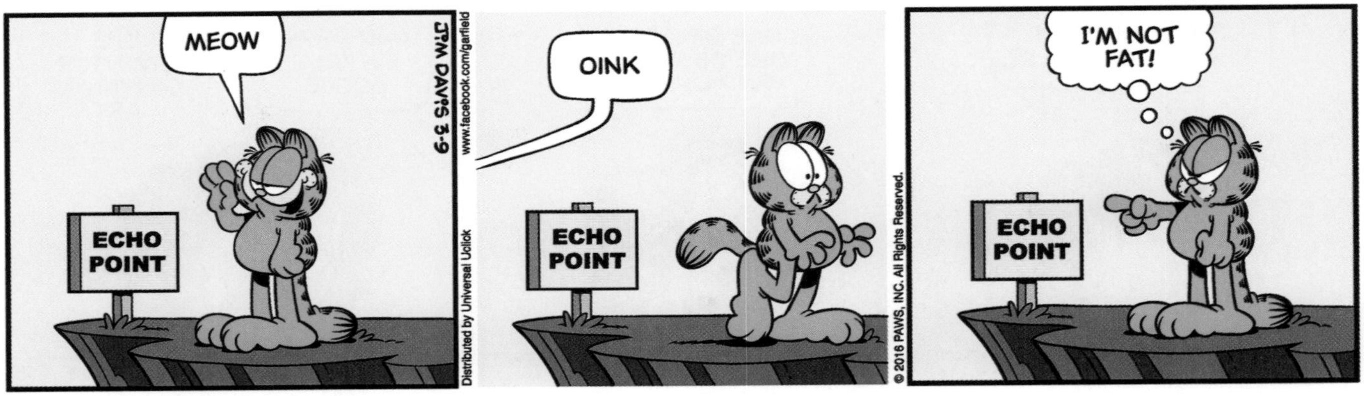
MEOW
ECHO POINT
JIM DAVIS 3-9
Distributed by Universal Uclick www.facebook.com/garfield
OINK
ECHO POINT
© 2016 PAWS, INC. All Rights Reserved.
I'M NOT FAT!
ECHO POINT

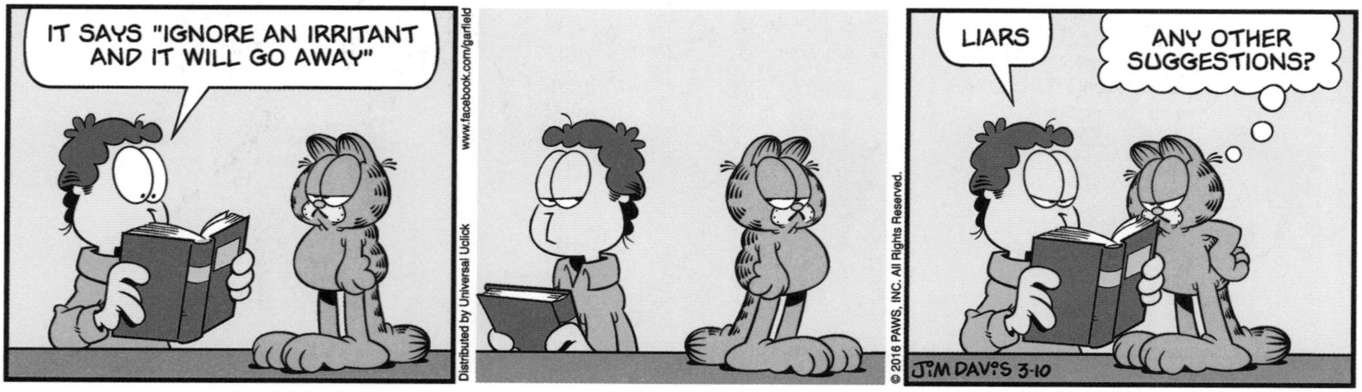
IT SAYS "IGNORE AN IRRITANT AND IT WILL GO AWAY"
Distributed by Universal Uclick www.facebook.com/garfield
LIARS
ANY OTHER SUGGESTIONS?
© 2016 PAWS, INC. All Rights Reserved.
JIM DAVIS 3-10

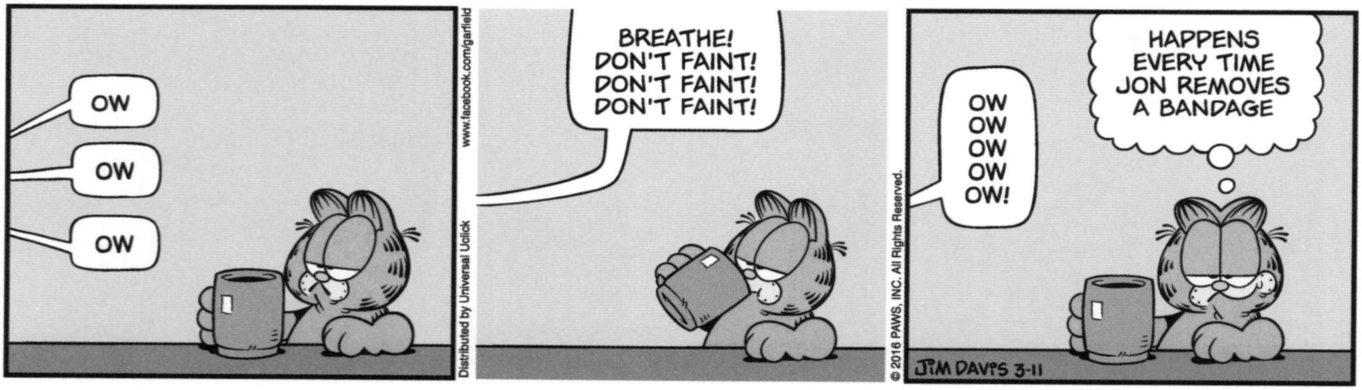
OW
OW
OW
Distributed by Universal Uclick www.facebook.com/garfield
BREATHE! DON'T FAINT! DON'T FAINT! DON'T FAINT!
OW OW OW OW OW!
HAPPENS EVERY TIME JON REMOVES A BANDAGE
© 2016 PAWS, INC. All Rights Reserved.
JIM DAVIS 3-11

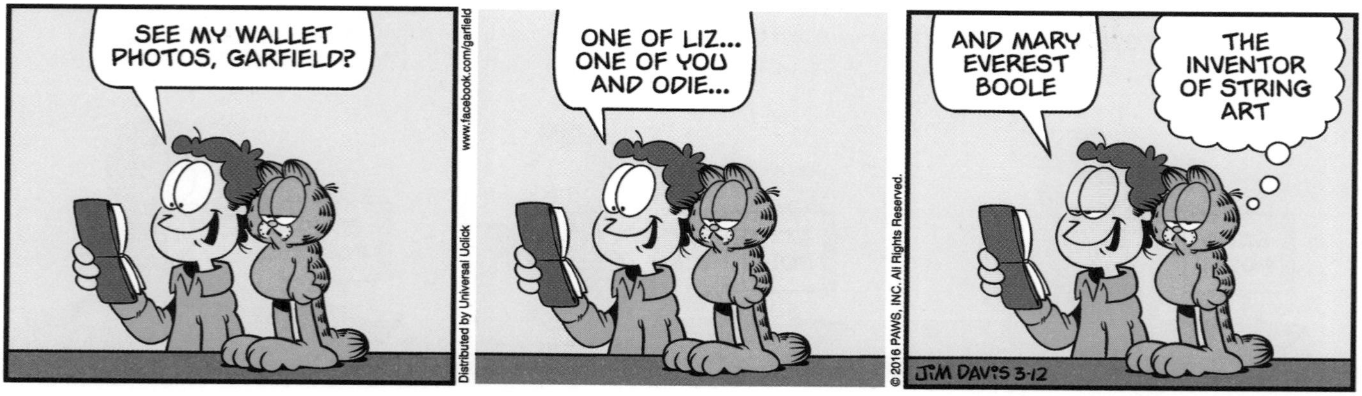
SEE MY WALLET PHOTOS, GARFIELD?
Distributed by Universal Uclick www.facebook.com/garfield
ONE OF LIZ... ONE OF YOU AND ODIE...
AND MARY EVEREST BOOLE
THE INVENTOR OF STRING ART
© 2016 PAWS, INC. All Rights Reserved.
JIM DAVIS 3-12

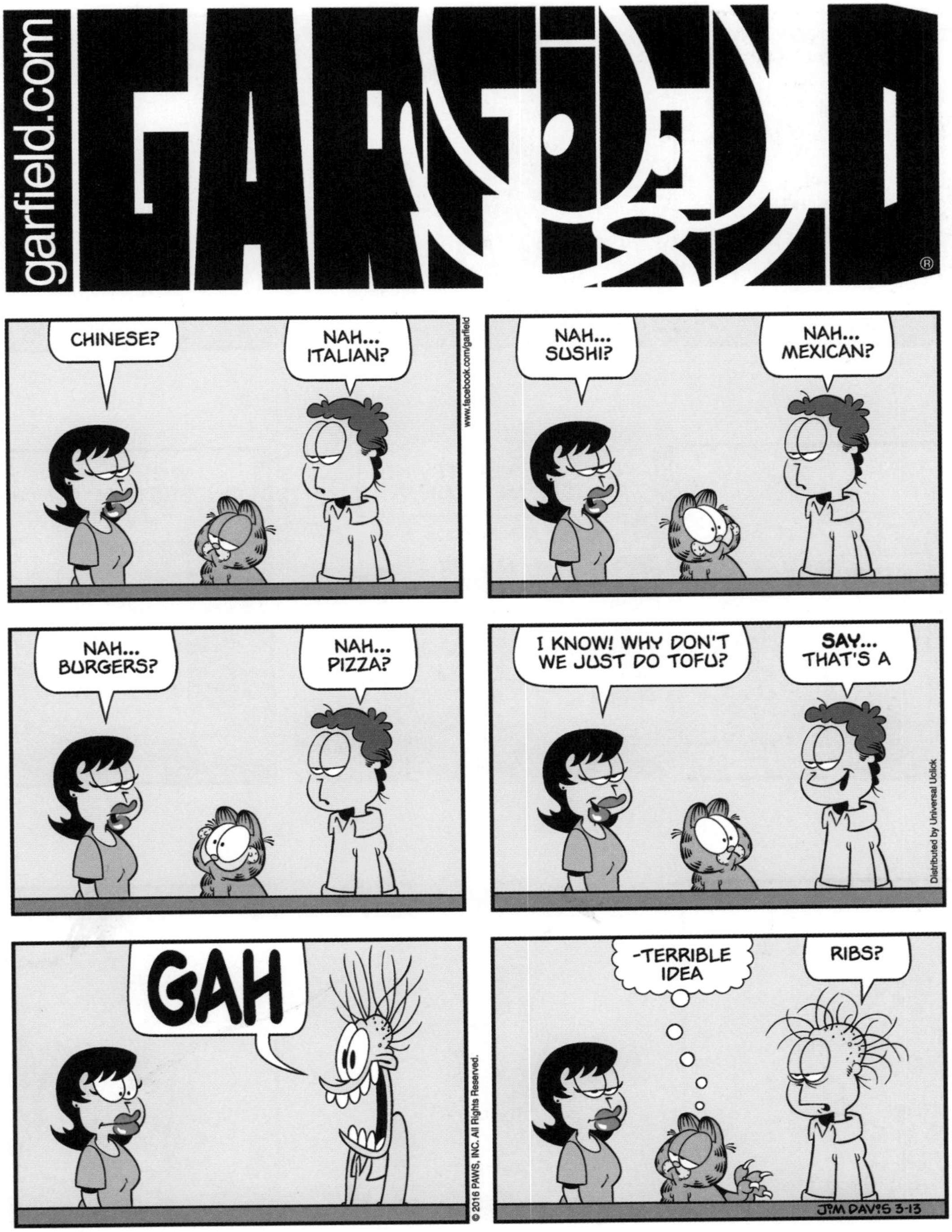
garfield.com
GARFIELD
CHINESE?
NAH... ITALIAN?
www.facebook.com/garfield
NAH... SUSHI?
NAH... MEXICAN?
NAH... BURGERS?
NAH... PIZZA?
I KNOW! WHY DON'T WE JUST DO TOFU?
SAY... THAT'S A
Distributed by Universal Uclick
GAH
© 2016 PAWS, INC. All Rights Reserved.
-TERRIBLE IDEA
RIBS?
JIM DAVIS 3-13

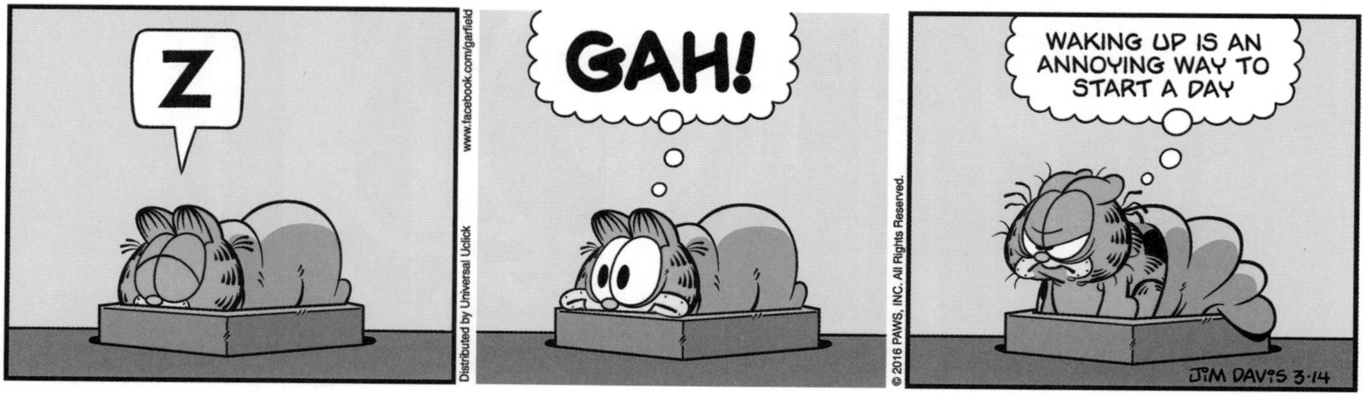
Z
GAH!
WAKING UP IS AN ANNOYING WAY TO START A DAY
JIM DAVIS 3-14
Distributed by Universal Uclick
www.facebook.com/garfield
© 2016 PAWS, INC. All Rights Reserved.

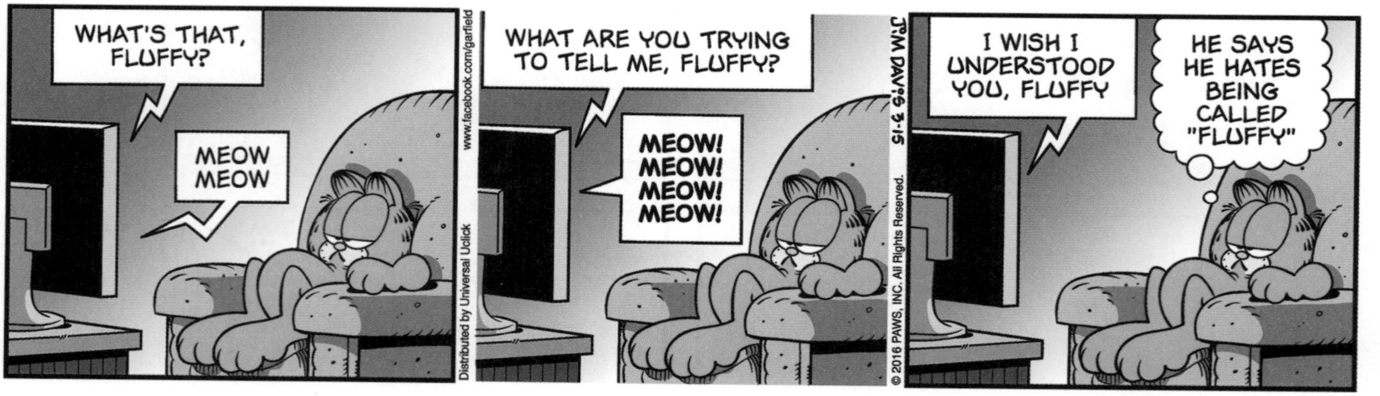
WHAT'S THAT, FLUFFY?
MEOW MEOW
WHAT ARE YOU TRYING TO TELL ME, FLUFFY?
MEOW! MEOW! MEOW! MEOW!
I WISH I UNDERSTOOD YOU, FLUFFY
HE SAYS HE HATES BEING CALLED "FLUFFY"
JIM DAVIS 3-15
Distributed by Universal Uclick
www.facebook.com/garfield
© 2016 PAWS, INC. All Rights Reserved.

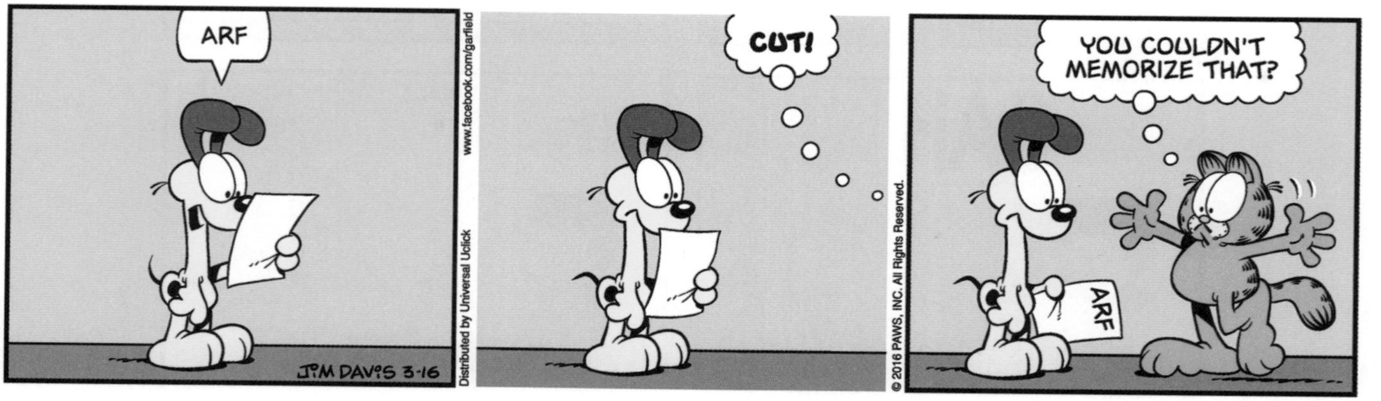
ARF
CUT!
YOU COULDN'T MEMORIZE THAT?
ARF
JIM DAVIS 3-16
Distributed by Universal Uclick
www.facebook.com/garfield
© 2016 PAWS, INC. All Rights Reserved.

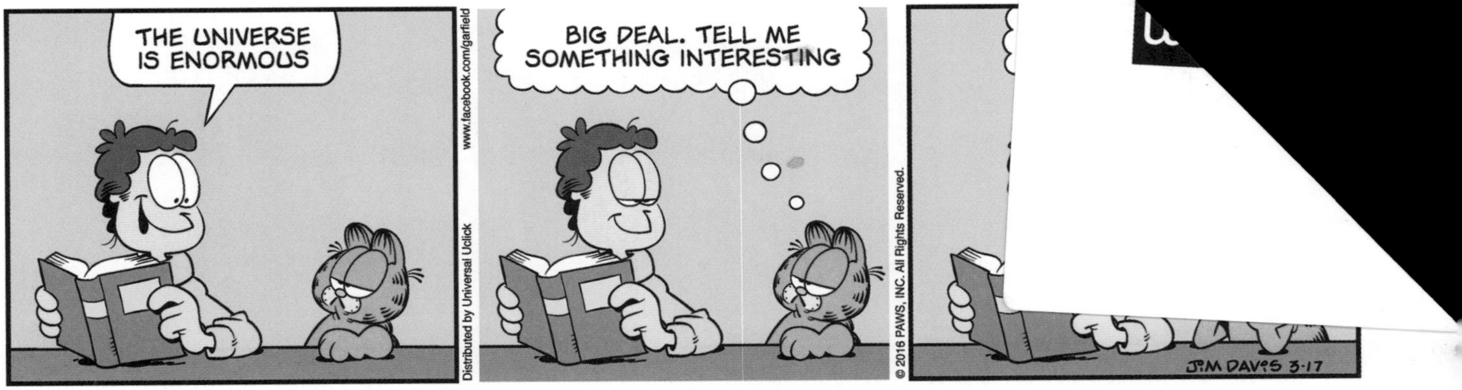
THE UNIVERSE IS ENORMOUS
BIG DEAL. TELL ME SOMETHING INTERESTING
JIM DAVIS 3-17
www.facebook.com/garfield
Distributed by Universal Uclick
© 2016 PAWS, INC. All Rights Reserved.

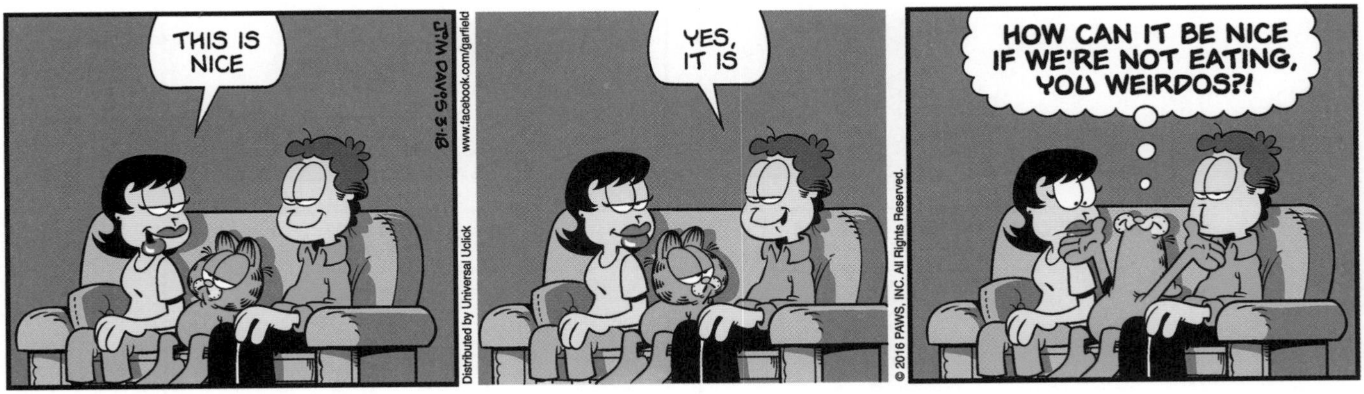
THIS IS NICE
YES, IT IS
HOW CAN IT BE NICE IF WE'RE NOT EATING, YOU WEIRDOS?!
JIM DAVIS 3-18
www.facebook.com/garfield
Distributed by Universal Uclick
© 2016 PAWS, INC. All Rights Reserved.

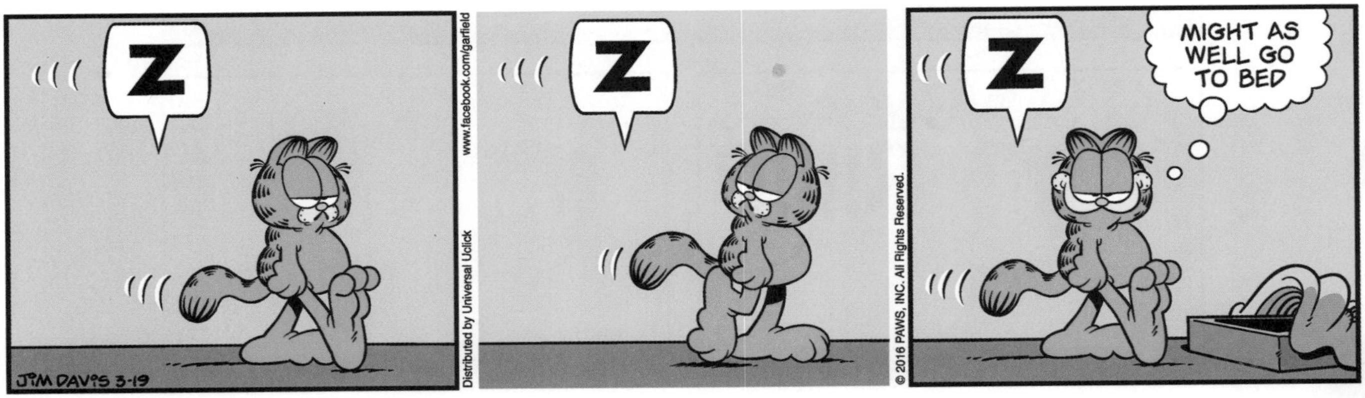
Z
Z
Z
MIGHT AS WELL GO TO BED
JIM DAVIS 3-19
www.facebook.com/garfield
Distributed by Universal Uclick
© 2016 PAWS, INC. All Rights Reserved.

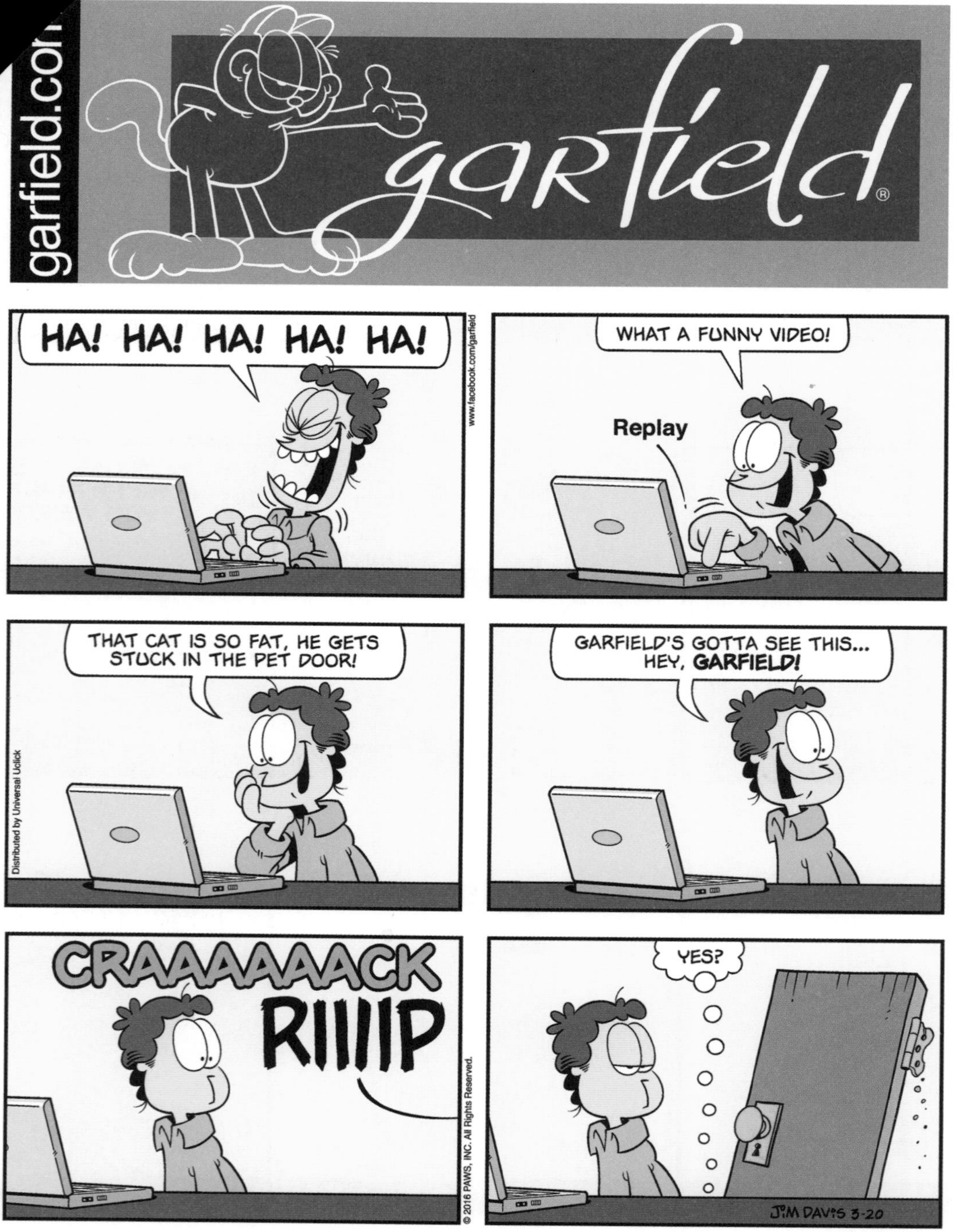

garfield.com
garfield
HA! HA! HA! HA! HA!
www.facebook.com/garfield
WHAT A FUNNY VIDEO!
Replay
THAT CAT IS SO FAT, HE GETS STUCK IN THE PET DOOR!
Distributed by Universal Uclick
GARFIELD'S GOTTA SEE THIS... HEY, GARFIELD!
CRAAAAAACK
RIIIIP
© 2016 PAWS, INC. All Rights Reserved.
YES?
JIM DAVIS 3-20

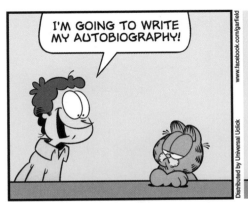

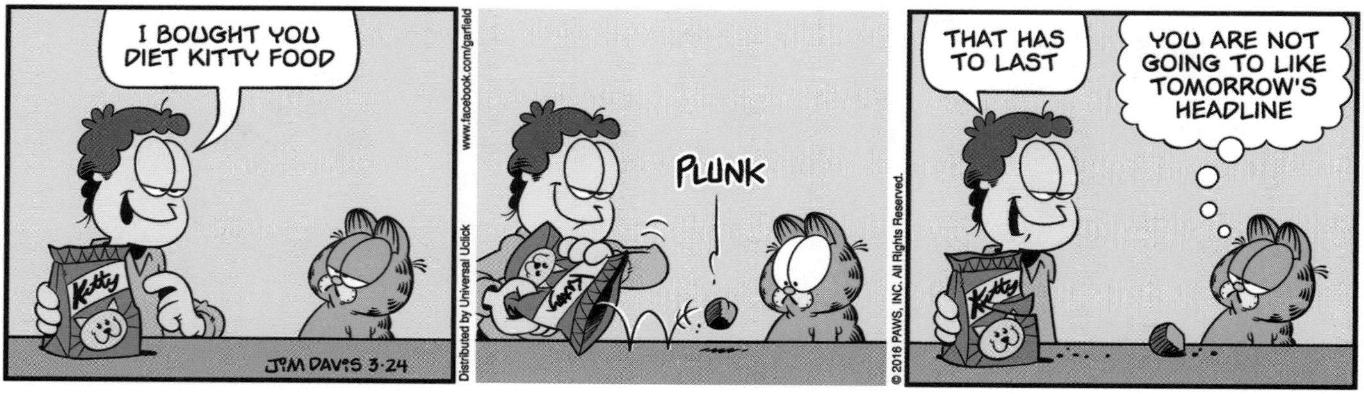
I BOUGHT YOU DIET KITTY FOOD
Kitty
JIM DAVIS 3-24
www.facebook.com/garfield
Distributed by Universal Uclick
PLUNK
THAT HAS TO LAST
YOU ARE NOT GOING TO LIKE TOMORROW'S HEADLINE
Kitty
© 2016 PAWS, INC. All Rights Reserved.

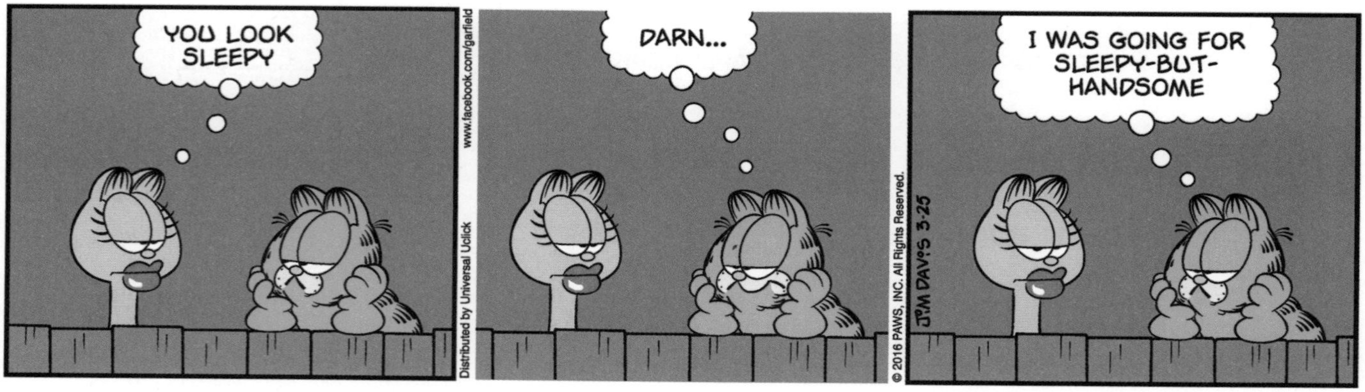
YOU LOOK SLEEPY
www.facebook.com/garfield
Distributed by Universal Uclick
DARN...
© 2016 PAWS, INC. All Rights Reserved.
JIM DAVIS 3-25
I WAS GOING FOR SLEEPY-BUT-HANDSOME

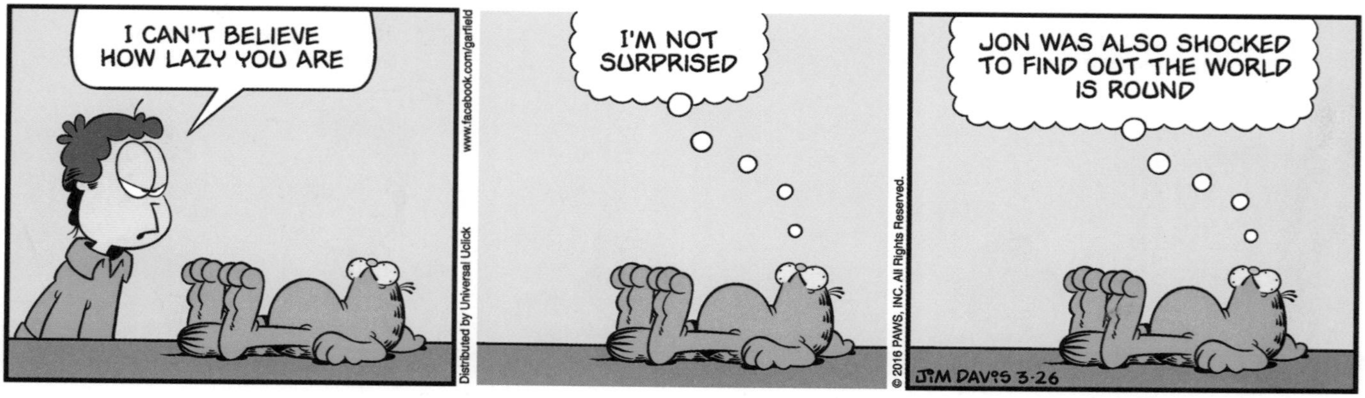
I CAN'T BELIEVE HOW LAZY YOU ARE
www.facebook.com/garfield
Distributed by Universal Uclick
I'M NOT SURPRISED
© 2016 PAWS, INC. All Rights Reserved.
JON WAS ALSO SHOCKED TO FIND OUT THE WORLD IS ROUND
JIM DAVIS 3-26

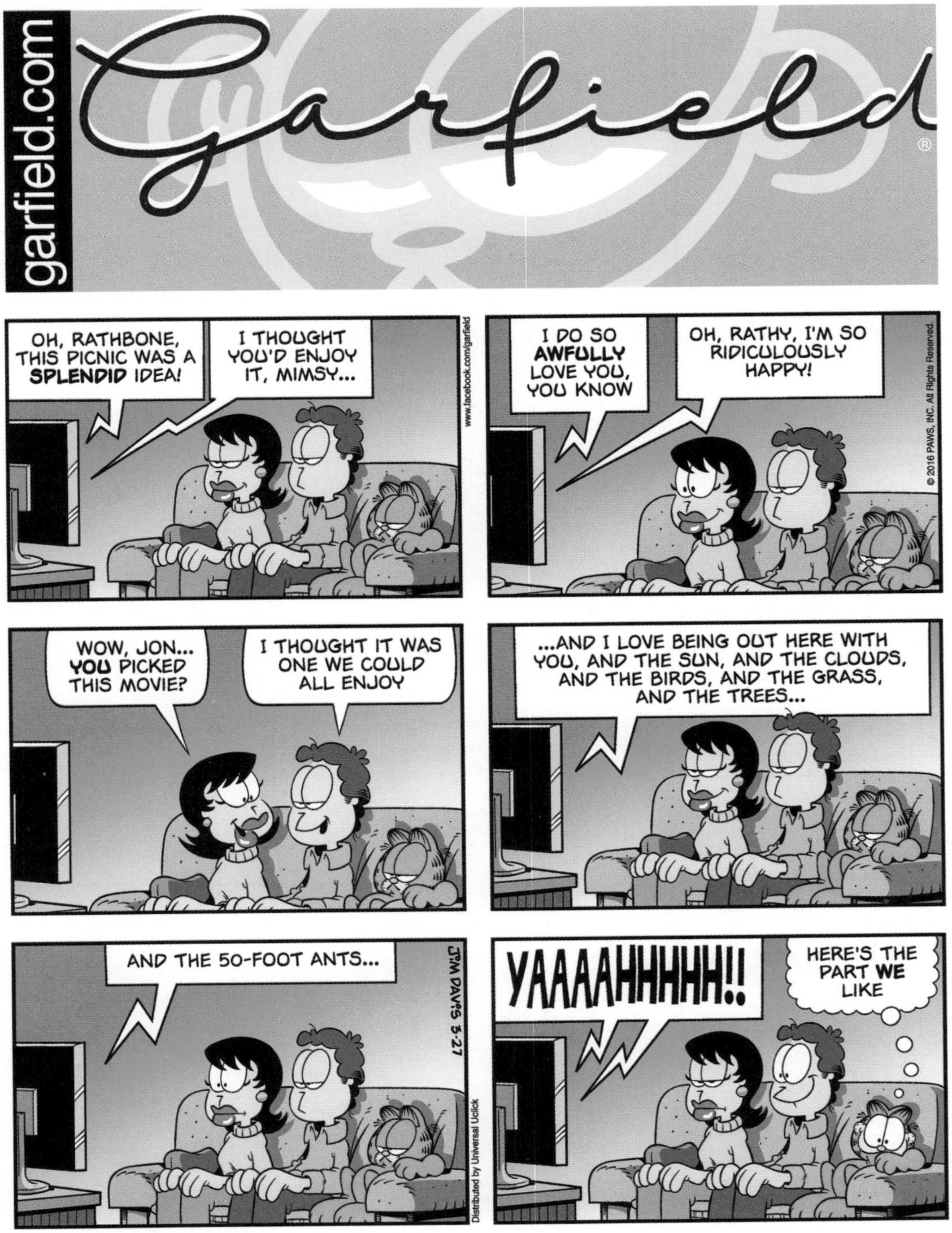

garfield.com
Garfield
OH, RATHBONE, THIS PICNIC WAS A SPLENDID IDEA!
I THOUGHT YOU'D ENJOY IT, MIMSY...
www.facebook.com/garfield
I DO SO AWFULLY LOVE YOU, YOU KNOW
OH, RATHY, I'M SO RIDICULOUSLY HAPPY!
© 2016 PAWS, INC. All Rights Reserved.
WOW, JON... YOU PICKED THIS MOVIE?
I THOUGHT IT WAS ONE WE COULD ALL ENJOY
...AND I LOVE BEING OUT HERE WITH YOU, AND THE SUN, AND THE CLOUDS, AND THE BIRDS, AND THE GRASS, AND THE TREES...
AND THE 50-FOOT ANTS...
JIM DAVIS 3-27
Distributed by Universal Uclick
YAAAAHHHHH!!
HERE'S THE PART WE LIKE

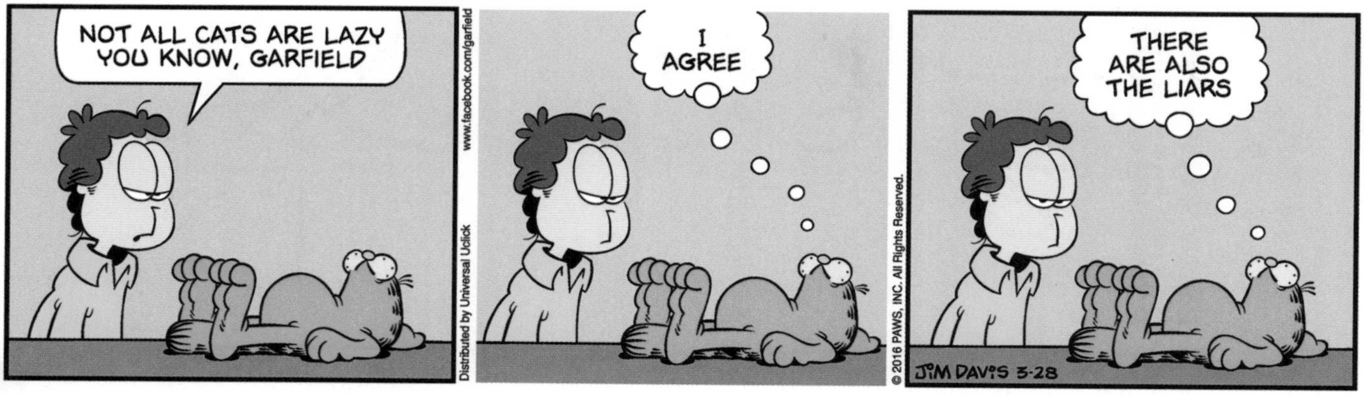
NOT ALL CATS ARE LAZY YOU KNOW, GARFIELD
Distributed by Universal Uclick
www.facebook.com/garfield
I AGREE
THERE ARE ALSO THE LIARS
© 2016 PAWS, INC. All Rights Reserved.
JIM DAVIS 3-28

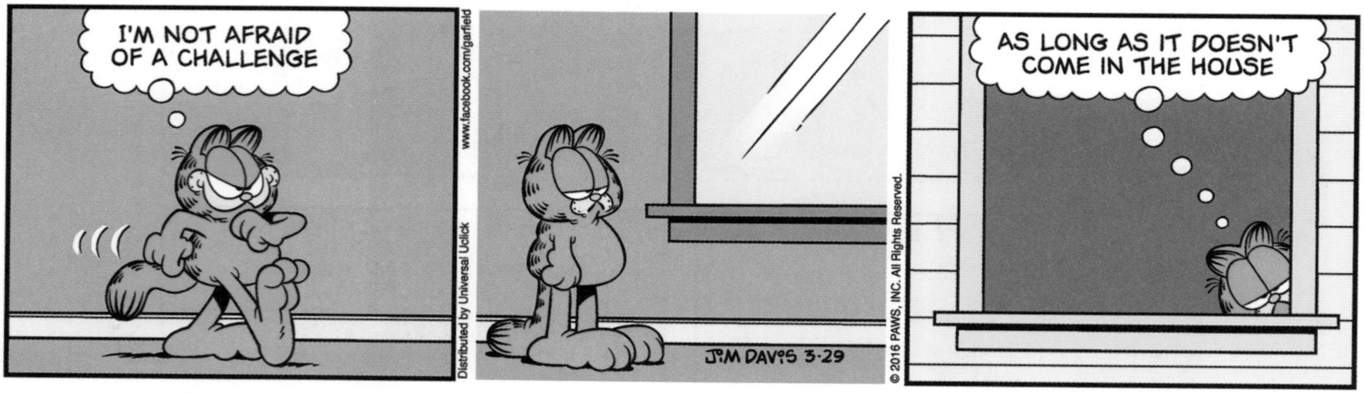
I'M NOT AFRAID OF A CHALLENGE
Distributed by Universal Uclick
www.facebook.com/garfield
JIM DAVIS 3-29
© 2016 PAWS, INC. All Rights Reserved.
AS LONG AS IT DOESN'T COME IN THE HOUSE

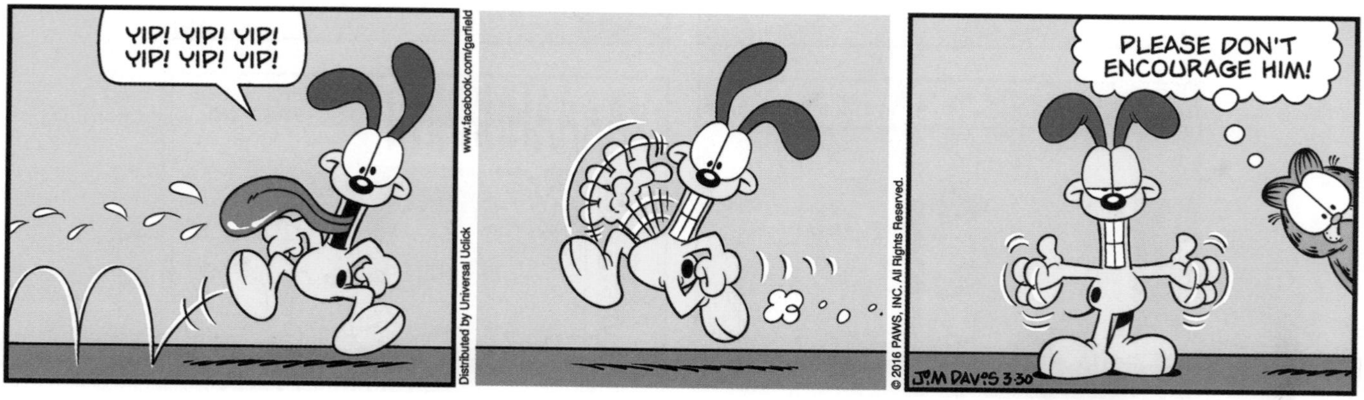
YIP! YIP! YIP! YIP! YIP! YIP!
Distributed by Universal Uclick
www.facebook.com/garfield
© 2016 PAWS, INC. All Rights Reserved.
PLEASE DON'T ENCOURAGE HIM!
JIM DAVIS 3-30

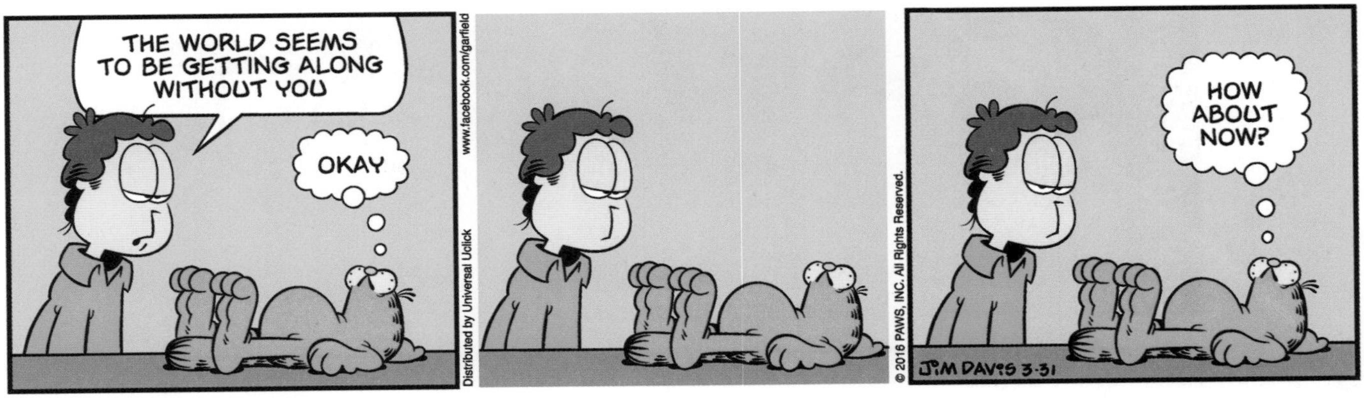
THE WORLD SEEMS TO BE GETTING ALONG WITHOUT YOU
OKAY
HOW ABOUT NOW?
JIM DAVIS 3-31
Distributed by Universal Uclick www.facebook.com/garfield
© 2016 PAWS, INC. All Rights Reserved.

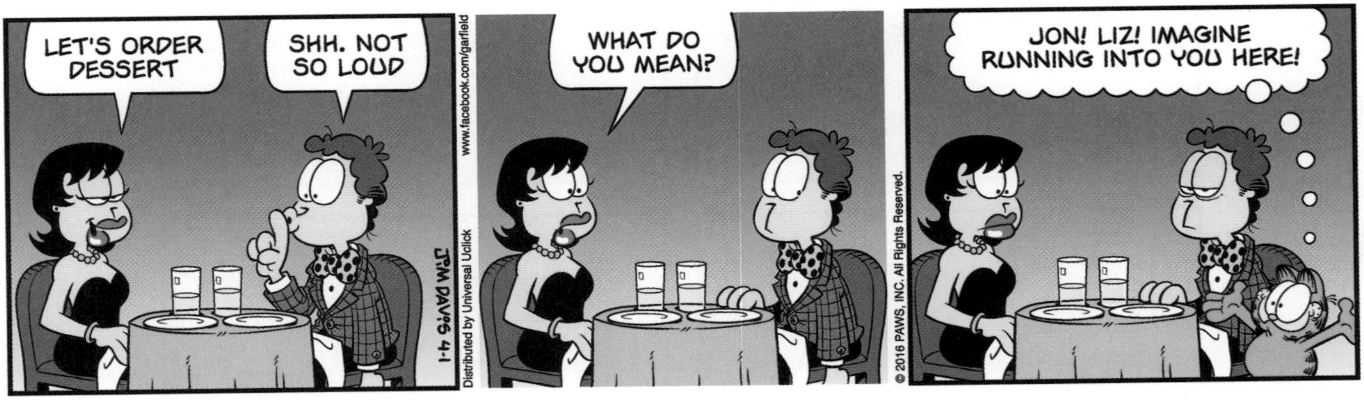
LET'S ORDER DESSERT
SHH. NOT SO LOUD
JIM DAVIS 4-1
WHAT DO YOU MEAN?
JON! LIZ! IMAGINE RUNNING INTO YOU HERE!
Distributed by Universal Uclick www.facebook.com/garfield
© 2016 PAWS, INC. All Rights Reserved.

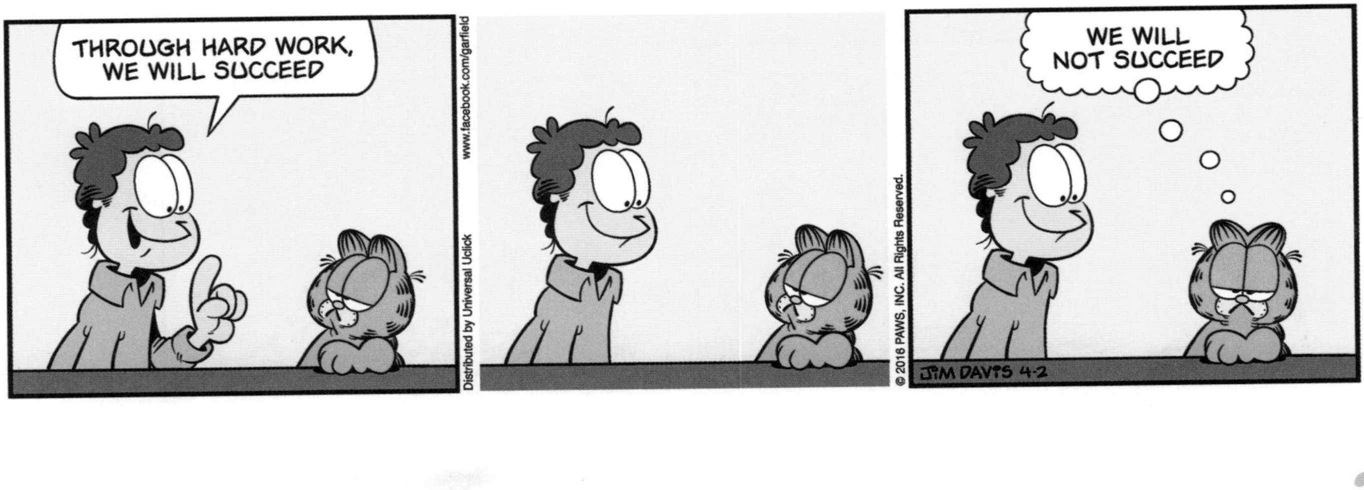
THROUGH HARD WORK, WE WILL SUCCEED
WE WILL NOT SUCCEED
JIM DAVIS 4-2
Distributed by Universal Uclick www.facebook.com/garfield
© 2016 PAWS, INC. All Rights Reserved.

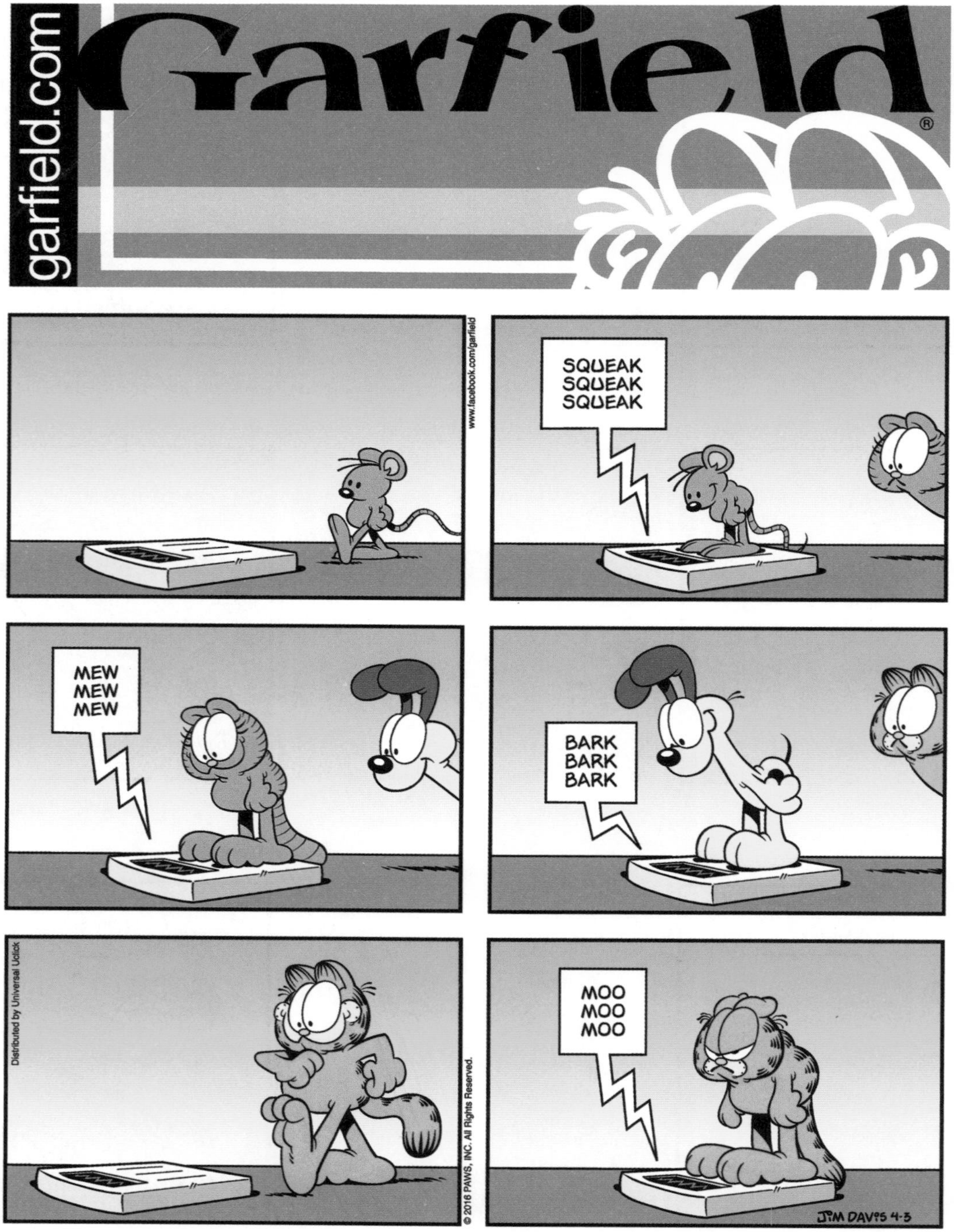

garfield.com
Garfield®
www.facebook.com/garfield
SQUEAK
SQUEAK
SQUEAK
MEW
MEW
MEW
BARK
BARK
BARK
Distributed by Universal Uclick
© 2016 PAWS, INC. All Rights Reserved.
MOO
MOO
MOO
JIM DAVIS 4-3

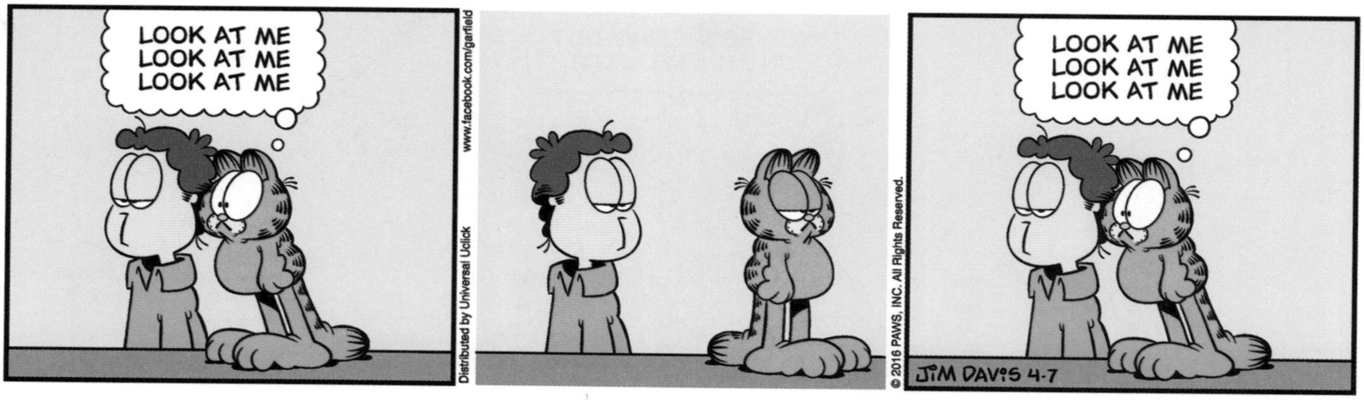
LOOK AT ME
LOOK AT ME
LOOK AT ME
www.facebook.com/garfield
Distributed by Universal Uclick
LOOK AT ME
LOOK AT ME
LOOK AT ME
© 2016 PAWS, INC. All Rights Reserved.
JIM DAVIS 4-7

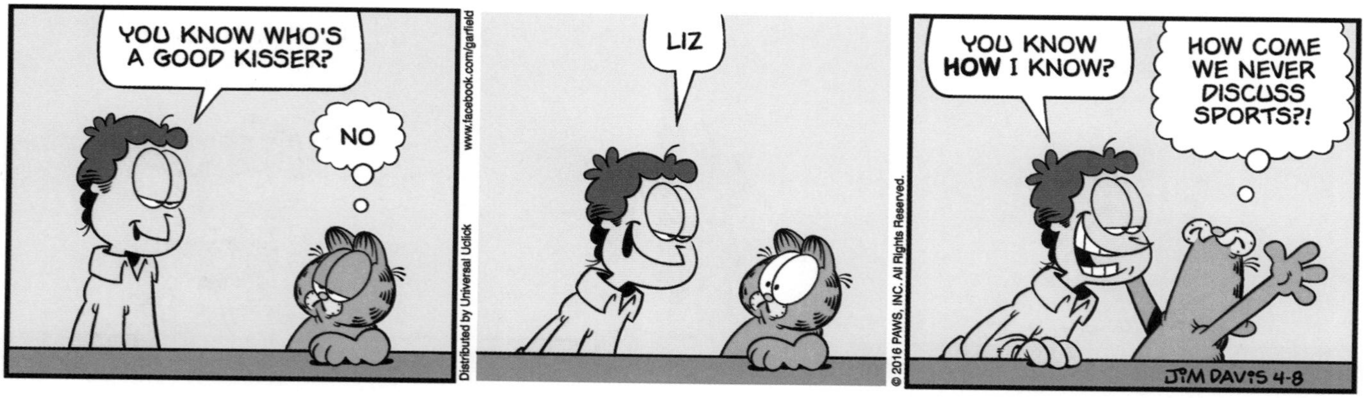
YOU KNOW WHO'S
A GOOD KISSER?
NO
www.facebook.com/garfield
Distributed by Universal Uclick
LIZ
YOU KNOW
HOW I KNOW?
HOW COME
WE NEVER
DISCUSS
SPORTS?!
© 2016 PAWS, INC. All Rights Reserved.
JIM DAVIS 4-8

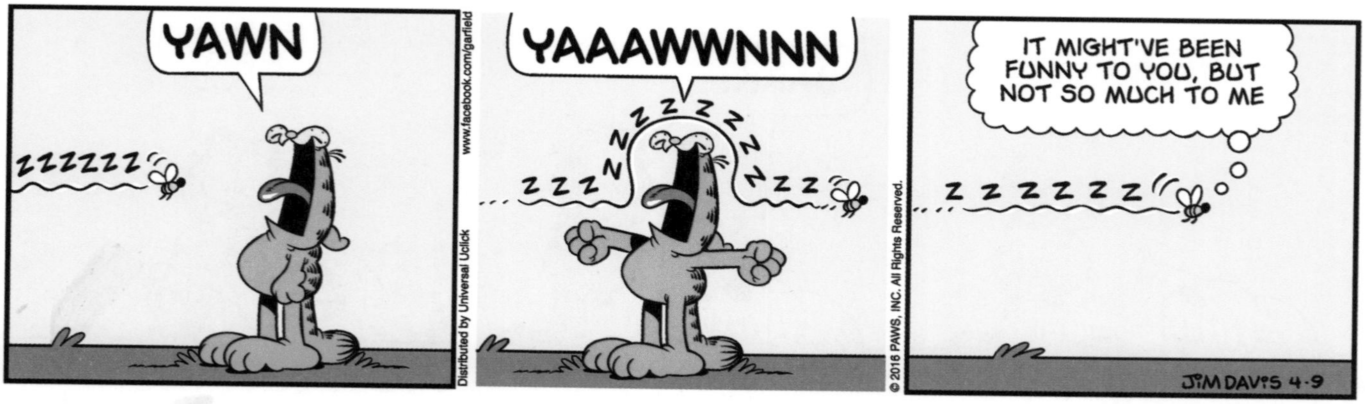
YAWN
ZZZZZZ
www.facebook.com/garfield
Distributed by Universal Uclick
YAAAWWNNN
Z Z Z Z Z Z Z Z Z Z Z Z Z Z
IT MIGHT'VE BEEN
FUNNY TO YOU, BUT
NOT SO MUCH TO ME
Z Z Z Z Z Z
© 2016 PAWS, INC. All Rights Reserved.
JIM DAVIS 4-9

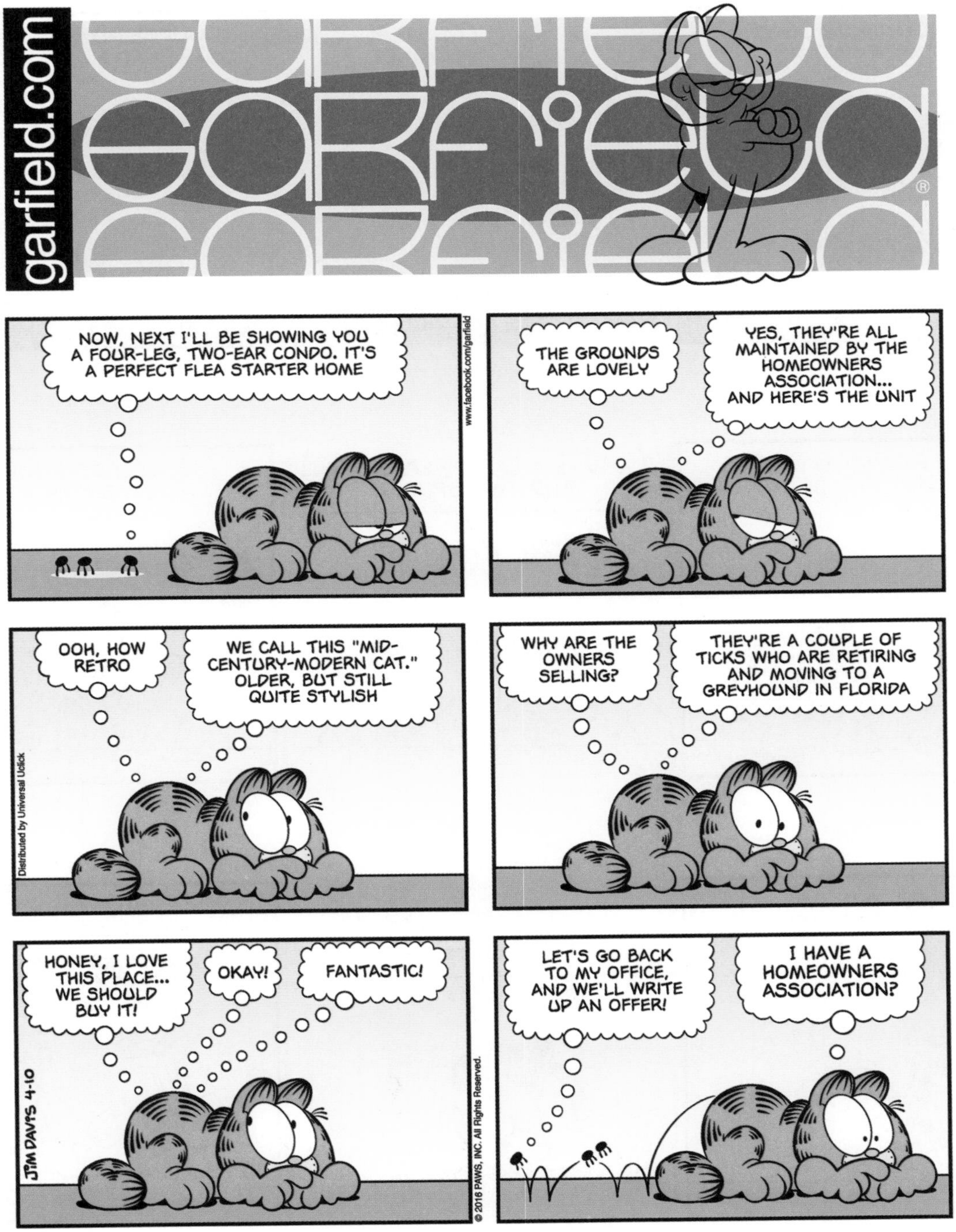
garfield.com
GARFIELD®
NOW, NEXT I'LL BE SHOWING YOU A FOUR-LEG, TWO-EAR CONDO. IT'S A PERFECT FLEA STARTER HOME
www.facebook.com/garfield
THE GROUNDS ARE LOVELY
YES, THEY'RE ALL MAINTAINED BY THE HOMEOWNERS ASSOCIATION... AND HERE'S THE UNIT
Distributed by Universal Uclick
OOH, HOW RETRO
WE CALL THIS "MID-CENTURY-MODERN CAT." OLDER, BUT STILL QUITE STYLISH
WHY ARE THE OWNERS SELLING?
THEY'RE A COUPLE OF TICKS WHO ARE RETIRING AND MOVING TO A GREYHOUND IN FLORIDA
JIM DAVIS 4-10
HONEY, I LOVE THIS PLACE... WE SHOULD BUY IT!
OKAY!
FANTASTIC!
© 2016 PAWS, INC. All Rights Reserved.
LET'S GO BACK TO MY OFFICE, AND WE'LL WRITE UP AN OFFER!
I HAVE A HOMEOWNERS ASSOCIATION?

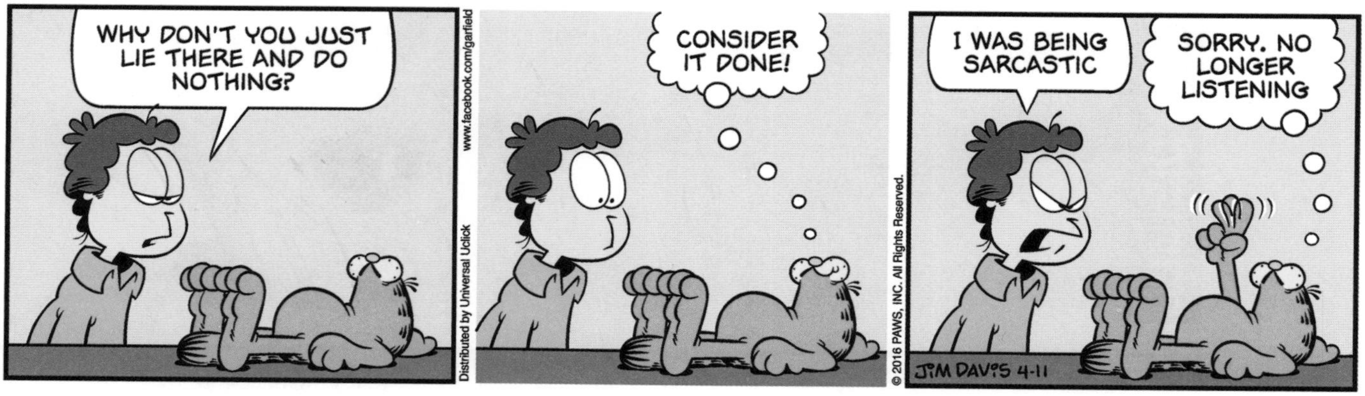
WHY DON'T YOU JUST LIE THERE AND DO NOTHING?
Distributed by Universal Uclick www.facebook.com/garfield
CONSIDER IT DONE!
I WAS BEING SARCASTIC
SORRY. NO LONGER LISTENING
© 2016 PAWS, INC. All Rights Reserved.
JIM DAVIS 4-11

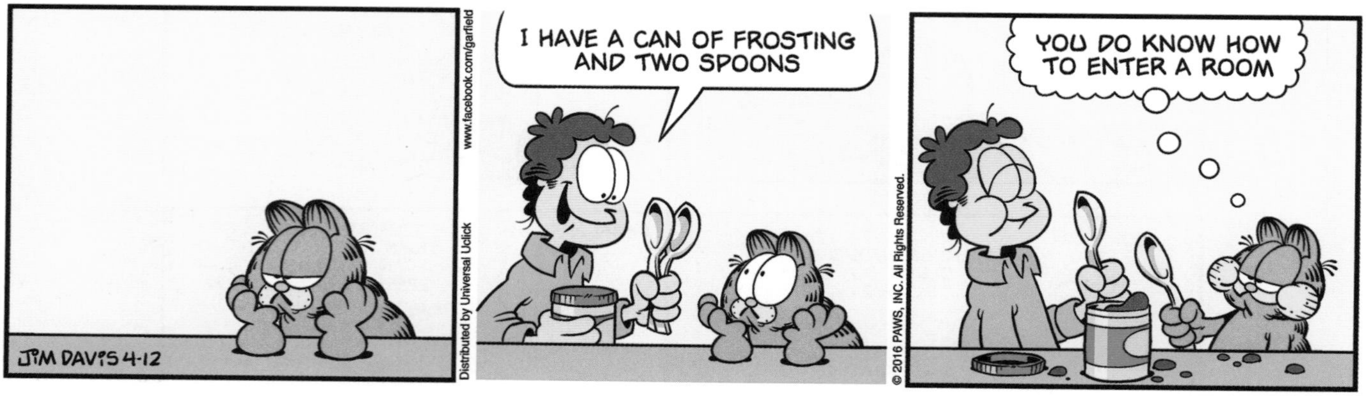
JIM DAVIS 4-12
Distributed by Universal Uclick www.facebook.com/garfield
I HAVE A CAN OF FROSTING AND TWO SPOONS
© 2016 PAWS, INC. All Rights Reserved.
YOU DO KNOW HOW TO ENTER A ROOM

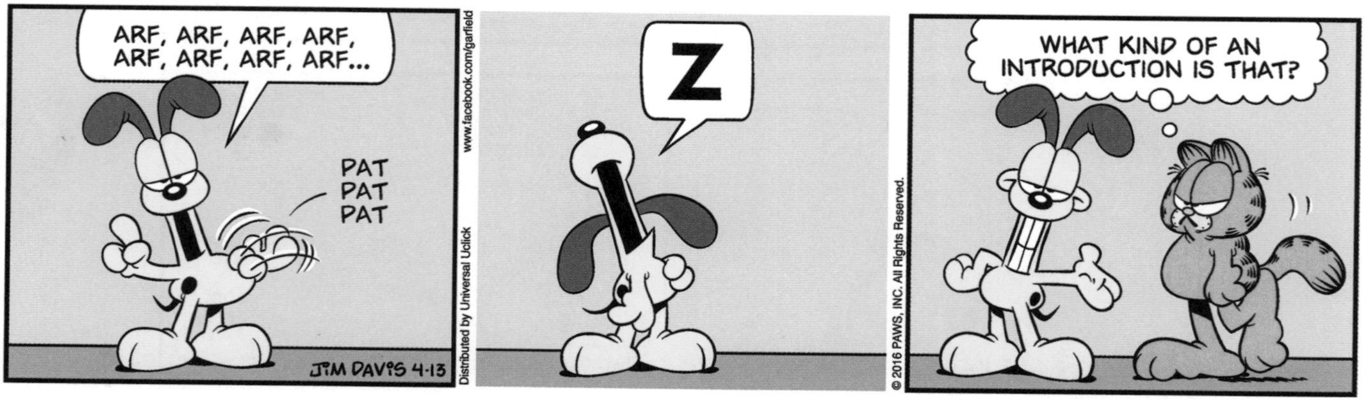
ARF, ARF, ARF, ARF, ARF, ARF, ARF, ARF...
PAT PAT PAT
JIM DAVIS 4-13
Distributed by Universal Uclick www.facebook.com/garfield
Z
© 2016 PAWS, INC. All Rights Reserved.
WHAT KIND OF AN INTRODUCTION IS THAT?

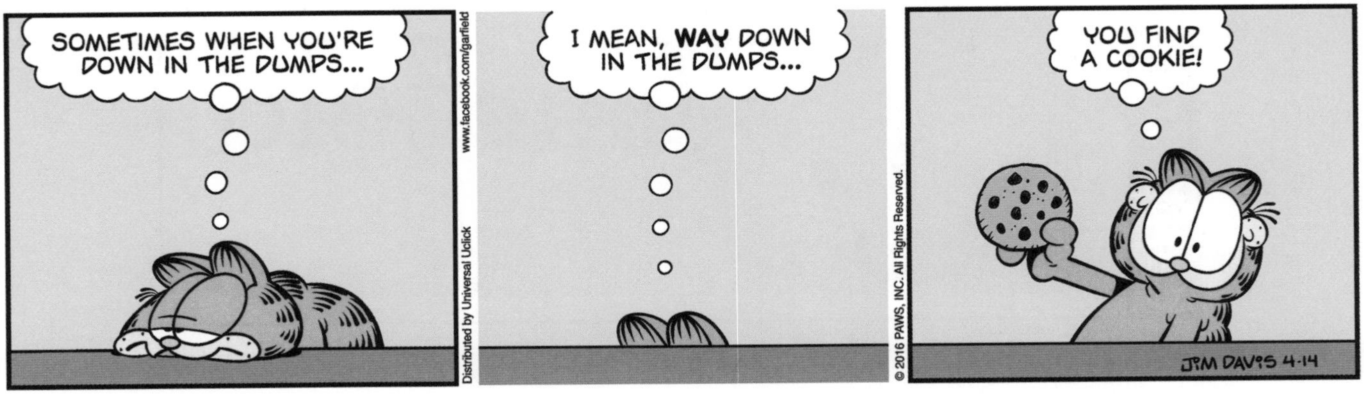
SOMETIMES WHEN YOU'RE DOWN IN THE DUMPS...
I MEAN, **WAY** DOWN IN THE DUMPS...
YOU FIND A COOKIE!
JIM DAVIS 4-14
www.facebook.com/garfield
Distributed by Universal Uclick
© 2016 PAWS, INC. All Rights Reserved.

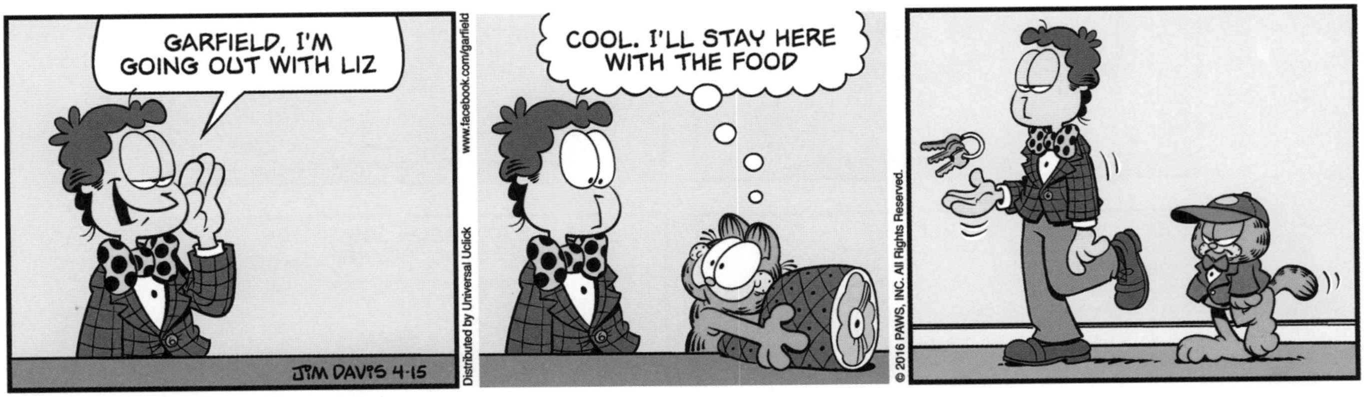
GARFIELD, I'M GOING OUT WITH LIZ
COOL. I'LL STAY HERE WITH THE FOOD
JIM DAVIS 4-15
www.facebook.com/garfield
Distributed by Universal Uclick
© 2016 PAWS, INC. All Rights Reserved.

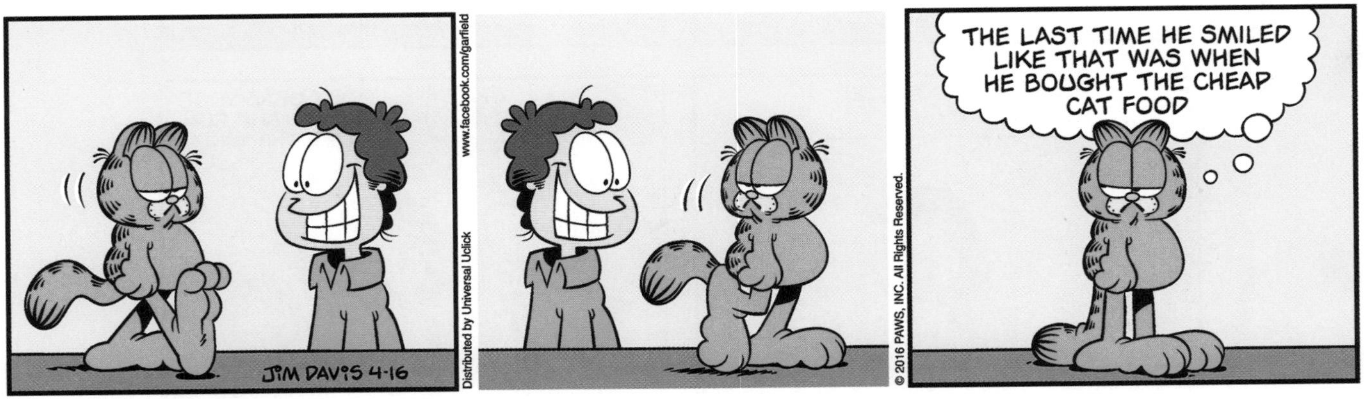
THE LAST TIME HE SMILED LIKE THAT WAS WHEN HE BOUGHT THE CHEAP CAT FOOD
JIM DAVIS 4-16
www.facebook.com/garfield
Distributed by Universal Uclick
© 2016 PAWS, INC. All Rights Reserved.

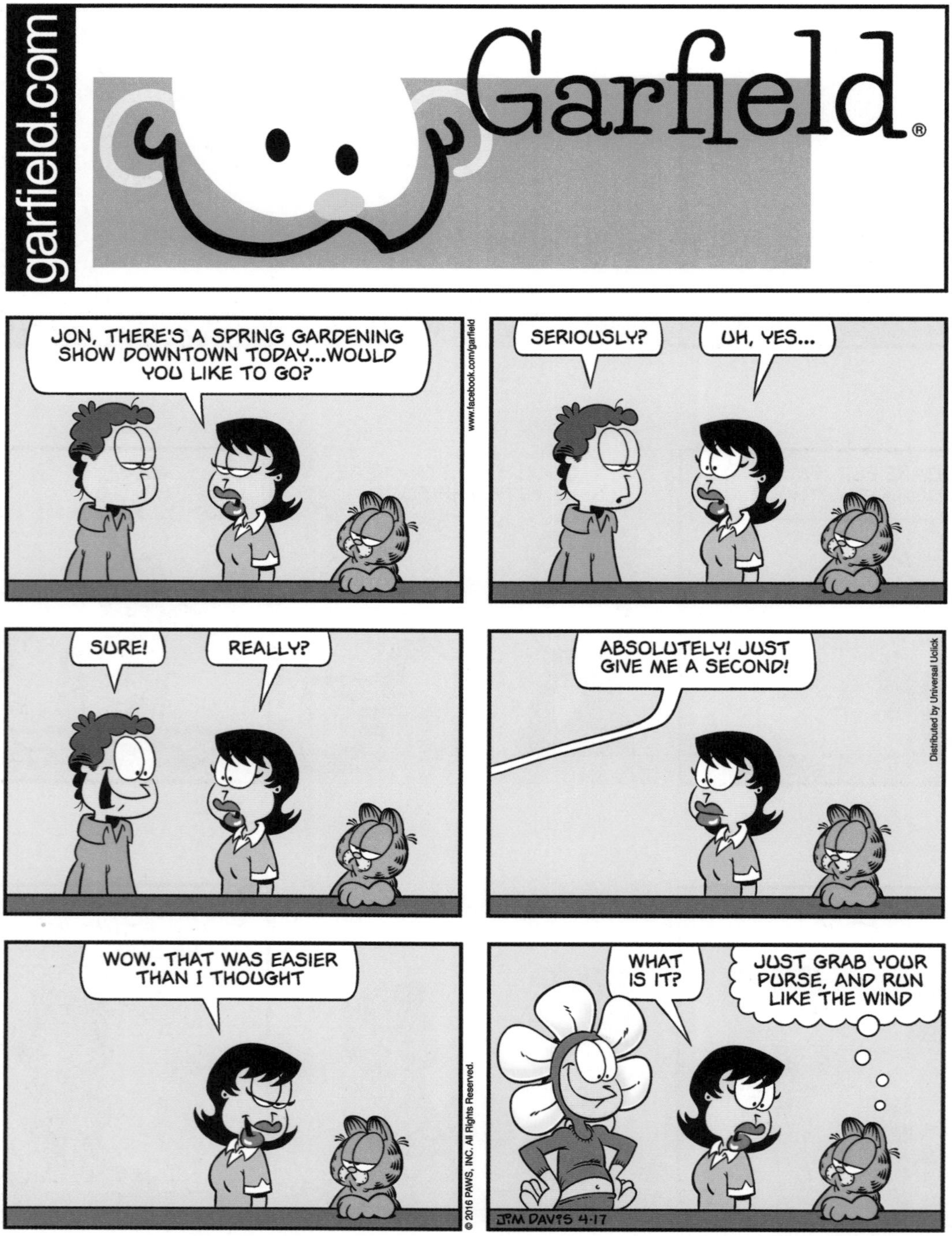
garfield.com
Garfield®
JON, THERE'S A SPRING GARDENING SHOW DOWNTOWN TODAY...WOULD YOU LIKE TO GO?
www.facebook.com/garfield
SERIOUSLY?
UH, YES...
SURE!
REALLY?
ABSOLUTELY! JUST GIVE ME A SECOND!
Distributed by Universal Uclick
WOW. THAT WAS EASIER THAN I THOUGHT
© 2016 PAWS, INC. All Rights Reserved.
WHAT IS IT?
JUST GRAB YOUR PURSE, AND RUN LIKE THE WIND
JIM DAVIS 4-17

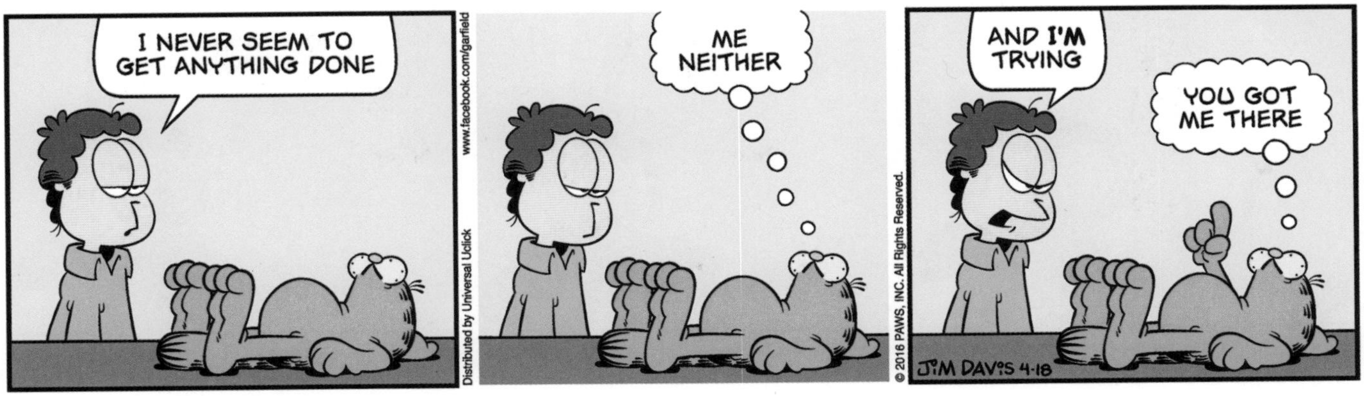
I NEVER SEEM TO GET ANYTHING DONE
ME NEITHER
AND I'M TRYING
YOU GOT ME THERE
JIM DAVIS 4-18

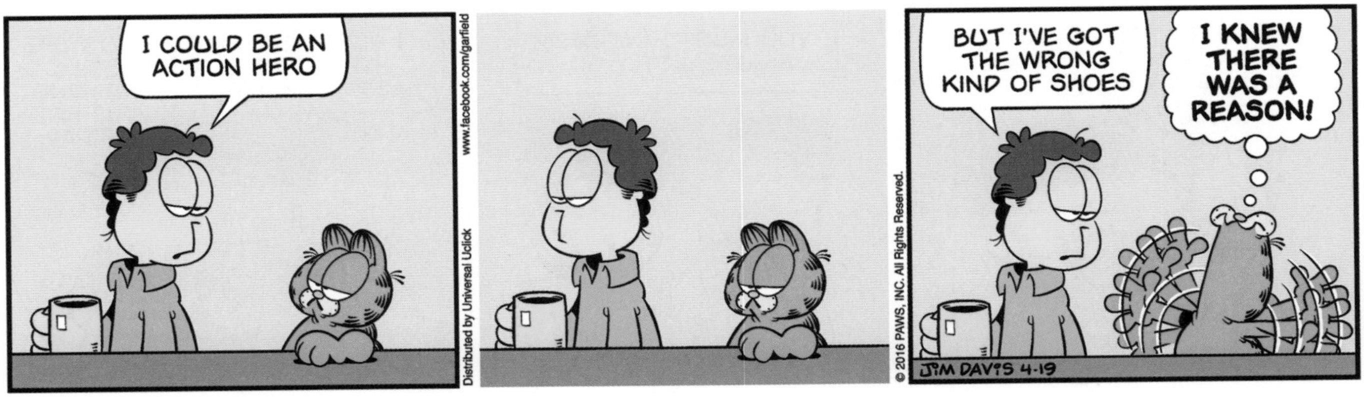
I COULD BE AN ACTION HERO
BUT I'VE GOT THE WRONG KIND OF SHOES
I KNEW THERE WAS A REASON!
JIM DAVIS 4-19

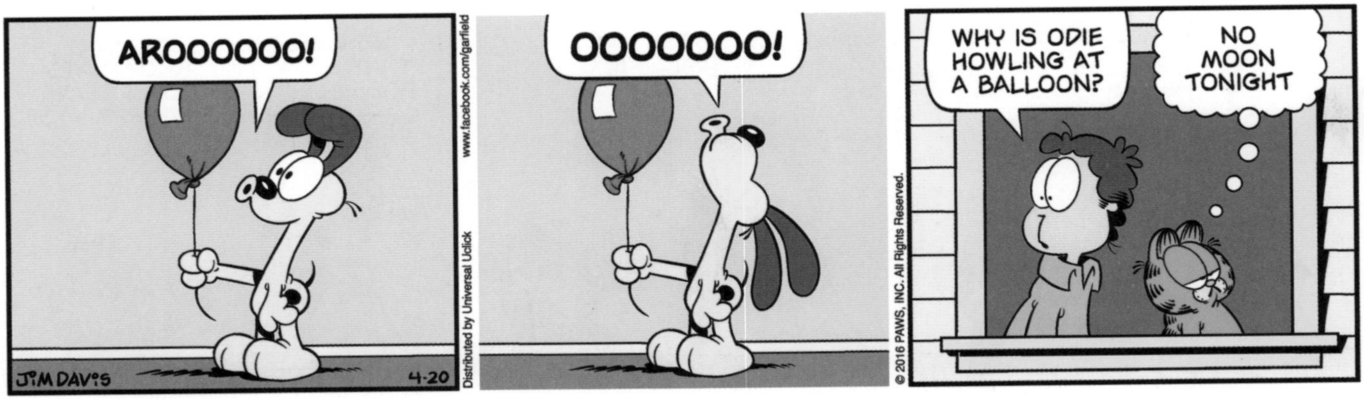
AROOOOOO!
JIM DAVIS 4-20
OOOOOOO!
WHY IS ODIE HOWLING AT A BALLOON?
NO MOON TONIGHT

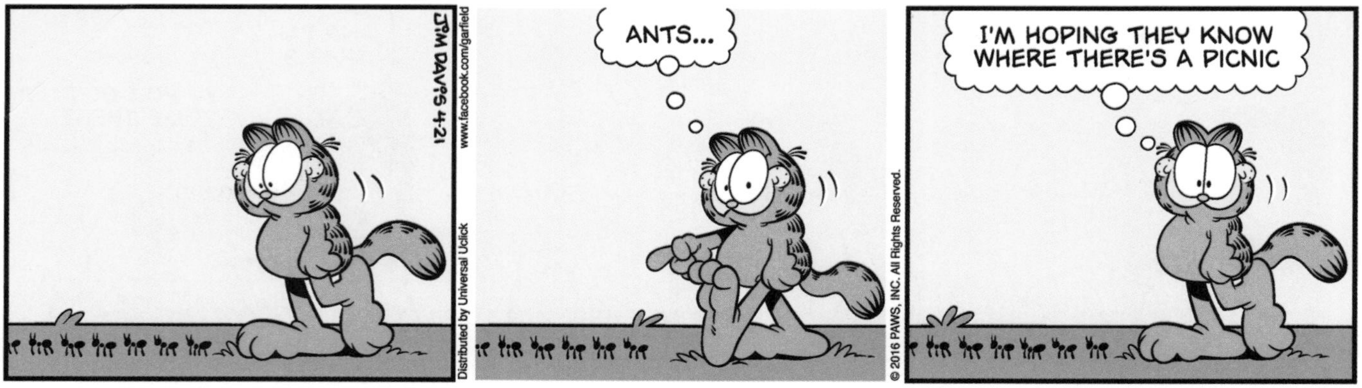
JIM DAVIS 4-21
www.facebook.com/garfield
Distributed by Universal Uclick
ANTS...
© 2016 PAWS, INC. All Rights Reserved.
I'M HOPING THEY KNOW WHERE THERE'S A PICNIC

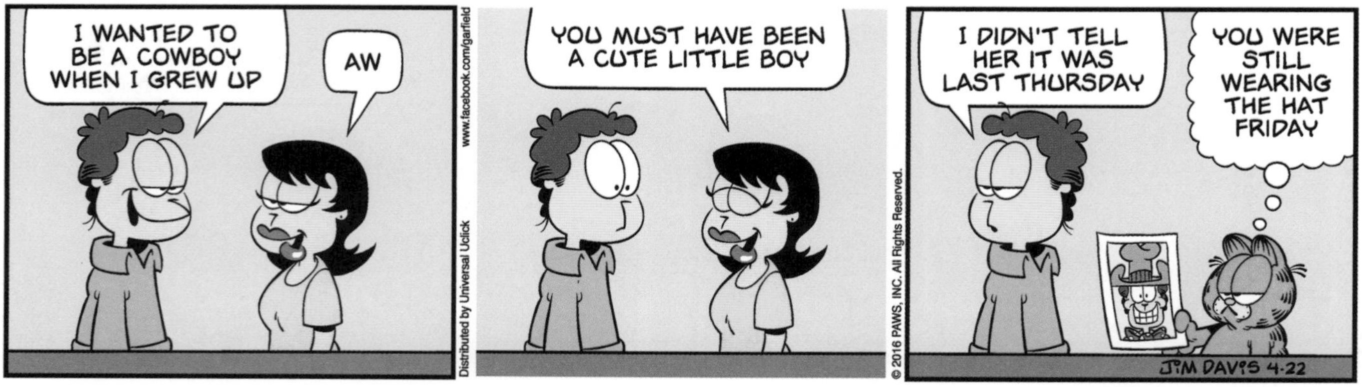
I WANTED TO BE A COWBOY WHEN I GREW UP
AW
www.facebook.com/garfield
Distributed by Universal Uclick
YOU MUST HAVE BEEN A CUTE LITTLE BOY
© 2016 PAWS, INC. All Rights Reserved.
I DIDN'T TELL HER IT WAS LAST THURSDAY
YOU WERE STILL WEARING THE HAT FRIDAY
JIM DAVIS 4-22

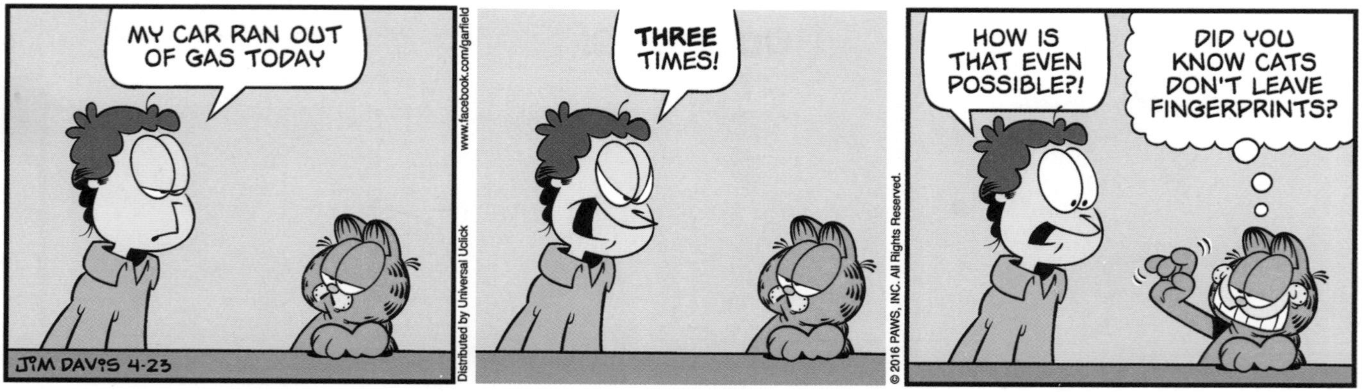
MY CAR RAN OUT OF GAS TODAY
JIM DAVIS 4-23
www.facebook.com/garfield
Distributed by Universal Uclick
THREE TIMES!
© 2016 PAWS, INC. All Rights Reserved.
HOW IS THAT EVEN POSSIBLE?!
DID YOU KNOW CATS DON'T LEAVE FINGERPRINTS?

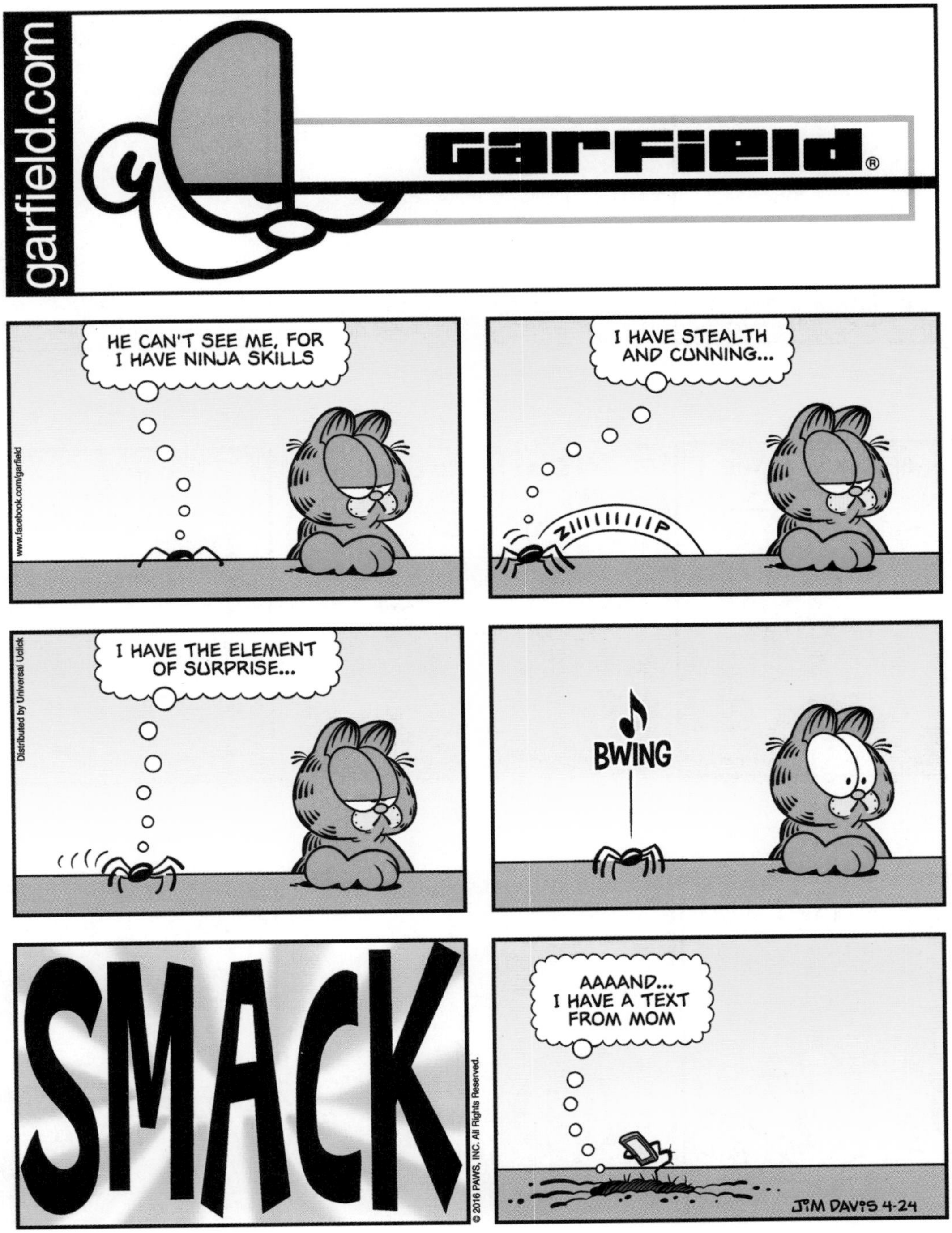
garfield.com
GARFIELD®
HE CAN'T SEE ME, FOR I HAVE NINJA SKILLS
www.facebook.com/garfield
I HAVE STEALTH AND CUNNING...
ZIIIIIIIIP
Distributed by Universal Uclick
I HAVE THE ELEMENT OF SURPRISE...
BWING
SMACK
© 2016 PAWS, INC. All Rights Reserved.
AAAAND... I HAVE A TEXT FROM MOM
JIM DAVIS 4-24

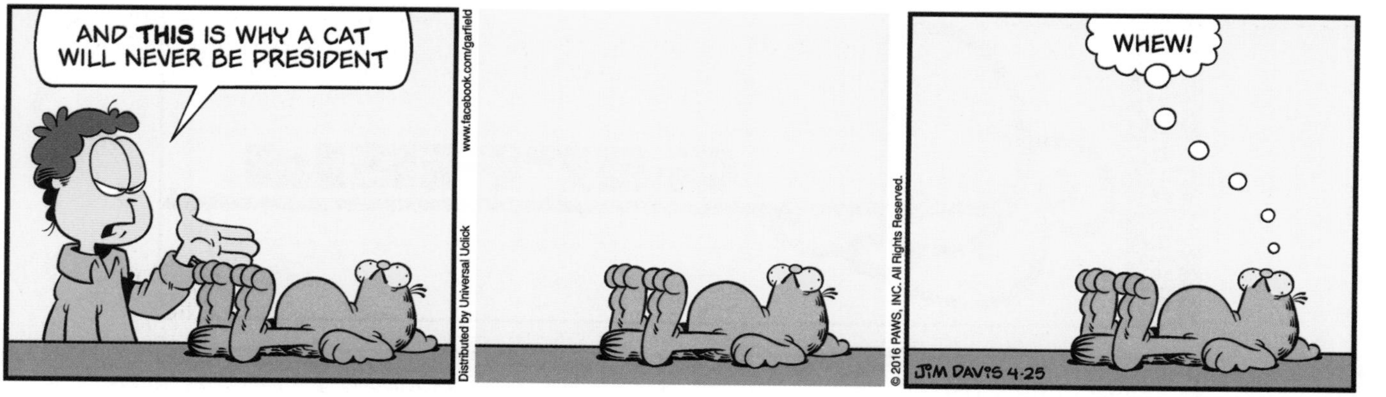
AND **THIS** IS WHY A CAT WILL NEVER BE PRESIDENT
www.facebook.com/garfield
Distributed by Universal Uclick
© 2016 PAWS, INC. All Rights Reserved.
WHEW!
JIM DAVIS 4-25

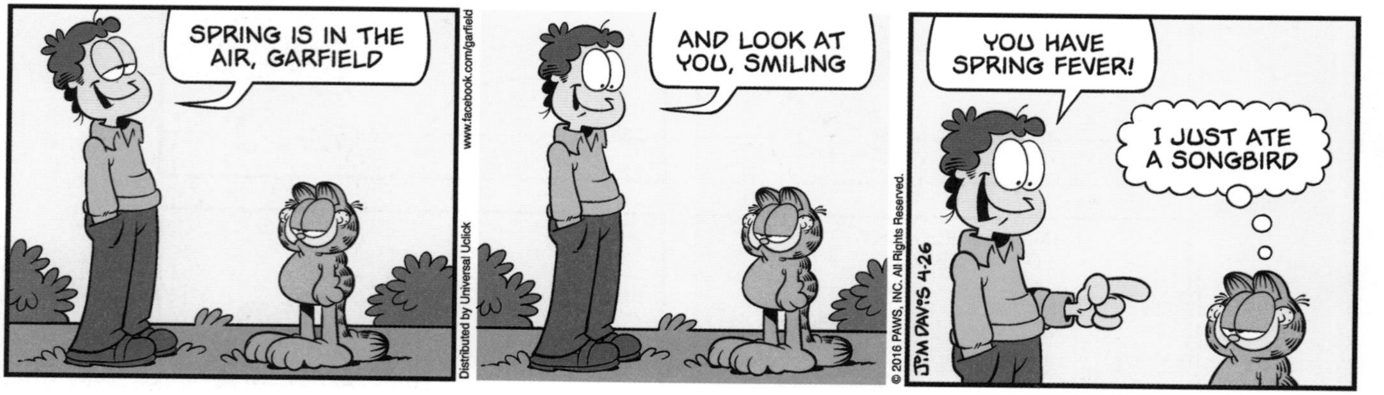
SPRING IS IN THE AIR, GARFIELD
www.facebook.com/garfield
Distributed by Universal Uclick
AND LOOK AT YOU, SMILING
© 2016 PAWS, INC. All Rights Reserved.
JIM DAVIS 4-26
YOU HAVE SPRING FEVER!
I JUST ATE A SONGBIRD

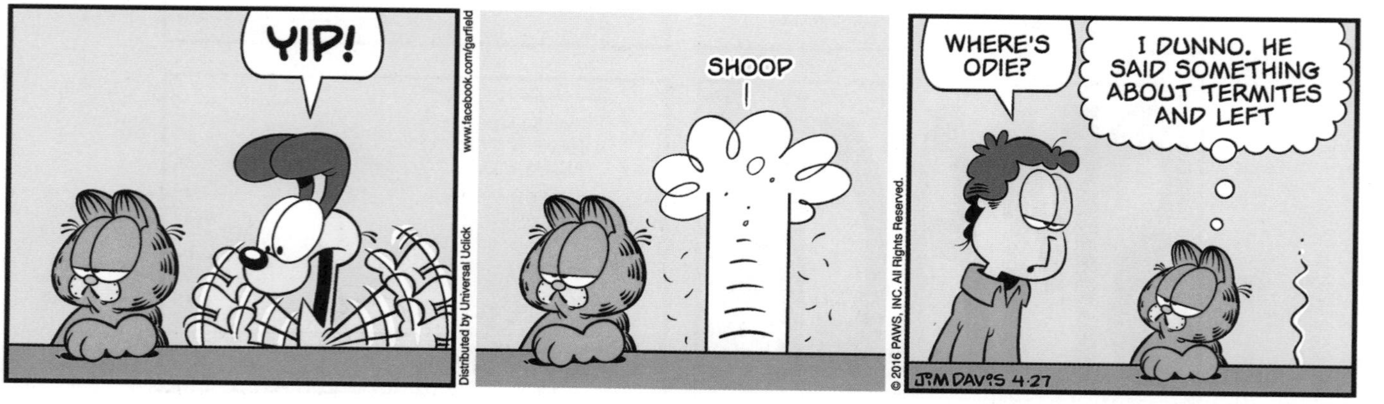
YIP!
www.facebook.com/garfield
Distributed by Universal Uclick
SHOOP
© 2016 PAWS, INC. All Rights Reserved.
WHERE'S ODIE?
I DUNNO. HE SAID SOMETHING ABOUT TERMITES AND LEFT
JIM DAVIS 4-27

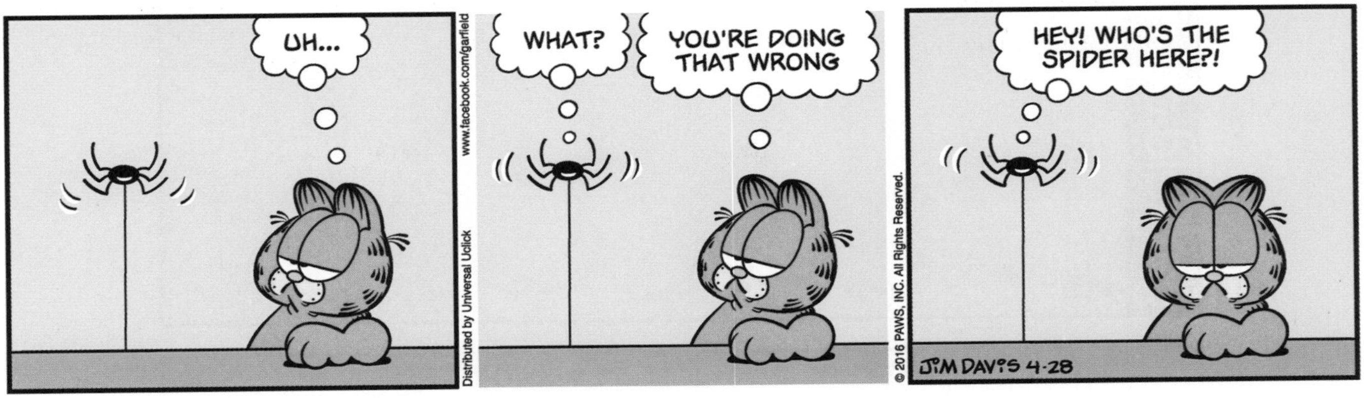
UH...
www.facebook.com/garfield
Distributed by Universal Uclick
WHAT?
YOU'RE DOING THAT WRONG
© 2016 PAWS, INC. All Rights Reserved.
HEY! WHO'S THE SPIDER HERE?!
JIM DAVIS 4-28

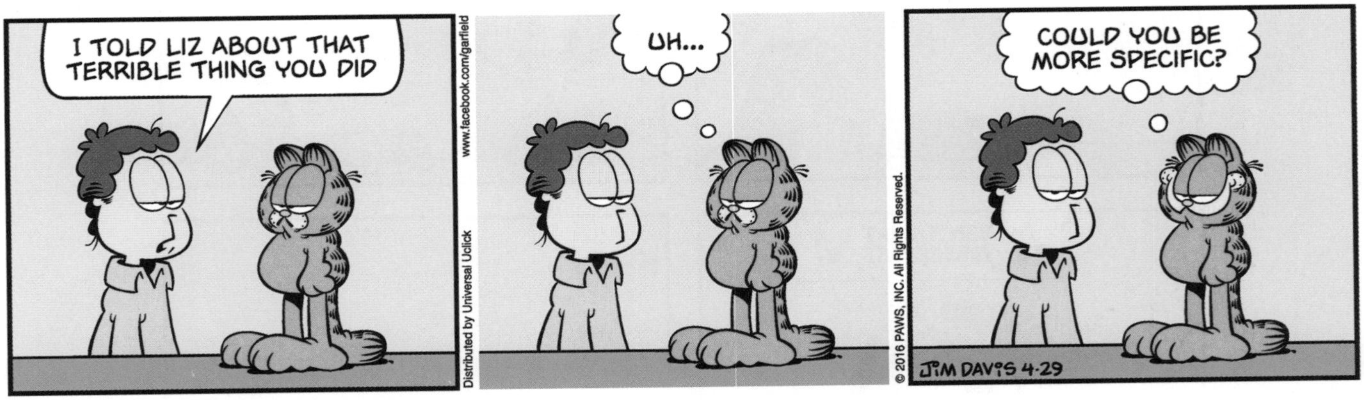
I TOLD LIZ ABOUT THAT TERRIBLE THING YOU DID
www.facebook.com/garfield
Distributed by Universal Uclick
UH...
© 2016 PAWS, INC. All Rights Reserved.
COULD YOU BE MORE SPECIFIC?
JIM DAVIS 4-29

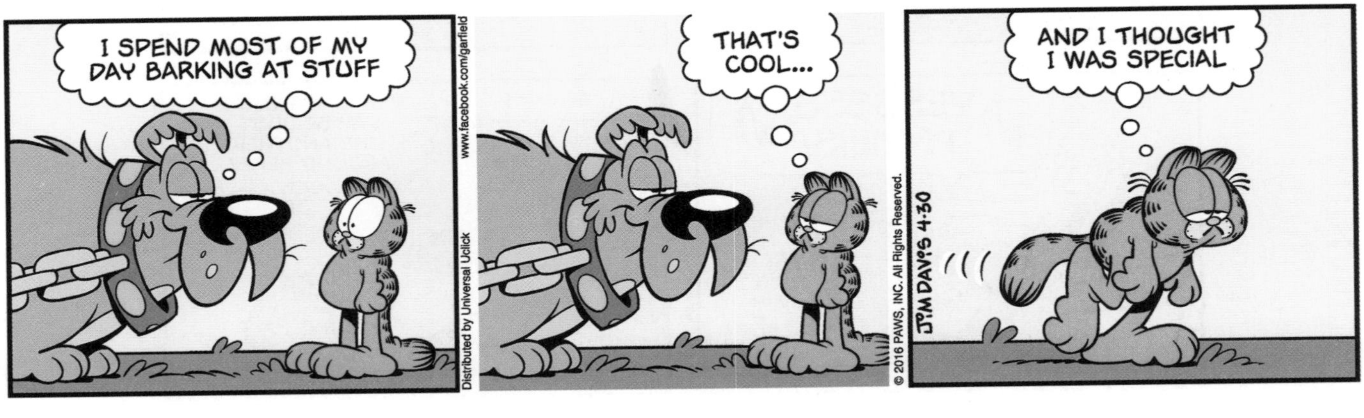
I SPEND MOST OF MY DAY BARKING AT STUFF
www.facebook.com/garfield
Distributed by Universal Uclick
THAT'S COOL...
© 2016 PAWS, INC. All Rights Reserved.
JIM DAVIS 4-30
AND I THOUGHT I WAS SPECIAL

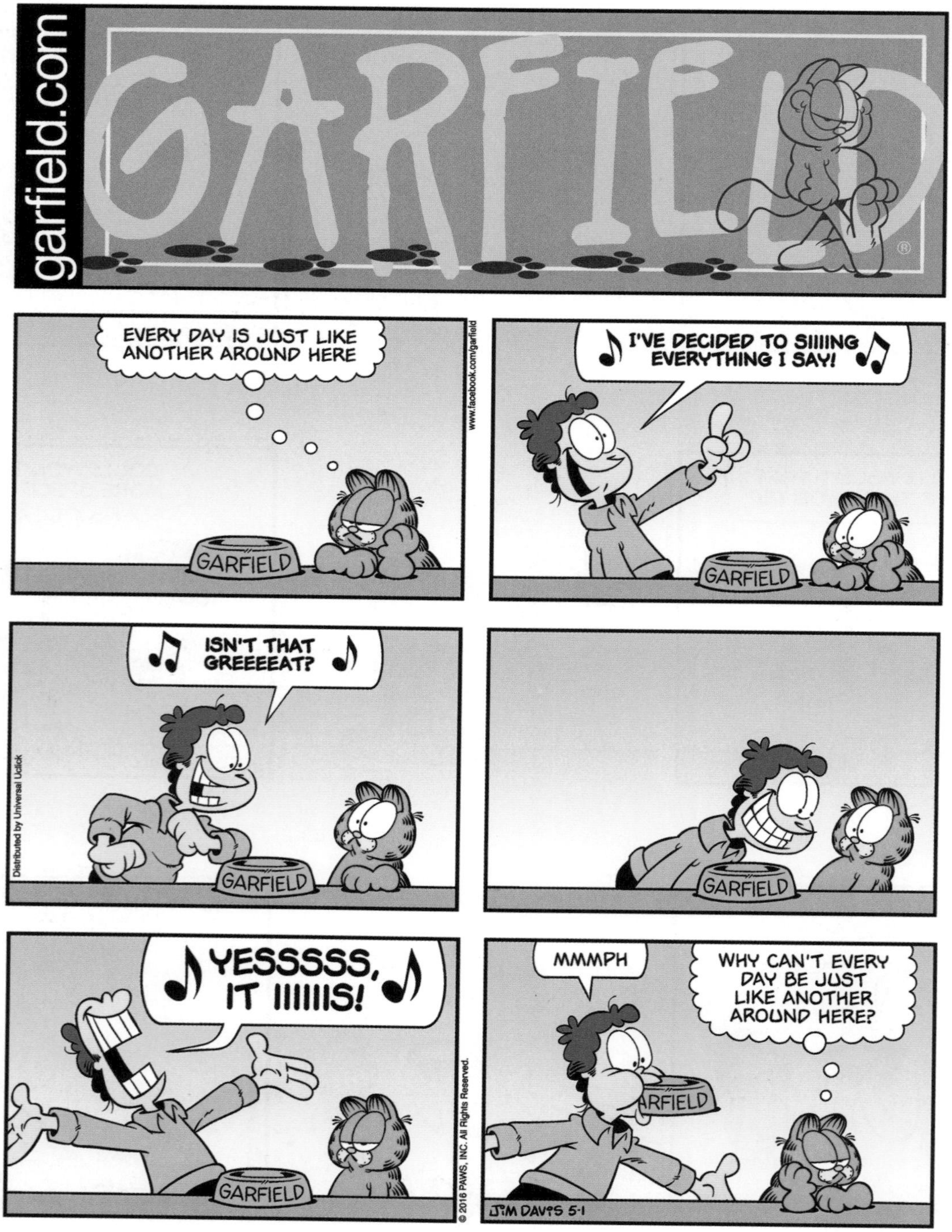
garfield.com
GARFIELD
EVERY DAY IS JUST LIKE ANOTHER AROUND HERE
GARFIELD
www.facebook.com/garfield
I'VE DECIDED TO SIIIING EVERYTHING I SAY!
GARFIELD
ISN'T THAT GREEEEAT?
GARFIELD
Distributed by Universal Uclick
GARFIELD
YESSSSS, IT IIIIIIS!
GARFIELD
© 2016 PAWS, INC. All Rights Reserved.
MMMPH
WHY CAN'T EVERY DAY BE JUST LIKE ANOTHER AROUND HERE?
JIM DAVIS 5-1

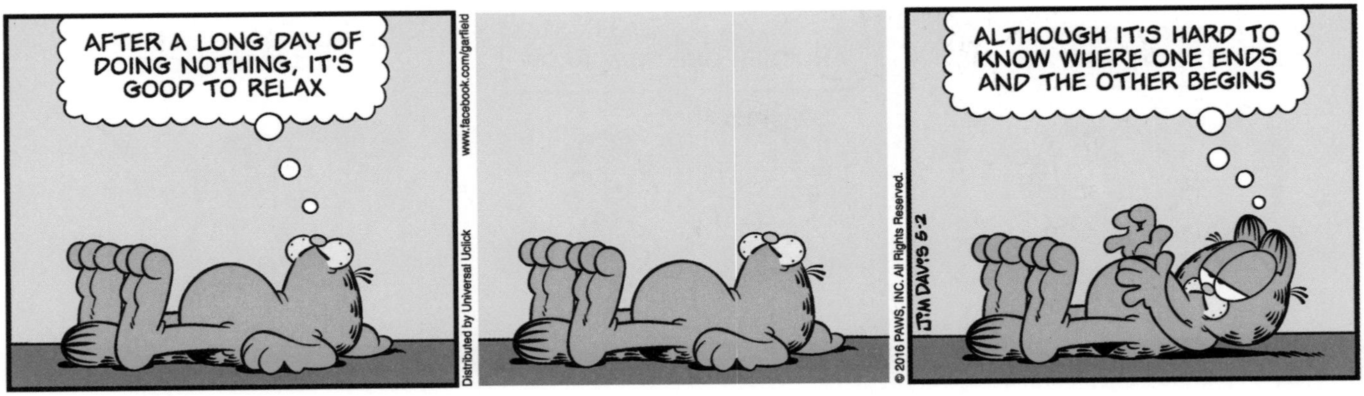
AFTER A LONG DAY OF DOING NOTHING, IT'S GOOD TO RELAX
ALTHOUGH IT'S HARD TO KNOW WHERE ONE ENDS AND THE OTHER BEGINS
JIM DAVIS 5-2
Distributed by Universal Uclick www.facebook.com/garfield
© 2016 PAWS, INC. All Rights Reserved.

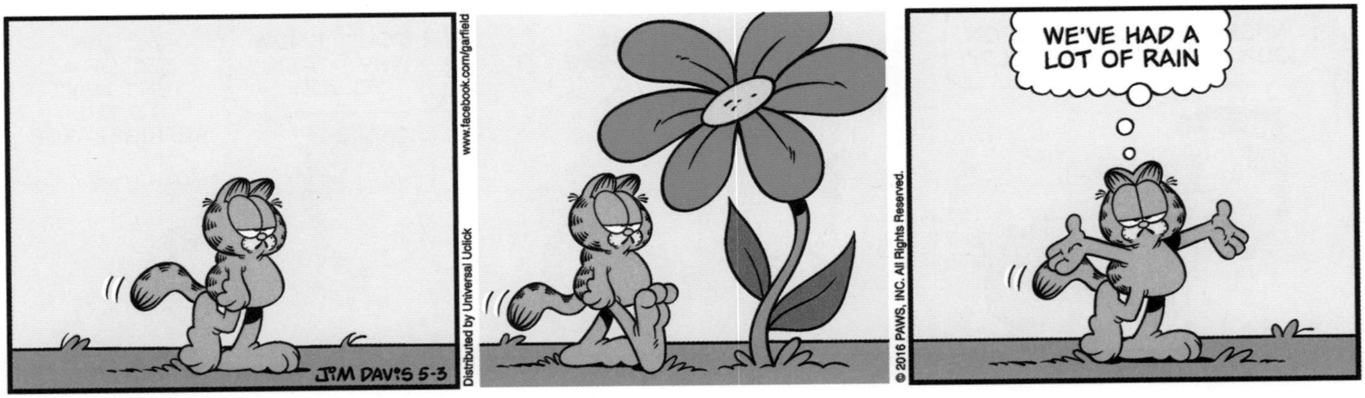
JIM DAVIS 5-3
WE'VE HAD A LOT OF RAIN
Distributed by Universal Uclick www.facebook.com/garfield
© 2016 PAWS, INC. All Rights Reserved.

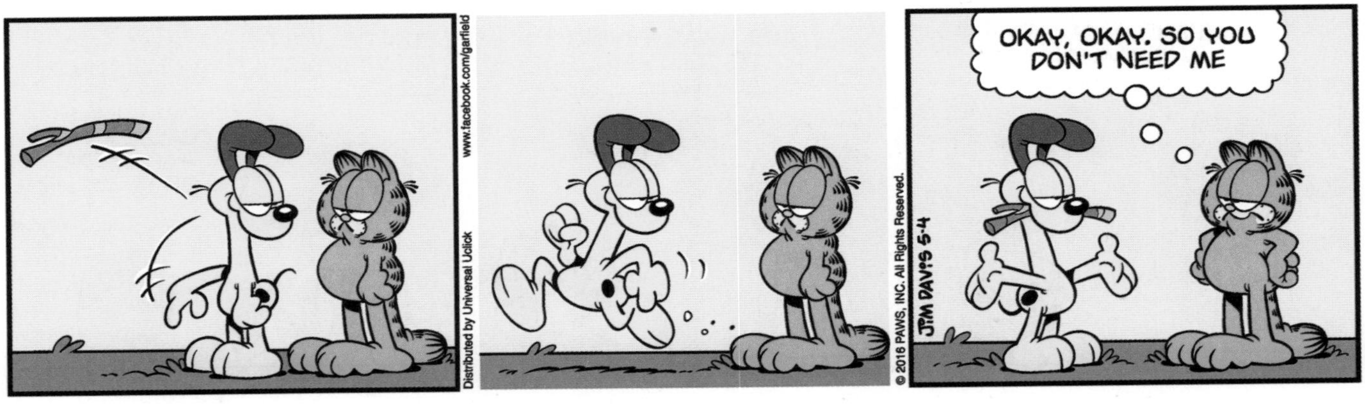
OKAY, OKAY. SO YOU DON'T NEED ME
JIM DAVIS 5-4
Distributed by Universal Uclick www.facebook.com/garfield
© 2016 PAWS, INC. All Rights Reserved.

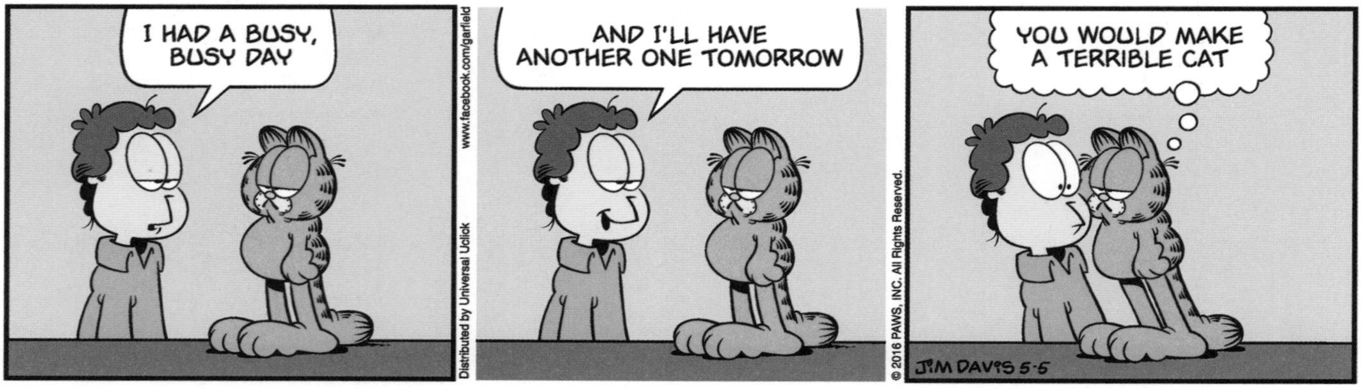
I HAD A BUSY, BUSY DAY
www.facebook.com/garfield
Distributed by Universal Uclick
AND I'LL HAVE ANOTHER ONE TOMORROW
© 2016 PAWS, INC. All Rights Reserved.
YOU WOULD MAKE A TERRIBLE CAT
JIM DAVIS 5-5

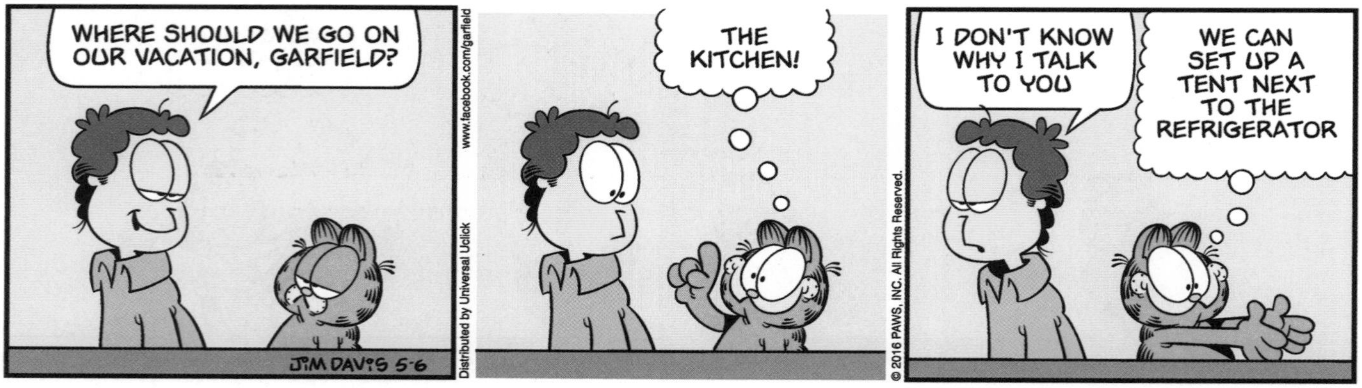
WHERE SHOULD WE GO ON OUR VACATION, GARFIELD?
JIM DAVIS 5-6
www.facebook.com/garfield
Distributed by Universal Uclick
THE KITCHEN!
© 2016 PAWS, INC. All Rights Reserved.
I DON'T KNOW WHY I TALK TO YOU
WE CAN SET UP A TENT NEXT TO THE REFRIGERATOR

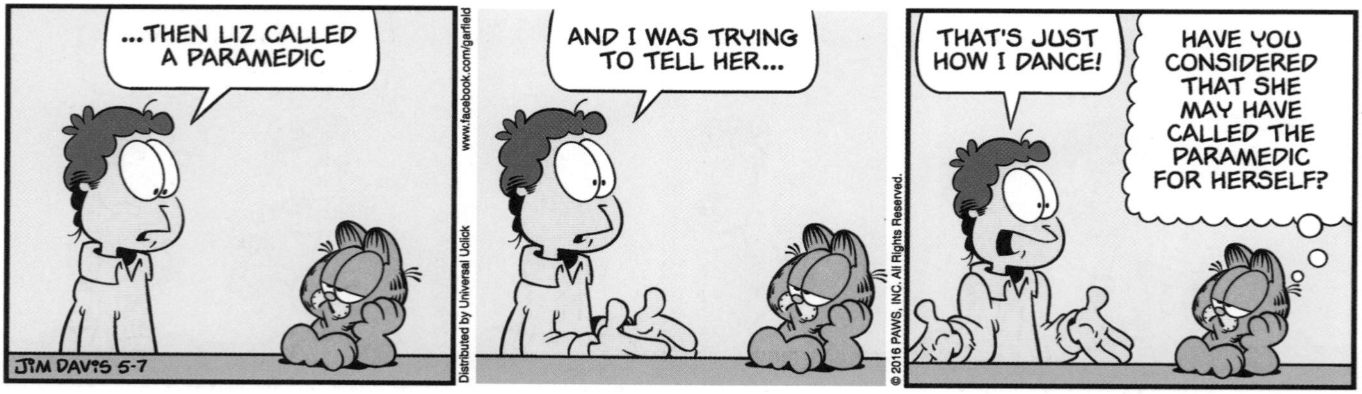
...THEN LIZ CALLED A PARAMEDIC
JIM DAVIS 5-7
www.facebook.com/garfield
Distributed by Universal Uclick
AND I WAS TRYING TO TELL HER...
© 2016 PAWS, INC. All Rights Reserved.
THAT'S JUST HOW I DANCE!
HAVE YOU CONSIDERED THAT SHE MAY HAVE CALLED THE PARAMEDIC FOR HERSELF?

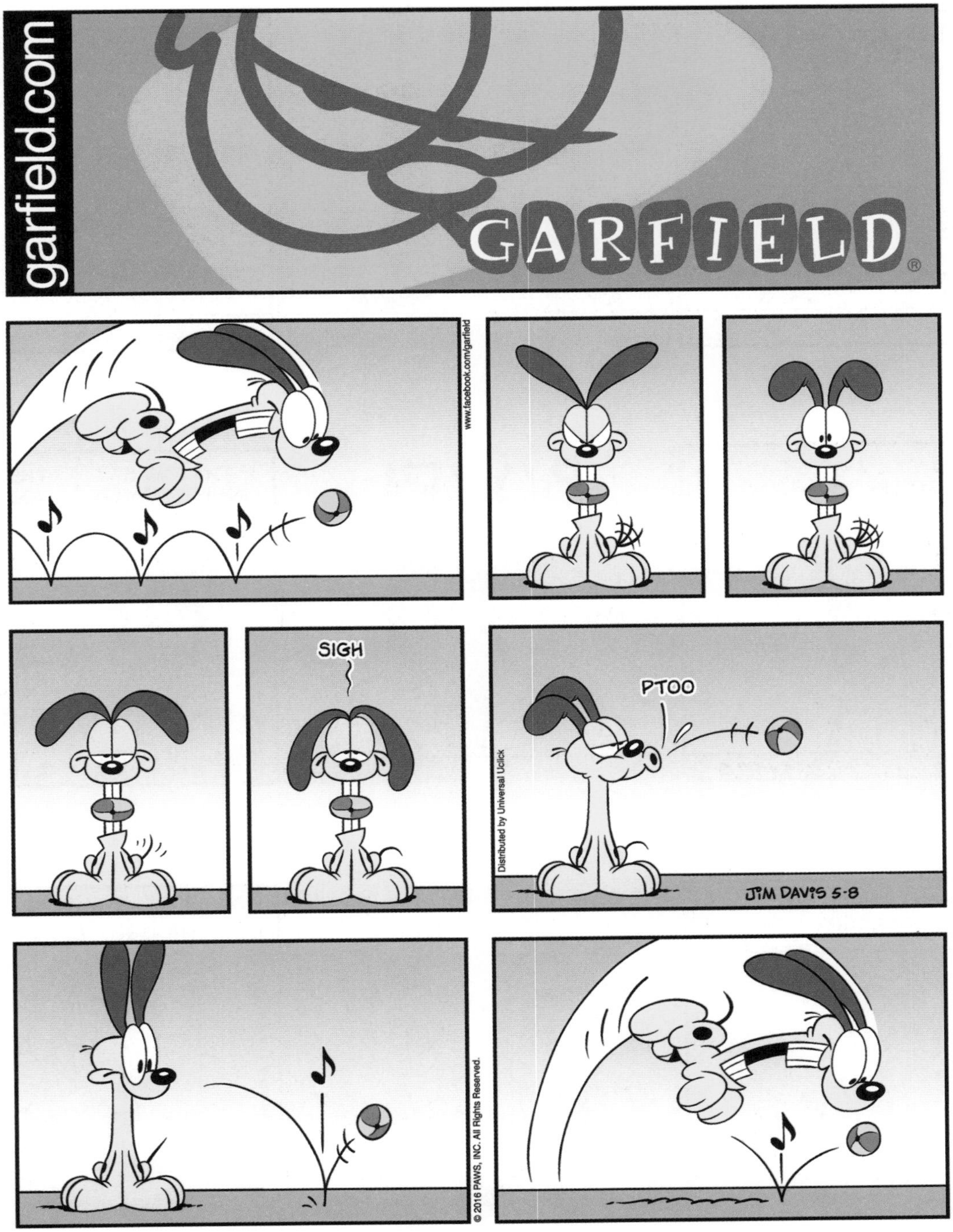
garfield.com
GARFIELD®
www.facebook.com/garfield
SIGH
Distributed by Universal Uclick
PTOO
JIM DAVIS 5-8
© 2016 PAWS, INC. All Rights Reserved.

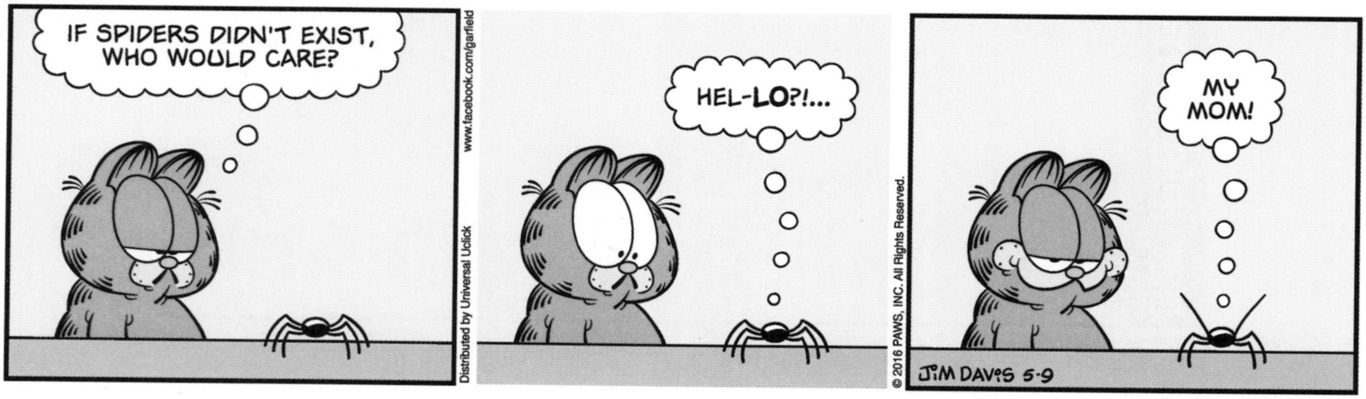
IF SPIDERS DIDN'T EXIST, WHO WOULD CARE?
Distributed by Universal Uclick www.facebook.com/garfield
HEL-LO?!...
© 2016 PAWS, INC. All Rights Reserved.
MY MOM!
JIM DAVIS 5-9

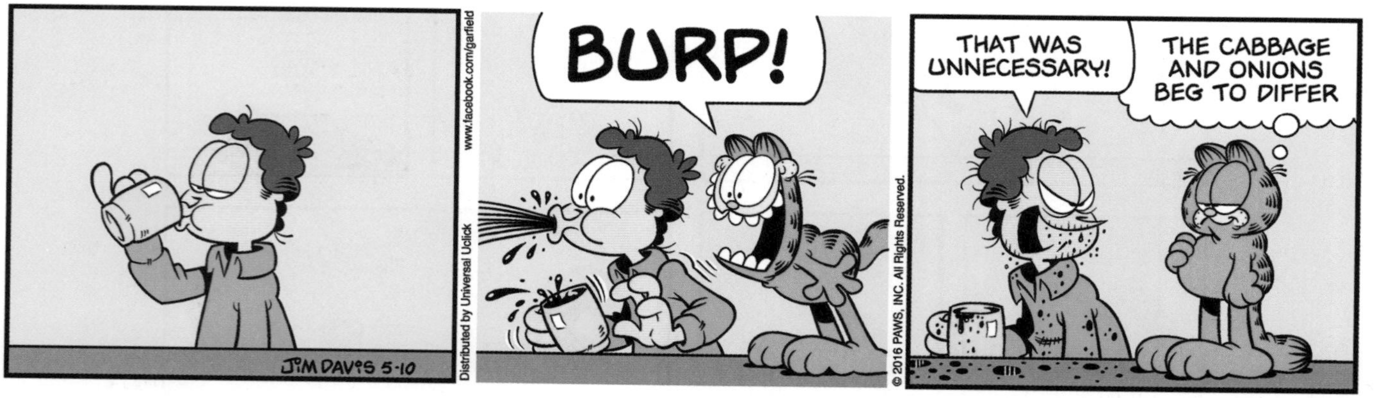
JIM DAVIS 5-10
Distributed by Universal Uclick www.facebook.com/garfield
BURP!
© 2016 PAWS, INC. All Rights Reserved.
THAT WAS UNNECESSARY!
THE CABBAGE AND ONIONS BEG TO DIFFER

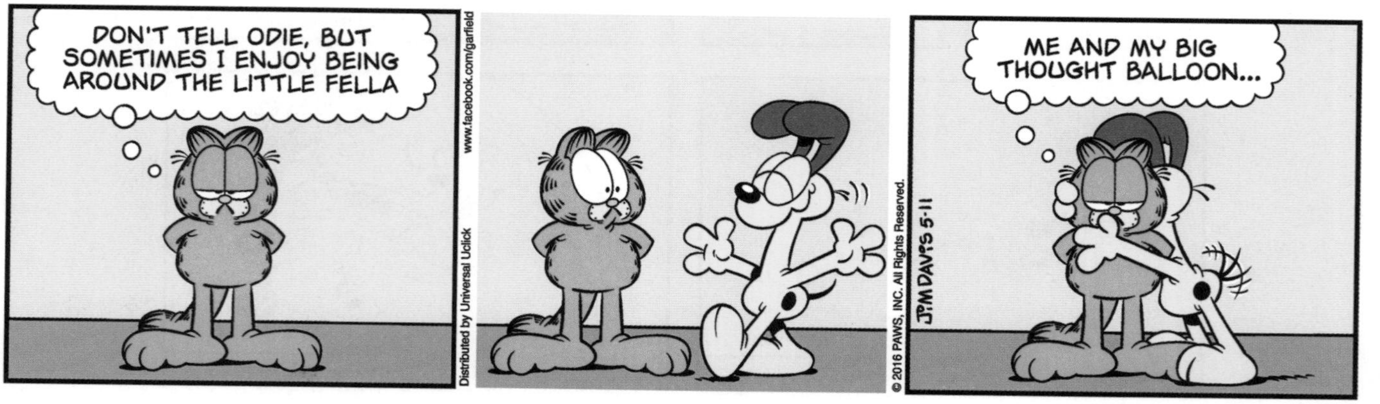
DON'T TELL ODIE, BUT SOMETIMES I ENJOY BEING AROUND THE LITTLE FELLA
Distributed by Universal Uclick www.facebook.com/garfield
© 2016 PAWS, INC. All Rights Reserved.
JIM DAVIS 5-11
ME AND MY BIG THOUGHT BALLOON...

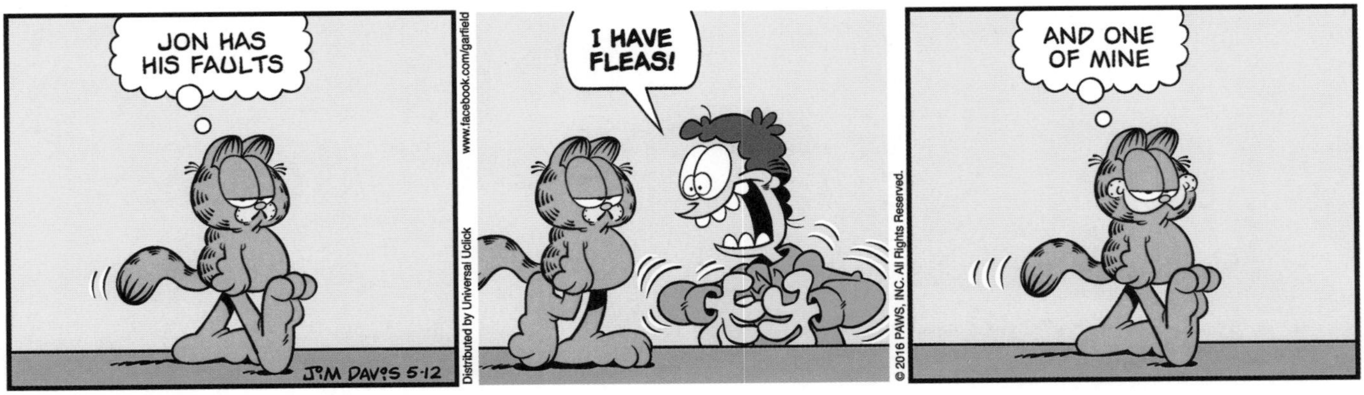
JON HAS HIS FAULTS
I HAVE FLEAS!
AND ONE OF MINE
JIM DAVIS 5-12
Distributed by Universal Uclick
www.facebook.com/garfield
© 2016 PAWS, INC. All Rights Reserved.

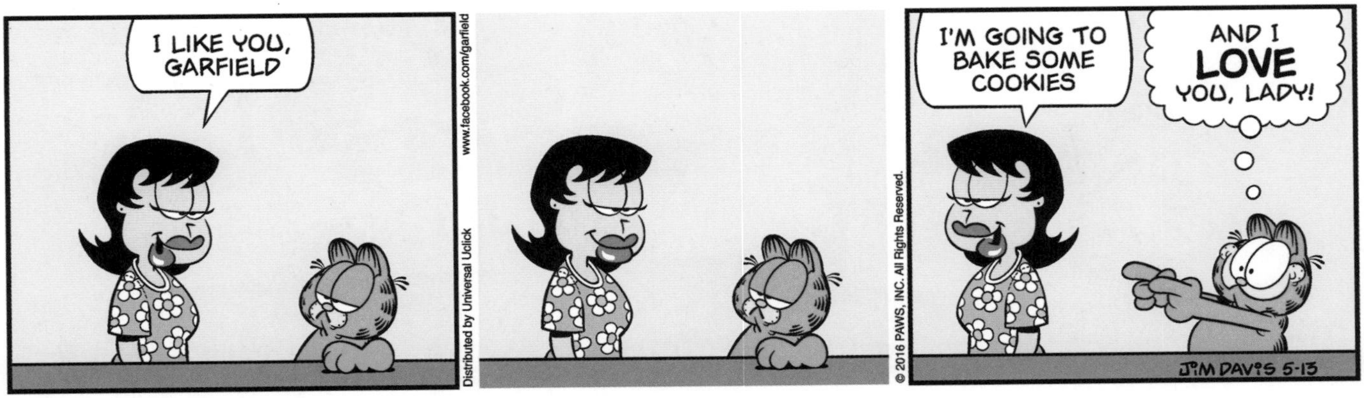
I LIKE YOU, GARFIELD
I'M GOING TO BAKE SOME COOKIES
AND I LOVE YOU, LADY!
JIM DAVIS 5-13
Distributed by Universal Uclick
www.facebook.com/garfield
© 2016 PAWS, INC. All Rights Reserved.

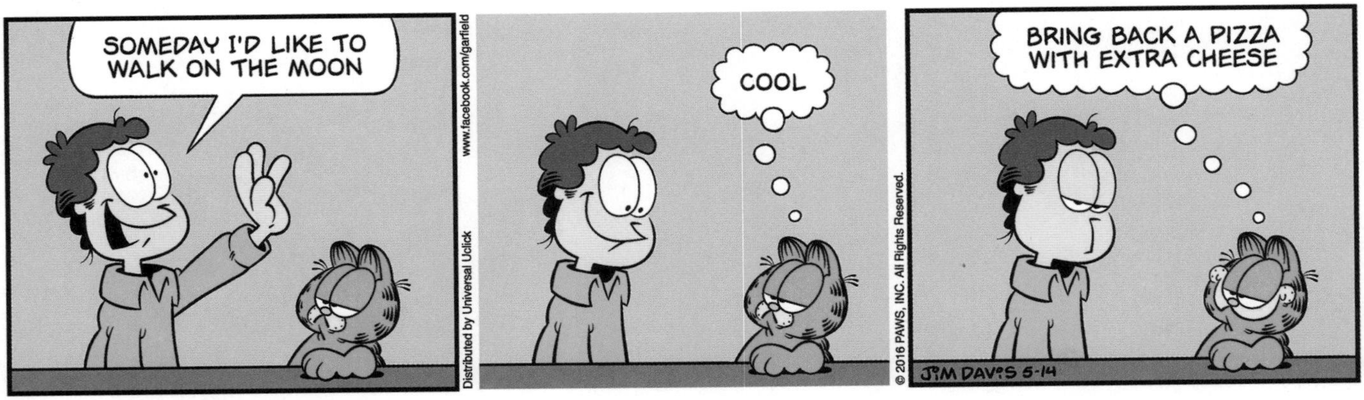
SOMEDAY I'D LIKE TO WALK ON THE MOON
COOL
BRING BACK A PIZZA WITH EXTRA CHEESE
JIM DAVIS 5-14
Distributed by Universal Uclick
www.facebook.com/garfield
© 2016 PAWS, INC. All Rights Reserved.

WORKING HARD...

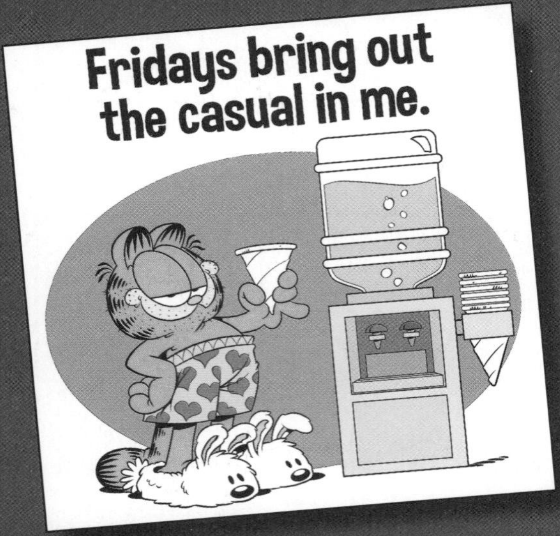
Fridays bring out the casual in me.

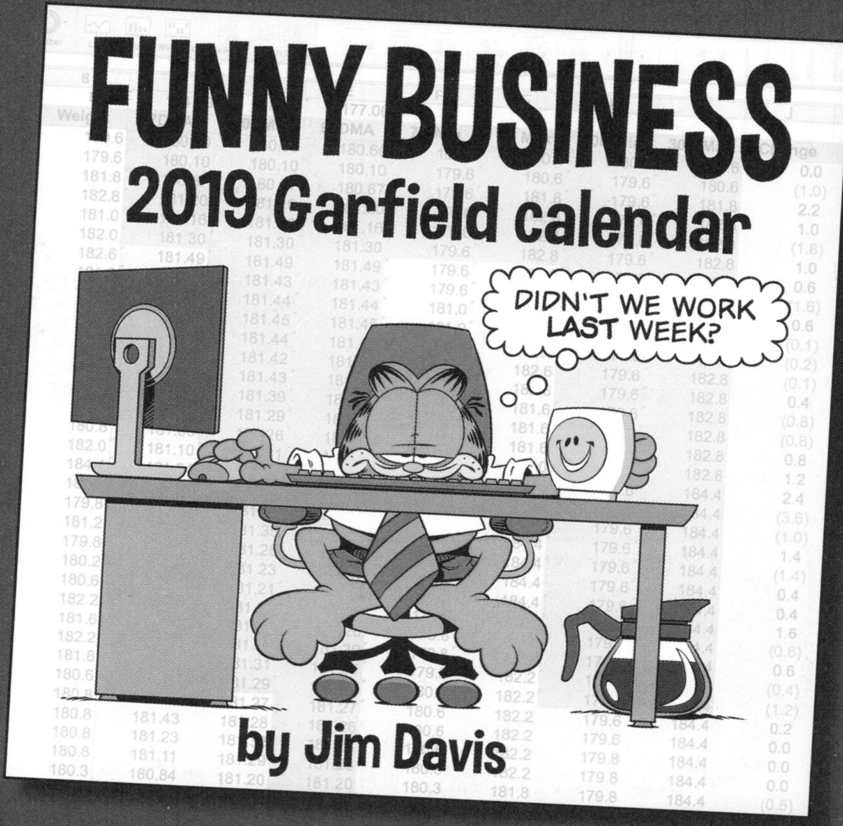
FUNNY BUSINESS
2019 Garfield calendar
DIDN'T WE WORK LAST WEEK?
by Jim Davis

OR HARDLY WORKING?

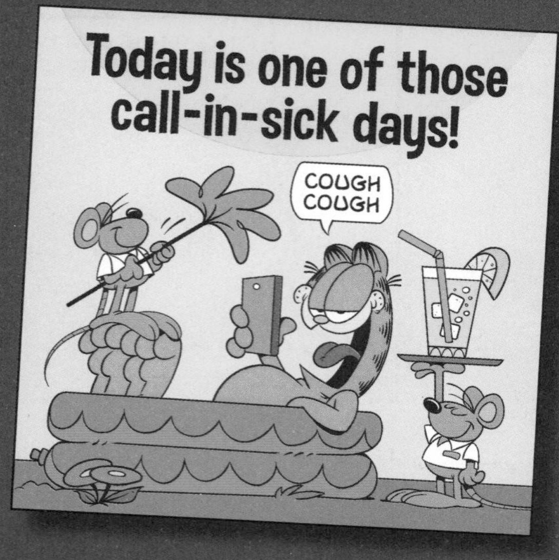
Today is one of those call-in-sick days!
COUGH COUGH

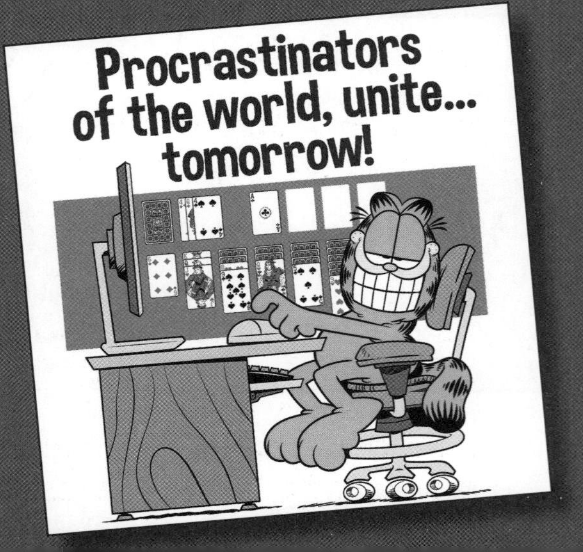
Procrastinators of the world, unite... tomorrow!

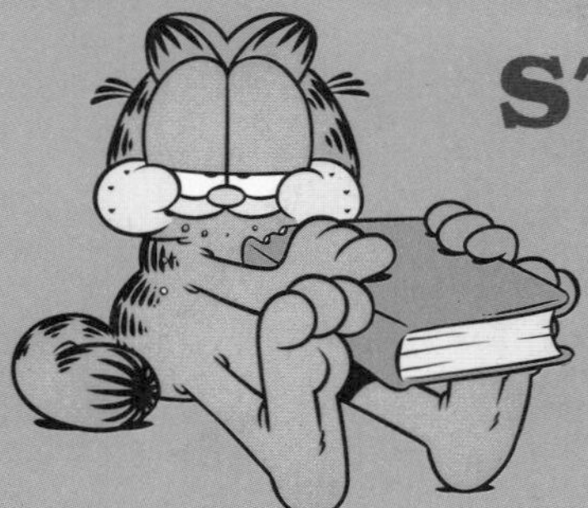

STRIPS, SPECIALS, OR BESTSELLING BOOKS . . . GARFIELD'S ON EVERYONE'S MENU.

Don't miss even one episode in the Tubby Tabby's hilarious series!

Title	No.	ISBN
GARFIELD AT LARGE	(#1)	978-0-345-44382-3
GARFIELD GAINS WEIGHT	(#2)	978-0-345-44975-7
GARFIELD BIGGER THAN LIFE	(#3)	978-0-345-45027-2
GARFIELD WEIGHS IN	(#4)	978-0-345-45205-4
GARFIELD TAKES THE CAKE	(#5)	978-0-345-44978-8
GARFIELD EATS HIS HEART OUT	(#6)	978-0-345-46459-0
GARFIELD SITS AROUND THE HOUSE	(#7)	978-0-345-46463-7
GARFIELD TIPS THE SCALES	(#8)	978-0-345-46909-0
GARFIELD LOSES HIS FEET	(#9)	978-0-345-46467-5
GARFIELD MAKES IT BIG	(#10)	978-0-345-46468-2
GARFIELD ROLLS ON	(#11)	978-0-345-47561-9
GARFIELD OUT TO LUNCH	(#12)	978-0-345-47562-6
GARFIELD FOOD FOR THOUGHT	(#13)	978-0-345-47563-3
GARFIELD SWALLOWS HIS PRIDE	(#14)	978-0-345-91386-9
GARFIELD WORLDWIDE	(#15)	978-0-345-91754-6
GARFIELD ROUNDS OUT	(#16)	978-0-345-49169-5
GARFIELD CHEWS THE FAT	(#17)	978-0-345-49170-1
GARFIELD GOES TO WAIST	(#18)	978-0-345-49173-2
GARFIELD HANGS OUT	(#19)	978-0-345-49174-9
GARFIELD TAKES UP SPACE	(#20)	978-0-345-49178-7
GARFIELD SAYS A MOUTHFUL	(#21)	978-0-345-49179-4
GARFIELD BY THE POUND	(#22)	978-0-345-52558-1
GARFIELD KEEPS HIS CHINS UP	(#23)	978-0-345-52559-8
GARFIELD TAKES HIS LICKS	(#24)	978-0-345-52587-1
GARFIELD HITS THE BIG TIME	(#25)	978-0-345-52589-5
GARFIELD PULLS HIS WEIGHT	(#26)	978-0-345-52594-9
GARFIELD DISHES IT OUT	(#27)	978-0-345-52595-6
GARFIELD LIFE IN THE FAT LANE	(#28)	978-0-345-52600-7
GARFIELD TONS OF FUN	(#29)	978-0-345-52601-4
GARFIELD BIGGER AND BETTER	(#30)	978-0-345-52605-2
GARFIELD HAMS IT UP	(#31)	978-0-345-52606-9
GARFIELD THINKS BIG	(#32)	978-0-425-28516-9
GARFIELD THROWS HIS WEIGHT AROUND	(#33)	978-0-425-28559-6
GARFIELD LIFE TO THE FULLEST	(#34)	978-0-425-28564-0
GARFIELD FEEDS THE KITTY	(#35)	978-0-425-28569-5
GARFIELD HOGS THE SPOTLIGHT	(#36)	978-0-345-43922-2
GARFIELD BEEFS UP	(#37)	978-0-345-44109-6
GARFIELD GETS COOKIN'	(#38)	978-0-345-44582-7
GARFIELD EATS CROW	(#39)	978-0-345-45201-6
GARFIELD SURVIVAL OF THE FATTEST	(#40)	978-0-345-46458-3
GARFIELD OLDER AND WIDER	(#41)	978-0-345-46462-0
GARFIELD PIGS OUT	(#42)	978-0-345-46466-8
GARFIELD BLOTS OUT THE SUN	(#43)	978-0-345-46615-0
GARFIELD GOES BANANAS	(#44)	978-0-345-91346-3
GARFIELD LARGE & IN CHARGE	(#45)	978-0-345-49172-5
GARFIELD SPILLS THE BEANS	(#46)	978-0-345-49177-0
GARFIELD GETS HIS JUST DESSERTS	(#47)	978-0-345-91387-6
GARFIELD WILL EAT FOR FOOD	(#48)	978-0-345-49176-3
GARFIELD WEIGHS HIS OPTIONS	(#49)	978-0-345-49181-7
GARFIELD POTBELLY OF GOLD	(#50)	978-0-345-52244-3
GARFIELD SHOVELS IT IN	(#51)	978-0-345-52419-5
GARFIELD LARD OF THE JUNGLE	(#52)	978-0-345-52584-0
GARFIELD BRINGS HOME THE BACON	(#53)	978-0-345-52586-4
GARFIELD GETS IN A PICKLE	(#54)	978-0-345-52590-1
GARFIELD SINGS FOR HIS SUPPER	(#55)	978-0-345-52593-2
GARFIELD CAUTION: WIDE LOAD	(#56)	978-0-345-52596-3
GARFIELD SOUPED UP	(#57)	978-0-345-52598-7
GARFIELD GOES TO HIS HAPPY PLACE	(#58)	978-0-345-52602-1
GARFIELD THE BIG CHEESE	(#59)	978-0-345-52604-5
GARFIELD CLEANS HIS PLATE	(#60)	978-0-345-52608-3
GARFIELD CHICKENS OUT	(#61)	978-0-425-28515-2
GARFIELD LISTENS TO HIS GUT	(#62)	978-0-425-28557-2
GARFIELD COOKS UP TROUBLE	(#63)	978-0-425-28562-6
GARFIELD FEEDS HIS FACE	(#64)	978-0-425-28567-1
DVD TIE-INS		
GARFIELD AS HIMSELF		978-0-345-47805-4
GARFIELD HOLIDAY CELEBRATIONS		978-0-345-47930-3
GARFIELD TRAVEL ADVENTURES		978-0-345-48087-3
AND DON'T MISS . . .		
GARFIELD AT 25: IN DOG YEARS I'D BE DEAD		978-0-345-45204-7
GARFIELD'S JOKE ZONE/INSULTS		978-0-345-46263-3
GARFIELD FAT CAT 3-PACK/ VOL. 1		978-0-345-46455-2
GARFIELD FAT CAT 3-PACK/ VOL. 2		978-0-345-46465-1
GARFIELD FAT CAT 3-PACK/ VOL. 3		978-0-345-48088-0
GARFIELD FAT CAT 3-PACK/ VOL. 4		978-0-345-49171-8
GARFIELD FAT CAT 3-PACK/ VOL. 5		978-0-345-49180-8
GARFIELD FAT CAT 3-PACK/ VOL. 6		978-0-345-52420-1
GARFIELD FAT CAT 3-PACK/ VOL. 7		978-0-345-52588-8
GARFIELD FAT CAT 3-PACK/ VOL. 8		978-0-345-52599-4
GARFIELD FAT CAT 3-PACK/ VOL. 9		978-0-345-52607-6
GARFIELD FAT CAT 3-PACK/ VOL. 10		978-0-425-28558-9
GARFIELD FAT CAT 3-PACK/ VOL. 11		978-0-425-28566-4
GARFIELD FAT CAT 3-PACK/ VOL. 13		978-0-345-46460-6
GARFIELD FAT CAT 3-PACK/ VOL. 14		978-0-345-49175-6
GARFIELD FAT CAT 3-PACK/ VOL. 15		978-0-345-52585-7
GARFIELD FAT CAT 3-PACK/ VOL. 16		978-0-345-52592-5
GARFIELD FAT CAT 3-PACK/ VOL. 17		978-0-345-52603-8
GARFIELD FAT CAT 3-PACK/ VOL. 18		978-0-399-59440-3
GARFIELD FAT CAT 3-PACK/ VOL. 19		978-0-425-28561-9
GARFIELD FAT CAT 3-PACK/ VOL. 20		978-0-425-28571-8
SEASON'S EATINGS: A VERY MERRY GARFIELD CHRISTMAS		978-0-345-47560-2
GARFIELD'S GUIDE TO EVERYTHING		978-0-345-46461-3
ODIE UNLEASHED!		978-0-345-46464-4
GARFIELD'S BOOK OF CAT NAMES		978-0-345-48516-8
THE GARFIELD JOURNAL		978-0-345-46469-9
LIGHTS, CAMERA, HAIRBALLS!: GARFIELD AT THE MOVIES		978-0-345-49134-3
30 YEARS OF LAUGHS AND LASAGNA		978-0-345-50379-4
GARFIELD MINUS GARFIELD		978-0-345-51387-8
GARFIELD FROM THE TRASH BIN		978-0-345-51881-1
GARFIELD LEFT SPEECHLESS		978-0-345-53058-5
MY LAUGHABLE LIFE WITH GARFIELD		978-0-345-52591-8
GARFIELD'S SUNDAY FINEST		978-0-345-52597-0

New larger, full-color format! (#1–#35)